T5-ANA-255

Dreaming
SUBURBIA

AFRICAN AMERICAN LIFE SERIES

A complete listing of the books in this series can be found online at http://wsupress.wayne.edu

SERIES EDITORS

MELBA JOYCE BOYD
Department of Africana Studies
Wayne State University

RONALD BROWN
Department of Political Science
Wayne State University Press

Dreaming SUBURBIA

Detroit and the Production of Postwar Space and Culture

AMY MARIA KENYON

DETROIT WAYNE STATE UNIVERSITY PRESS

Manufactured in the United States of America.
08 07 06 05 04 5 4 3 2 1

Library of Congress Cataloging-in-Publication Data

Kenyon, Amy Maria.
Dreaming suburbia : Detroit and the production of postwar space and culture / Amy Maria Kenyon.
p. cm. — (African American life series)
Includes bibliographical references and index.
ISBN 0-8143-3228-5 (pbk. : alk. paper)
1. Suburban life—United States—History—20th century. 2. City and town life—United States—History—20th century. 3. Suburban life in popular culture—United States. 4. Suburban life in literature. 5. United States—Social conditions—1945– 6. Detroit Metropolitan Area (Mich.)—Social conditions—20th century. 7. Detroit Metropolitan Area (Mich.)—Race relations. 8. Riots—Michigan—Detroit. I. Title. II. Series.
HT352.U62D485 2004
307.76'0973—dc22 2004015479

∞The paper used in this publication meets the minimum requirements of the American National Standard for Information Sciences—
Permanence of Paper for Printed Library Materials, ANSI Z39.48-1984.

FOR MY PARENTS

Raymond and Shirley Kenyon

Contents

Introduction

Postmodernism was once described as being "about how the world dreams itself to be 'American.'"[1] This statement might be read as an allusion to the logic and practice of "American" consumption and its contribution to the global capitalist culture that we have recently termed "postmodern." In the "brief American century" (1945–73), that is, that "hothouse of the new system" of late capitalism, Fredric Jameson locates a related cultural break at the end of the 1950s.[2] In Jameson's account, the 1950s represent the "stability and prosperity of a *pax Americana* but also the first naïve innocence of the countercultural impulses" of postmodernity.[3] The 1950s may be considered as a prelude to the cultural processes of postmodernism, but also, for our purposes, as a last *domestic* American context, in which *Americans* dreamed themselves to be American.

In this book, I propose that the postwar settlement of American capitalism involved a particular configuration and *spatialization* of the American dream as both white and suburban. After the war, the production and distribution of suburban space was indispensable to the corporate-liberal settlement. Suburbanization was part of the immediate social and economic recovery, and it also helped to secure the long-term interests of capital. Yet if suburbia was a physical place, it was also an integral part of the postwar imaginary. In that imaginary, a white, middle-class suburban lifestyle was commodified and equated with "America" and with "American national identity." Although the American dream had always incorporated images of movement and frontier expansion alongside those of home and place, such images were newly combined and invoked in a range of cultural representations of the postwar suburban boom. Suburbia was marketed with significant success to suburbanites and nonsuburbanites alike. And indeed, those who could, chose suburbia in vast numbers. At the same time, suburbanization provided the material space for the postwar consolidation of capital *and* for the marked exclusion of certain groups from the American dream.

My central argument is that the changing fortunes and relations of city and suburb must be understood as belonging to local and larger processes of socioeconomic and cultural disinvestment. Disinvestment is viewed here as the redistribution of resources, rights, and cultural-political authority away from the city and along racist and spatially exclusive lines. I further argue that the success of postwar suburbanization depended on a kind of cultural dreaming, on a mystification of processes of disinvestment *in and through* culture. We might have dreamed ourselves to be American; now we dreamed ourselves to be suburban. Any social divisions and exclusions underpinning the produced space of postwar suburbia were effectively hidden.

A Motel in Detroit

When we try to understand the arrangement of social space, we typically begin with an attraction to place: *our* place. This research began as an attempt to understand the extraordinary complexity of suburban Detroit, the place of my childhood. To study a place is to return to the specific events, acts, and conditions that engage people's lives. I wanted to examine a particular, remembered event that took place in Detroit, during the riots of July 1967—the killing of three black men by members of the Detroit police at the Algiers Motel—an occurrence that became known as the Algiers Motel incident. This was an event that resisted private and public understanding from the moment it occurred, one that immediately connected to the history of race in America, through a series of difficult local histories about space and violence, about place and narrative. *Dreaming Suburbia: Detroit and the Production of Postwar Space and Culture* opens and closes with this historically and geographically specific material, with local histories that, as I will argue, engage with the larger project of this book.

That project is to situate postwar suburbia as a *cultural* phenomenon, but one that can only be understood as occurring in a historically specific configuration of social, political, and economic conditions. To ground these complex and often abstract phenomena, I provide an analysis of Detroit and its suburbs in order to examine exemplary local evidence of processes of disinvestment in the postwar production of space and culture. As a city in which industrial development had a close and early link with suburbanization, Detroit also provides historical and ongoing evidence that urban and suburban identities are profoundly related and politically charged. But while there is a wealth of local, historical material concerning the larger themes of this book, my work does *not* treat Detroit as *representative* of universal conclusions about American suburbia. Detroit's manufacturing and employment history brought about singular economic and demographic changes that make its experience unique. Moreover, although segregation and exclusion can be identified in most metropolitan areas, in Detroit these processes have been arguably more extreme and more persistent and have centered more on a black-white divide than elsewhere.[4] My purpose, then, is to examine Detroit, its specific history of industry, suburbanization, and race, and the heightened events of 1967 *alongside* a more general study of suburban culture in order to demonstrate that work on the one might inform and illuminate the other. The very fact of Detroit's specificity and its difference suggest that to work on a place, *any* place, is to embrace the complexity of relations between the local and the particular and the more abstract material on space and culture.

In chapter 1, the Algiers Motel is introduced as the site of a material act of violence—the murder of three young African Americans in Detroit—and as the imaginary of a narrative crisis about postwar space and culture. In a narrow sense, I use the term "narrative crisis" to describe a crisis in telling, writing, and explaining the Algiers Motel incident—a crisis that occurred from the moment it happened, and one that persists. Moreover, this crisis applied to the "riots" of July 1967, to the politics of naming and describing these events, and to the individual and collective acts of remembering. In a larger sense, though always in relation to local issues, the term "narrative crisis" refers to historical problems of narration and interpretation concerning postwar suburban space. Each subsequent chapter works toward the (at least) partial resolution of the narrative crisis by relating it to the larger material and metaphorical map upon which we might locate the Algiers

Motel incident. Each chapter thus contributes to a progressive understanding of the wider cultural, historical, and geographical context of the 1967 riot.

In chapter 2, I begin the work of contextualization with a historical examination of the political and cultural economy of the suburban boom. The aim is to identify the importance of suburbanization to the postwar settlement of American capitalism. This chapter is an introductory work of demystification, a broad look at the material processes that suburbanized American social space and put race firmly at the center of our geographical identities.

Chapters 3, 4, and 5 provide an analysis of a range of cultural representations of American suburbia. Virginia Woolf once remarked that "where the truth is important, I prefer to write fiction."[5] These chapters conduct a work of historical interpretation by drawing from a selection of those fictions or cultural narratives that pertain to the lived spatial experience of the postwar suburbanizing nation. Each chapter is organized around a group of cultural representations—texts, utterances, practices—situated in broad historical context. My work is therefore, by necessity, interdisciplinary in its combined use of cultural and sociohistorical materials. Indeed, I move freely from social and historical studies to novels, film, and other cultural forms. Although it must be recognized that a novelist has different goals and observes different rules than those followed by the social or economic historian, I would argue that, in this study, each is brought into play to inform and deepen the other as a *chronicler* of suburbia. One cannot deliver a cultural analysis of suburban space without engaging in a productive integration of these materials.

Accordingly, chapter 3 draws on film, television, and early popular novels of suburbia in order to interrogate the ideological project of suburbanization. I argue here that the success of suburbia relies precisely on its action as a space of *detachment*—a separated and instrumental space, mystified and emptied of historical reference to the city. Specifically, the material growth of the postwar suburb rested upon a collective cultural dreaming in which detachment, separation, and exclusion might be *reframed* as attachment, consensus, and inclusion. The processes of disinvestment—of the redistribution of power and resources away from the city—might be literally and poetically disappeared from the suburban mind's eye.

The violence of segregation and social division that underpinned the produced space of suburbia might also be effectively removed from our collective memory.

It might be argued that the reframing of detachment as attachment was so successful that suburbia came to be seen by many as the locus of a reinvented American identity, one that would soon be critiqued as a suburban conformity. Indeed it was the problem of conformity, rather than detachment or race exclusion, that attracted the first critical appraisals of suburbia. Chapter 4 is the first of two chapters that examine the various postwar critiques of suburbia, beginning with an assessment of the mass culture debates. If the urban intelligentsia argued that mass culture encouraged conformity, then suburbia provided critics with a perfect, *located* target. I argue that these early critiques of suburbia were trapped within the frame of reference set by the mass culture debates, producing a dream critique from without, one that ignored both the problem of disinvestment *and* the lived experience of suburbia. Although the issue of disinvestment remained largely invisible to the mass culture critics, the lived space of suburbia was being partially recovered in a range of popular cultural texts of the period. These texts are more frequently seen as interrogating general issues of conformity and difference in cold war America. However, I will argue that a number of postwar films and novels mapped domestic incarnations of cold war "otherness" onto suburban locations.

Chapter 5 develops the work of the previous chapter by interrogating an exemplary group of writings that extend the critique of suburbia by treating it at the intersection of space, subjectivity, and everyday life. Here, Henri Lefebvre's argument that everyday life is the site of both alienation and disalienation is developed in relation to specific novels and short stories in which suburban subjectivities and estrangement feature as central themes. The theme of estrangement is deployed in order to explore the suburban experience of the pressures and cracks in the ideological project of the suburban dream and to treat the problem of conformity with greater complexity. Moreover, and in particular texts treated in this chapter, one can begin to trace a more explicitly stated suburban malaise relating to the city and to the problem of disinvestment.

The themes in these three middle chapters are closely related, so much so that the cultural representations treated in any one of the chapters might easily find a point of reference in the other two. The themes of detachment, conformity, and estrangement cannot ultimately be disentangled. That said, each of these chapters does privilege one of these themes and reads its selected texts accordingly. Moreover, by the order in which they appear, the three themes map a general direction in which an increasing complexity of cultural representation is posited.

A recurring issue in almost all of the texts treated in the middle chapters concerns city-suburb relations. Not surprisingly, these texts (and particularly those studied in chapter 5) belie a suburban ambivalence, if not a more explicitly stated sense of guilt or anxiety about the city. Chapter 6 is a return to the city of Detroit and its suburbs, beginning with a historical interrogation of a series of texts and events associated with the Ford Motor Company. Specifically, this chapter inspects city-suburb relations by drawing on selected narratives relating to Detroit's automotive history, industrial and residential suburbanization, and the politics of race.

Back to the Algiers Motel

The last chapter opens with a specific analysis of the Detroit suburb of Garden City. Drawing upon the insights gained in chapter 6, the rapid postwar growth of one suburb is examined in relation to developments in Detroit during the same period. This positions us to consider the violence of 1967 and the Algiers Motel incident in its greater spatial and contextual complexity. I argue that the postwar production of space, and its cultural expression in the suburban dream, provide an archive for our reading of the Algiers Motel incident. This book's analysis of selected historical moments and texts of postwar America and Detroit will enable me to better *locate* the Algiers incident as a time and a place in the cultural geography of disinvestment and race. In chapter 7, then, it is possible to provide a detailed analytical account of this significant moment of violence and its political aftermath. But I also consider the ways in which the Algiers deaths and the 1967 riot produced a radical cultural politics that contested the place and meaning of violence itself. Indeed the response of black activists provided an early indication that after 1967 Detroiters would find effective and creative ways to build a black political power base in an urban community increasingly abandoned by whites. Although the post-1967 history of Detroit falls outside the scope of this book, the memory of the events of 1967 continued to inform political culture and black activism in the city.[6]

At the same time, the Algiers Motel incident and the response of local activists provide an evocative illustration and indication of the explanatory power of Henri Lefebvre's theoretical work on space. Lefebvre's studies of postwar capitalism and its "survival" through the production of space have given us a frequently tragic picture of modernity. Yet his work was animated by a self-professed utopianism combined with an attention to concrete political and cultural practices. This book, and the studies of Detroit in particular, benefit throughout from Lefebvre's expressly stated commitment to the narratives and direct participation of the "users" of space in cultural and political practice. What Lefebvre termed "the right to the city" could not be separated from his utopian vision of human agency and heterogeneity. Urban life was, for Lefebvre, a metaphor for the politics of difference, the politics of space.

As a cultural geographical manifestation of the reconsolidation of capital, the postwar suburb may appear to those who spent their childhood there as a space frozen in a lingering optimism of late modernity. This was a space in which the sheer repetition of tract house, car, and street design might invoke a profound experience of safety. Yet it can be argued that a suburban suspicion and premonition of violence run through many of the representations of suburbia treated in this book. Is anywhere ever really safe? Is it possible to inhabit such a space without a nagging memory of some hidden violence embedded in that space itself?

We travel to suburbia in order to think about the violence of 1967 and the Algiers incident. We revisit the Algiers and Detroit in order to better understand the violence of disinvestment that underpinned suburban development. Specifically, we can situate suburbia as a political economy with profound implications for cities and for postwar configurations of American racism. We might also locate in the postwar production of suburban space and culture a collective dream haunted by a trace memory of violence.

1 Rumors from a Motel in Detroit

In late summer 1967, waves of rumors moved across metropolitan Detroit, announcing a series of race divisions across the city and between city and suburb. There were conflicting accounts about events at the Algiers Motel in the early hours of July 26 of that year. In many downtown neighborhoods, it was said that three young black men—Carl Cooper, Auburey Pollard, and Fred Temple—had been murdered in an act of police brutality. In white suburbia it was widely believed that the three men had died in a sniper battle with police. This last rumor was known to have its origins in police statements made in the days following the incident.[1]

In the nature of their mobility and in their content, these and other rumors mapped a physical and psychological geography of Detroit at a highly charged historical moment—for the events at the Algiers Motel had occurred during the worst urban uprising in American history. At around 4 A.M. on July 23, the police raided a Twelfth Street "blind pig" (the local term for an illegal after-hours club) where a party was being held to celebrate the return of a black serviceman from Vietnam. With more than eighty clients apprehended, police took more than an hour to complete the arrests, during which time a crowd of local residents had formed. As anger at police actions grew, onlookers began throwing bottles and setting fires. By the end of the day, the incident had escalated into a full-scale riot, with both the state police and the National Guard deployed on city streets. On July 24, city and state officials appealed for federal help, and President Johnson ordered in nearly five thousand paratroopers.

The riot was marked by extreme violence and devastation. With 43 deaths (33 black, 10 white), 2,000 injured, and 7,000 people arrested, Detroit's riot figures were not surpassed until the 1992 Los Angeles riot (52 deaths, 2,383 injured, 16,291 arrested).[2] Along with

Watts and Newark, the Detroit riot received national and international attention in what was in fact a period of frequent and widespread urban unrest. The National Commission on the Causes and Prevention of Violence identified 239 urban riots between 1963 and 1968. In what Paul Gilje has termed a "contagion of disorder," the Commission cited some 200,000 participants, 8,000 injuries, and 190 deaths.[3]

These were highly favorable conditions for the transmission of rumor. In any situation of social disorder in which people are on the streets and talking, rumor takes on a particularly tangible and uncontrolled spatiality. It travels by word of mouth; it spreads unpredictably and opportunistically. It transgresses the borders of received wisdom and subverts official channels of communication. In the days and weeks following the July upheaval, the rumors about the Algiers incident provided just a small sample of a wider range of differing and frequently contradictory rumors across city and suburb. These rumors included the following: the police were training white suburbanites, preparing to incite a riot, and then launch an armed invasion of ghetto areas.[4] Black activists were mining the expressways and planning to shoot white suburbanites as they drove to their downtown offices. Or, by rolling down gas drums, they would set fire to the expressways.[5] Concentration camps in secret sites across the United States were being readied for a massive displacement and incarceration of black inner-city populations. Or the ghetto itself might be cordoned off into a concentration camp.[6] Black mobile killer squads would roam suburbia, kidnapping and murdering a white boy from each Detroit suburb.[7] Black maids were organizing to poison white households in the wealthier suburbs.[8]

By autumn, the escalation of rumor, along with a strike by the city's two largest newspapers, produced a crisis in the very telling, description, naming, and interpretation of the deaths at the Algiers and of the riot itself. This was, then, a narrative crisis in metropolitan Detroit, one that had material effects, such as the local arms race that occurred as city dwellers and suburbanites bought large quantities of rifles and handguns. Finally, the mayor set up a "Rumor Control" Center, with the express purpose of checking out rumors and countering falsehood with truth. On its first day the center received ninety-six calls, and the phones continued to ring for a month. By the time the wave of rumors had subsided, ten thousand calls had been taken. Most of the callers were "thought to be white."[9]

Occupying the northwest corner of Woodward Avenue and Virginia Park, the Algiers Motel might also be seen as a marker of Detroit's social divisions. Woodward Avenue drew the boundary between east and west with its corresponding race/class divide. In the late 1940s, increasing numbers of black middle- and upper-working-class Detroiters began to move out of the traditional black neighborhoods of the lower east side. Those who remained experienced increased isolation along race and class lines. Many of these would soon be forced into already crowded adjacent neighborhoods when freeway construction and "urban renewal" projects decimated their communities.[10] At one time Virginia Park was a leafy and prosperous street not far from the Twelfth Street area, the site of the first spark of violence in the 1967 uprising. Twelfth Street had undergone a rapid racial transition in the 1950s as black Detroiters began moving into this formerly Jewish neighborhood.[11]

The Algiers Manor House was a large annex to the motel with dormers, bay windows, and white pillars. Originally one of the imposing middle-class homes of Virginia Park, the Manor House had since been divided into fifteen kitchenette units. In the late 1960s, the Algiers Motel had a reputation as a trading post for a range of illegal economies including gambling, drugs, and prostitution. By October 1967, it was being investigated as a "public nuisance" and was the subject of a "padlocking" application. But looking back on the events of July, John Hersey remarked that these investigations and the threat of closure "could not possibly be construed as anything but a punishment of a locus of shame for the police force."[12]

To anybody still residing at the motel or the Manor House, the idea of a Rumor Control Center might have seemed laughable at a time when narrative certainties were being contested and shattered on a daily basis. The only available truth was that Detroit was full of stories. They were all about lived urban space, and they were all up for grabs. For example, what *was* the event of July 1967? A riot, a rebellion, an outing, a holiday, an insurrection, a new feeling? These were some of the terms used by participants and witnesses at the time. In these differing expressions, everyone staked some claim to the event: the families and friends of the forty-three people who died; the police; the inner city dwellers who burned, looted, and talked; the suburbanites who sat shocked in front of blue TV screens until downtown had been "made safe" by federal troops. Then they jumped into station wagons, locked the car doors, and went sightseeing in such numbers that the curfew had to be reinstated. In their disparate life paths, everyone searched for some narrative hold on events. Everyone figured in the local inscriptions and representations of power relations in space.

On a very concrete level, the long, hot summer was about people as *users* of space; it was about bodies and experience. It was about houses and streets, who owned them, who controlled them, and who occupied them. In the postwar period, rapid suburbanization had exacerbated an already profound dislocation of space and race. During the 1950s, nearly one out of every four white Detroiters moved to the suburbs. The increasing mechanization of industry in the American South, combined with the draw of Detroit as the automotive capital, meant that in the same period, the city's black population grew more than 50 percent.[13] However, commercial and industrial suburbanization increased almost simultaneously with these demographic movements, taking jobs out of the city, causing downtown property values to plummet, and the city tax base to shrink in a period of heightened social need. Together, Ford, General Motors, and Chrysler (Detroit's "Big Three" automakers) built twenty-five new plants in suburban areas between 1947 and 1958.[14]

Derelict houses, factories, and warehouses dotted the cityscape. The postriot suburban sightseeing may mark one of the few occasions that commuters ventured off the expressways into the neighborhoods marked by postwar disinvestment. In his radical historical geography of Fitzgerald, a neighborhood on the northwest side, William Bunge accused suburbanites of "sucking" money out of Detroit "like the lamprey eels suck the juices out of Michigan Lake trout."[15] In Bunge's account, freeway construction proved to be one of the many crucial acts of geographical disinvestment, providing a funnel for the suburban migration of commerce, industry, and residence. Moreover, freeway building was a tangibly spatial and visual act of segregation in that it removed entire city neighborhoods from the commuters' field of vision. Bunge put it more bluntly: "Suburbanites view the poor as commuter time necessary to pass through 'it.'"[16] If Detroit's inner-city neighborhoods could be reduced to the abstraction of a spatially experienced expense of travel time, then Detroit as a city in which people *lived* had become less and less real to suburbanites.

The demography of neighborhoods changed quickly, with the overall trend in living space moving toward increased black-white segregation, with black renters and home owners forced to occupy an aging urban housing stock left behind by departing whites. With the construction of public housing already kept to a minimum, African Americans were effectively excluded from the private real estate market by a range of discriminatory practices emanating from city realtors and lending institutions. These practices were facilitated by postwar federal housing policies and were consolidated "on the ground" by organized resistance on the part of white neighborhood "defense" groups.[17]

When black Detroiters succeeded in crossing the "color line," they regularly met with harassment and violence from their new neighbors. White resistance took a variety of forms, including demonstrations, effigy burning, arson, vandalism, and physical attacks.[18] On Eight Mile Road, a builder had erected a concrete wall six feet high and a half mile long to separate his development property from a small number of black residents living nearby. In spite of a gradual spatial expansion of black residence, visible and "invisible walls" continued to operate as a northern version of Jim Crow to contain, isolate, and limit the chances of African Americans.[19] In the Twelfth Street area, the population density was twenty-one thousand people to the square mile, more than twice the density of white districts.[20] Detroiters soon found that the integration narrative of the southern-based Civil Rights movement could not easily be transplanted to northern cities. Some black Detroiters invented their own narratives of space, ones that underlined the de facto apartheid of the North, in contrast to the South's de jure apartheid.

Detroit stories went like this: "We pay taxes so white people can live in the suburbs. No one attempted to compensate us for the freeways. We don't use them. But they have taken up land and reduced our tax base."[21] Suburbia is a "white noose."[22] "I work in Detroit and I live in Detroit, but I don't feel free. There are so many places closed to me."[23] In Motown, it was said, integration referred to no more than the period of time between the arrival of the first black on the block and the departure of the last white.[24] Or, as one of Toni Morrison's characters so aptly states, "I do believe my whole life is geography."[25]

Such were the descriptors used to define the racism inherent in the arrangement of space in postwar Detroit. Moreover, these developments in Detroit and its suburbs provide a local, exemplary image of Henri Lefebvre's work on the history of the production of space, in which he sought to write a spatial analysis into the historicist Marxist problematic and into post-Marxist social theory.[26] In Lefebvre's project, the history of the modes of production entails a connecting history of their spaces. But it is under late capitalism that the organization of space *directly* ensures the reproduction of the social relations of production. Capital no longer just takes possession of existing space. It produces its own space. Indeed, the production of space is indispensable to the "survival of capitalism."

In this scheme, urbanism is the literal and figurative replacement for industrialism in the spatial settlement of late capitalism. It is how capital maintains itself. Urbanism may still refer to the city, but it also extends to beyond the city, to the process whereby spatial arrangements sustain capital on both the local and global scales. Lefebvre's development of the term "abstract space" refers to that space produced and consumed according to the exigencies of capital. This is a space that creates an illusion of homogeneity, of the suppression of difference, and of the suppression of resistance. In this sense, abstract space has an instrumental homogeneity as its image and its goal.[27]

In his own work on the postwar organization of space, David Harvey gave a more narrowly economic explanation in which urbanism involved the concentration of surplus in "some version of the city."[28] Under late capitalism it is "*necessary* for urbanism to generate expanding consumption if the capitalist economy is to be maintained. Much of the expansion of GNP in capitalist societies is in fact bound up in the whole suburbanization process."[29] Here, American suburbanization is part of a space economy in which the production and consumption of "hierarchies of city types" ensure the continued safe circulation of surplus value.[30]

These processes of spatial change and suburbanization cannot be separated from the history of race in America. In Detroit as in other rust belt cities, middle-class whites were able to follow and add to the flow of investment away from the city. Many white workers had the means to move into tract houses in the blue-collar fringe developments located near suburban manufacturing plants. But persistent housing discrimination prevented any genuine possibility of black suburbanization and contributed to the development of a "spatial mismatch between urban African Americans and jobs."[31] The organization of postwar American space was the mapping that underpinned Malcolm X's assertion that "it's impossible for a white person to believe in capitalism and not believe in racism."[32] In Detroit, Auburey Pollard's father put it still more graphically: "What does this do with the Negro? It puts him in a circle. . . . They work in a circle. You can see the money moving."[33]

It was Pollard's father who first situated his son's death in the larger picture of lived urban experience in modern America. At the time of the Algiers Motel incident, Auburey Pollard Sr. was working his night job, loading trucks for the Detroit Public Works. When his foreman took him aside to say something had happened to one of his sons, Mr. Pollard phoned home, worrying that his third son, Tanner, had got into some kind of trouble. The news of Auburey's death was hard to take in, and all the way to the morgue he hoped against hope that it was all some kind of mistake. And then, as sometimes happens when we face the worst of all possibilities, time was merciful and stopped. Mr. Pollard got a brief reprieve, a contemplative delay:

> So the lady at the morgue, she was very nice, she was beautiful . . . she's a ageable lady, she's within knowledge of the world, she's no fifteen, sixteen, twenty, or twenty-two years, she's in her late forties or early fifties, right along there someplace. So we talked. We sit there and I bet you we talked for about thirty-five minutes, and we talked about youngsters, you know, how they communicate, how they do not if they want to be slick, you know—it's life, we talked about everyday life. And then she says, "You know . . . I've been living in this place so long, just to take out my trash I pay so much, just do little odds-and-ends different things I have to pay so much." So we sit there and talk, and she said, "Well, I see you want to see him." I

> said, "Sure." So I walked up. There he was. She take me over and showed me Auburey. I said, "That's my son."[34]

There were many unexpected encounters in the streets, jails, hospitals, and morgues of Detroit in the summer of 1967. Here two middle-aged people meet over Auburey Pollard's body, brought together by his violent and unaccountable death. Yet they choose to talk about the costs and repetitions of daily life, of "living in this place so long." Mr. Pollard and the "morgue lady" already know that a single event, in an old Detroit mansion turned rooming house, has no single explanation. There are only those tangled narratives, small explanations and large explanations, all equally rooted in a longer history of lived space.

The Algiers Motel incident belongs to a larger social mystery. Indeed, it might seem a minuscule point on a wide and shifting mosaic in which postwar American space was remapped. In July 1967 that point flared briefly, then went out. When it was over, no essential truth was laid bare. However, the flash of violence at the Algiers might illuminate the big map, the larger context to which I turn in this book's remaining chapters before a final consideration of the events of 1967. In the introduction to his study of the Fitzgerald neighborhood, Bunge sounds a hopeful if cautious note toward such localized analysis: "Is America really homogenous enough so that one square mile of it could contain the essential story of the nation itself? . . . Certainly it would be ridiculous to claim, 'as Fitzgerald goes, so goes the nation,' and such a claim is not being entered, but still, an uneasy feeling grips the author that if enough of the Fitzgeralds of America fall down, then could not the nation itself? For what is America other than a collection of Fitzgeralds?"[35]

Bunge's material on Fitzgerald was drawn from his own residence in the area, oral history interviews, meetings with local inhabitants, and an iconoclastic approach to mapping. The work pieced together a historical geography of a square mile of Detroit that was "no longer located in the wilderness as it was in the 1830s, or in the affluent suburban edge of Detroit as it was in the 1920s, but halfway between the suburbs and the slums."[36] *Fitzgerald* remains a powerful account of a local politics of space with far-reaching implications. As

Bunge stated, the study "attempts to learn big things from a little region."[37]

With the introduction of the Algiers Motel incident as an eruptive moment that raises questions about the historical geography of postwar America, I share Bunge's caution, hopeful nonetheless that an understanding of the local and the global will be better grasped by holding to the confusion of both. I also share Bunge's assertion that suburbanization had much to do with the subsequent state of America's "Fitzgeralds."

In the events of July 1967 we catch a glimpse of the relations between city and suburb, a usually veiled interdependence built upon a whole history of efforts to separate and exclude. Suburbia was founded on the premise and promise of segregation. Apart from an annual outing to a show or a ballgame, many suburbanites prided themselves on having escaped the city for green spaces and clean air. Yet the rumors of late summer 1967 suggest a play of mutual fascination and resentment between suburbanites and city dwellers. For middle-class whites, black skin figured increasingly as a nagging absence. By the time of the Algiers incident, James Baldwin had already warned that in the geography of northern cities, black was becoming invisible to white.[38] The absences created by segregation encouraged suburbanites to identify themselves as "sovereign subjects" in the postwar illusion of a "classless" and "color-blind" America.

But in the inner city, white remained visible to black, in the shape of the police, courts, lawmakers, city administrators, absentee landlords, the media—indeed in all the outward signs of WASP hegemony. Here we begin to track a persistent colonial trope in the Western metropolis. White had access to black homes and streets in a way that was not reciprocal. Incidents involving white police officers drew particular criticism from individual black residents and from the local NAACP. In a community that was nearly 50 percent black in 1965, just 2.8 percent of the police force was black.[39] Yet the Kerner Report found that the Detroit riot was not "interracial." In physical terms, black and white residents did not have sufficient proximity to fight each other. The events of 1967 "involved action against white society—authority and property—rather than against white persons."[40] The rebellion was "put down" by the police and by state and federal troops—the occupying forces of a white (and increasingly *suburban*) network of power.[41]

In the postwar period, suburbia provided a spatial greenhouse in which the laws of exchange and the commodity might come to rule space as a whole. The space of proliferating commodities becomes commodity itself. In this respect, abstract space is a mystified space from which difference and history have been removed. This is the great suburban "escape from the past" described by Jerry Herron in his study of Detroit as the "most historically representative city in America" and a city "so thoroughly humiliated by history, so emptied of the content, both material and human . . . that it becomes questionable whether the city still exists at all in any practical sense."[42]

The mystification occurs in the notion that suburbanization was a "natural" process, a "manifest destiny," a "meritocratic" expression of American movement, growth, and prosperity, and, finally, in the denial that every suburban act had consequences for the city. In the next chapter, I begin my investigation of the wider context within which the events of 1967 took place. This is a preliminary work of demystification, a broad look at the political and cultural economy of American suburbanization and at the material processes that decentralized social space and put race at the center of our geographical identities.

2 Mapping Postwar Space and Culture

The Suburbanization of American Space

There is no classic suburb, nor have representations of suburbia confirmed it as a good space, a bad space, or any particular point in between. Indeed the merits of suburbia have always been, and continue to be, hotly debated.[1] What can be stated with certainty is that in terms of its own growth, suburbia is an all-American success story. Between 1950 and 1980, the number of people residing in suburbia rose from 35.2 million to 101.5 million.[2] The 1970 Census showed that "for the first time in the history of the world, a nation-state counted more suburbanites than city-dwellers or farmers."[3] And by 1990 nearly half of all Americans resided in suburbia.[4] Like a snowball rolling downhill over a thirty-year period, suburbanization proceeded apace. Not everyone landed in Oz at the same time; and as later chapters will show, not everyone viewed the Emerald City through green spectacles.[5] But suburbia was, and is, a seemingly irreversible American project.

The postwar suburban boom had a staggering impact on the demography of both city and periphery. While the suburban population doubled between 1950 and 1970, eighteen of America's twenty-five largest cities suffered a net loss of population between 1950 and 1980.[6] Thomas Sugrue reports that, since 1950, Detroit has lost about a million people.[7] But there have been other boom periods for suburbia, each connected to a distinct set of conditions.[8] Indeed the 1920s boom put into place a number of elements that were important to postwar growth. As such, this particular period of growth forms a useful point of departure.

One notable effect of the 1920s automotive revolution was increased residential development in the suburbs. This was accompanied by a continuous decentralization of industry, consumption, and leisure. Industrial suburbanization is sometimes ignored in historical accounts of suburbia. But Kenneth Jackson finds that, in the decade between 1920 and 1930, "the proportion of factory employment located in central cities declined in every city of more than 100,000 residents."[9] After 1925, almost all new industrial building took place on the urban fringes. Suburban industrial districts appeared outside Boston, Chicago, Detroit, and other cities. Henry Ford located assembly plants in Highland Park, Northville, and River Rouge—all beyond the city line of Detroit. Department stores and vaudeville theaters also began to establish suburban sites. Most of these developments were still reliant on public transport systems to bring people to them. This trend began to change in 1920, when Country Club Plaza opened in Kansas City. Designed with the car in mind, it was the first planned regional shopping center and prefigured the suburban malls of the 1950s and 1960s.

By the mid-1920s, the great interwar era of subdividers had arrived. The cost of real estate was lower in areas only accessible by car than in areas served by public transport. In the new automobile suburbs, developers worked on large-scale tracts of land usually divided into forty by one hundred foot lots.[10] Zoning regulations were used to counter the rank roadside commercial growth that accompanied the oncoming car culture. Industrial, commercial, and residential zones were identified and kept separate, thus ensuring the eventual predominance of the bedroom community as residential suburb. "Away went barbershops, luncheonettes, candy stores, garages, poolrooms and cheap movie houses—banished to thoroughfares zoned "'commercial' on the edges of subdivisions."[11]

Joel Schwartz notes that whereas 35 municipalities had comprehensive zoning ordinances before 1920, 438 adopted them in the next five years.[12] All of these changes favored the large-scale subdivider, who could offer low-density living to a growing number of private car owners. Henry Ford predicted, "The city is doomed. . . . We shall solve the city problem by leaving the city."[13] Throughout the 1920s, Ford's statement seemed to have hit the mark. While automobile registrations rose by 150 percent, the suburbs of the ninety-six largest U.S. cities grew twice as fast as the central cities.[14]

The best-known and most extreme example of the subdivider's power was in Los Angeles. By manipulating the city's water politics, developers had managed to create a massive monopoly over the subdivision of Hollywood and the San Fernando Valley.[15] In what Margaret Marsh has termed "the new exclusionary virulence of the 1920s," zoning and restrictive covenants in suburban Los Angeles set the racial and economic homogeneity that would continue into the postwar era.[16] Low-density home ownership favored white, middle-class nuclear families, and publicists equated suburban residence with "American citizenship . . . American patriotism."[17]

The Los Angeles property boom provided James Cain with the material for his sordid suburban tales told in *Double Indemnity* (1936) and *Mildred Pierce* (1941). But Cain's stories are set across the Depression decade, which, in Los Angeles in particular, saw the ruin of many lesser property speculators who had latched on to the 1920s boom. One of Cain's characters, Bert Pierce, a developer in Glendale, embodies the story of many of these unfortunate speculators. In the 1920s,

> almost overnight, with his three hundred acres that were located in the exact spot where people wanted to build, he became a subdivider . . . a man of vision, a big shot. He and the three gentlemen formed a company, called Pierce Homes, Inc., with himself as president. He named a street after himself. . . . But then came Black Thursday of 1929, and his plunge into ruin was so rapid he could hardly see Pierce Homes disappear on his way down.[18]

According to Mike Davis, it was the "depression-crazed middle classes of Southern California" who became the original lead characters in noir fiction. "Noir was like a transformational grammar turning each charming ingredient of the boosters' arcadia into a sinister equivalent."[19] Noir writers may have been busily recording the seedy underside of the city, but by the time of the Crash, developers had pioneered a "technology of decentralization," making Los Angeles the prototypical postmodern city later celebrated by

Jean Baudrillard.[20] Los Angeles was becoming a "suburban metropolis," which has since prompted one historian to remark that there "suburbia had redefined the modern city in its own image."[21]

In Los Angeles and other places, real estate developers had already plotted out subdivisions that, due to the economic collapse, were not completed until the postwar decades. Detroit, for example, had 1,250,000 empty lots. "Within several spring seasons, depression weeds had grown tall enough to cover stakes pounded in with such hope months before."[22] The building industry all but ground to a halt during the Depression. Between 1929 and 1933, the construction of residential property dropped to an average annual rate of 34 percent.[23] In 1933, half of all home mortgages were in default, with foreclosures running at more than a thousand per day.[24] In the Depression decade, suburban population growth nearly kept pace with overall population growth.[25]

The economic shakeup reached across the class structure, with many middle-class families experiencing impoverishment for the first time. By the end of the decade, mass unemployment brought homelessness, bread lines, and a resurgence in working-class and radical activism. In Detroit, for example, the Communist Party and the Committee for Industrial Organization (C.I.O.) made gains among autoworkers, including black workers. The 1932 Ford Hunger March resulted in greater activism after marchers died under police fire. In 1933, there was a series of strikes throughout the industry.[26] By the end of the decade, the new United Auto Workers Union (U.A.W.) had one of its first and most celebrated victories in the 1937 Flint sit-down strike.[27]

The period's literature produced a series of "social concern" novels.[28] These novels mounted a critique of the political order, combined with a celebration of "the people." One of the most ambitious of these works was John Dos Passos's *U.S.A.*, a trilogy published between 1930 and 1936. *U.S.A.* was an epic assessment of America in the first quarter of the century, but its techniques and critical angle belonged to the 1930s. In its use of documentary material and biographies of working-class heroes and capitalist villains, *U.S.A.* presents a cultural survey of the nation that gradually uncovers the gaps between myth and reality under capitalism. In the opening pages of the first book, Dos Passos maps out his project by pitting a Michelet-like rendering of "the people" against the images and contradictions of capitalism. An anonymous young man recalls the nation's speech:

> In his mother's words telling about longago, in his father's telling about when I was a boy, in the kidding stories of uncles in the lies the kids told at school, the hired man's yarns, the tall tales the doughboys told after taps; it was the speech that clung to the ears, the link that tingled in the blood; U.S.A. U.S.A. is the slice of a continent. U.S.A. is a group of holding companies, some aggregations of trade unions, a set of laws bound in calf, a radio network . . . a column of stockquotations rubbed out and written in by a Western Union boy on a blackboard, a public library full of old newspapers and dogeared historybooks with protests scrawled on the margins in pencil. . . . U.S.A. is the world's greatest river valley fringed with mountains and hills. U.S.A. is a set of bigmouthed officials with too many accounts. . . . U.S.A. is the letters at the end of an address when you are away from home. But mostly U.S.A. is the speech of the people.[29]

Alongside its modernist experimentation, *U.S.A.* was an attempt to articulate a belief in history as process, which Dos Passos had recovered through his involvement with the Communist movement. To some extent, this was a fading discourse. *U.S.A.* ends on a pessimistic note, with the execution of Sacco and Vanzetti, the misery of striking miners, and finally a return to the anonymous young man, now homeless, hungry, and on the road.

Contemporaneous to the articulations of *U.S.A.* was the emergence of a new discourse. In his study of social modernism in postwar America, Anthony Woodiwiss identifies the key signs of what he terms a "modernizing discourse": "self-reliance," "responsible unionism," "opportunity," "loyalty," and "modernity."[30] While Woodiwiss sees these signs as consolidating the *postwar* settlement, he locates their sources in the 1930s. In particular, he sees New Deal legislation as announcing the new discourse.

According to Woodiwiss, the passage of the 1935 Social Security Act was the first clear signal of a changing climate. Old age insurance was the only scheme to emerge with any semblance of a "social democratic tinge."[31] For the rest, permanent and universal public assistance was rejected. The whole bill was "declared inapplicable to agricultural labor, domestic labor and the self-employed, or in other words to approximately fifty per cent of the total labor force and most of its African-American component."[32]

The Wagner Act of the same year announced a "new deal for labor—provided it was 'responsible.'" This latter notion was reinforced in 1947 with the Taft-Hartley Act, passed on a postwar wave of anti–New Deal sentiment in Congress. This act outlawed the closed shop and ruled that Union leaders could not be Communists. Employer rights were reaffirmed, and it was decided that certain strikes could be temporarily halted by presidential order.[33]

Woodiwiss summarizes the message of the Social Security Act as follows:

> America would continue to be a society that aspired to provide "opportunity" rather than "equality" for its citizens. In addition, its administration, by requiring that every citizen or bonafide resident be issued with a social security number, created a basis upon which a distinction could be drawn between licit and illicit presences within the population, a distinction that was later to be repeated on a different basis as that between the loyal and the disloyal.[34]

This is the emergent discourse against which Dos Passos's portrayal of social conflict may be set. Here historical process and challenges to the rule of capital are seen to be giving way to the "corporate liberalism" associated with the 1950s. The tension generated by this changing discourse can be seen in Sugrue's delineation of two competing interpretations of the New Deal ethos and legislation—one calling for support to the "have-nots," the other protecting the resources of the "haves." Sugrue finds that in Detroit these competing interpretations took on a particular vehemence in relation to housing policy. Public housing advocates fought home owners, each claiming to be guided by New Deal principles.[35]

Can we relate any of these developments to the postwar suburban boom? We have already seen that suburbanization in the 1920s put into place a number of characteristics now associated with postwar fringe building: low-density projects dependent on new road building and zoning regulations that kept industrial, commercial, and residential suburbanization separate. As stated earlier, zoning and restrictive covenants already were establishing the white middle-class homogeneity we now associate with the postwar suburb. The promoters' marketing of family togetherness and green safe spaces for childrearing was predominant.[36] In Margaret Marsh's description, the upheavals of the Depression experience served eventually to reinforce rather than undermine these trends: "By the end of the 1920s there had developed an image of suburbia that was to remain fixed in the landscape of the American mind for decades to come. . . . The Depression dashed the plans of many intended suburbanites, but a number of programs of the Roosevelt administration explicitly embodied suburban values. It may not go too far to say that the New Deal institutionalized the suburban vision."[37]

Herbert Hoover had set the agenda, in 1931, when he convened a national conference on building and home ownership. The rhetoric of the conference was support for home ownership for those "of sound character and industrious habits."[38] Acting on Hoover's statement that private home ownership was the expression of "individualism, of enterprise, of independence and of the freedom of spirit," the conference called for investment of private capital in order to avoid the alternative of public housing construction.[39] We can certainly see in this idea corporate, liberal notions of self-reliance, opportunity, responsibility, and loyalty to capital.

But as Marsh has stated, it remained for Roosevelt's New Deal to put these sentiments into practice. The Greenbelt Town Program failed in its implementation but was overt in its prioritization of suburb over city. The idea was to go outside the central cities, "pick up cheap land, build a whole community, and entice people into them. Then go back into the cities and tear down whole slums and make parks of them."[40] The Greenbelt Town plans also contained restrictions that would turn up formally or informally in postwar suburban developments. African Americans were excluded, and economic restrictions limited prospective residents to specific income levels. A working wife was an automatic disqualifier.[41]

But it would be two other New Deal schemes that would have a more enduring influence on the postwar period. Between them, the Home Owners Loan Corporation (HOLC) and the

Federal Housing Administration (FHA) established mortgage and construction practices that favored suburban development and that were furthered by the GI Bill of 1944.

The HOLC was introduced in 1933 and refinanced tens of thousands of endangered mortgages. It introduced the practice of long-term mortgages and a uniform system of property appraisal. This latter innovation included the practice known as "redlining." Redlining was a neighborhood rating system blatantly based on class, ethnic and race prejudice, as well as a more generalized anti-urbanism.

The HOLC rating system is worth describing in some detail because the practices it established endured in various forms well into the postwar period, in what Abrams has called "a racial policy that could well have been culled from the Nuremberg laws."[42] The system consisted of four categories of A through D, with corresponding colors. Grade A (green) areas were described as new and "homogenous," meaning "American business and professional men." Jewish neighborhoods were excluded on the grounds that Jews were not "American." Grade B (blue) went to older areas that were expected to remain unchanged for several years. Grade C (yellow) neighborhoods were "definitely declining." Grade D (red) areas *had* declined and invariably included black neighborhoods.[43] These codes were plotted onto "residential security maps" held in local HOLC offices.

Jackson cites a case study of St. Louis to illustrate how the rating system tended to work. Not surprisingly, the highest ratings went to the suburbs. In the suburb of Ladue, in 1940, "HOLC appraisers noted approvingly that the area's 4,535 acres, criss-crossed by streams, were 'highly restricted' and occupied by 'capitalists and other wealthy families.' Reportedly not the home of 'a single foreigner or negro, Ladue received a First Grade (green) rating."[44] As in the Greenbelt Town plans, a generalized anti-urbanism pervaded many HOLC appraisals. Neighborhoods were marked down for having smaller lots with houses close to the pavements, denser populations, and other characteristics of urban residential spaces.

The American predilection for detached housing (a staple of suburbia) was evident in all the appraisals.[45] As in the 1920s, the desire for a detached house was represented as an innate characteristic of Americanism. In Frank Capra's 1946 film *It's a Wonderful Life*, the young George Bailey tells his father that he wants to leave Bedford Falls and the "shabby little office" of Bailey's Building and Loan. George has a more grandiose (and urbane) aspiration to "design new buildings, plan modern cities." His father defends the Building and Loan in essentialist terms: "I feel that in a small way we're doing something important . . . satisfying a fundamental urge. It's deep in the race for a man to want his own roof and walls and fireplace. And we're helping him to get those things in our shabby little office."

Of course, George never leaves Bedford Falls, but stays on to build "Bailey Park," a suburban-type subdivision of modest detached houses with yards. *It's a Wonderful Life* (along with Capra's *Mr. Deeds Goes to Town* [1936] and *Mr. Smith Goes to Washington* [1939]) figures among the best examples of the "small-town film." Indeed, the persistent imagery of small-town life in cultural representations of suburbia is part of a more generalized anti-urbanism that accompanied suburban growth. Yet at the same time, towns like Bedford Falls represented a paradise lost, even for suburbanites.

Despite its anti-urban appraisal system, the HOLC did issue mortgage assistance in urban areas. But HOLC insistence that racial homogeneity be preserved lent government backing to local racist practices. In Detroit, white home owners "came to expect a vigilant government to protect their segregated neighborhoods."[46] Moreover, private lending associations discriminated against the red and yellow areas, in which city neighborhoods usually fell. Not only did private lenders have access to HOLC residential security maps, many continued the practice of redlining into the 1970s.

The FHA was established in 1934 in order to stimulate employment in the building industry. The idea was to launch at least one program that would encourage building through private capital. Government spending was to be avoided. So, like the Social Security Bill, the FHA was a New Deal intervention that sought to alleviate the effects of the Depression, while at the same time consolidating the rule of capital.

Most of the FHA's work was accomplished in partnership with the Veterans Administration (VA), which was created under the

Servicemen's Readjustment Act (GI Bill) in 1944. The combined workings of these two agencies contributed hugely to the postwar suburban boom. Between them, the two programs consolidated systems of long-term mortgage loans from private lenders for home construction and sale. Interest rates on government-insured loans were below the market rate, and down payments were for 5 percent or less.[47] Through a series of indemnities and protective measures, private lenders were encouraged to invest in residential development. The FHA set minimum construction standards, which helped to create uniform building practices.

All of these measures served to jump-start the building industry in the short term. Following the war, residential construction began to accelerate at an astonishing rate, particularly in the suburbs. Indeed the mechanics of the VA/FHA programs were such that it was often possible to own a family-sized, new suburban house for less than the cost of renting a central city apartment.[48]

The Experience of War and the Suburban Boom

Released in 1946, *The Best Years of Our Lives* was a Hollywood treatment of the experience of veterans in the immediate postwar period. Tapping into a cultural ethos in which returning soldiers were presented as "deserving better" following wartime sacrifices, the film follows the fortunes of three servicemen, each bearing his own combination of physical and emotional scars. One of them, Homer, was played by Harold Russell, an amateur actor who was himself an amputee. Homer returns to a devoted "girl next door," whereas Fred has to get acquainted with the "good-bye bride" he married just before enlistment. He tells Homer and Al: "All I want is a good job, a mild future, a little house big enough for me and my wife. Give me that much and I'm rehabilitated like that!"

Eventually, Fred finds a job taking apart war planes in order to salvage material for prefabricated houses. Al has returned to his position at the bank, where he is put in charge of administering GI loans. After being told to exercise caution in approving loans to GIs who have little collateral, Al gets drunk at a company banquet and makes a bitter speech about how he applied his banking skills to wartime experience:

> One day . . . a Major comes up to me. He says, "Stevenson, you see that hill?" I says, "Yes sir, I see it." He says, "You and your platoon will attack said hill and take it." So I said to the Major, "That operation involves considerable risk. We haven't sufficient collateral." "I'm aware of that," said the Major. "But the fact remains that there's the hill, and you are the guys who are going to take it." So I said to him: "I'm sorry Major. No collateral, no hill." So we didn't take the hill—and we *lost the war.*

This story is met with a hostile and embarrassed silence. But when Al proceeds to make a rousing plea for the bank to take the hill (approve risky loans) in order to ensure America's future prosperity, his colleagues—and his wife—are won over:

> I love the Cornbelt Loan and Trust Company. There are some who say that the old bank is suffering from hardening of the arteries—and the heart. I refuse to listen to such radical talk. I say that our bank is alive! It's generous! It's human! And we're going to have such a line of customers seeking—and getting—small loans, that people will think we're gambling with the depositors' money. And we will be. We'll be gambling on the future of this country.

The (white) pluralist vision of *The Best Years of Our Lives* should be set against the cutthroat competition for living space occurring at the time. Sugrue offers telling statements from two Detroit veterans, one white, one African American:

> Our boys are fighting in Europe, Asia and Africa to keep those people off our soil. If when these boys return they should become refugees who have to give up their homes because their own neighborhood with the help of our city fathers had been invaded and occupied by the Africans, it would be a shame which our city fathers could not outlive.

> We have won the war and are striving to win a complete peace. Each time Negroes are discriminated against, veterans or otherwise, a nail is driven into the coffin of peace.[49]

All of these articulations occurred in the context of a national preoccupation with what was a real housing shortage. The marriage and birth rates had begun a steep rise in 1940 and continued at high levels after the war. When servicemen came home to young families, there was an unprecedented demand for affordable housing that could not be absorbed by the existing market. In 1947, 6 million families were living with friends or relatives, and a half million more families were occupying temporary, makeshift housing. In Chicago, for example, 250 streetcars were converted into dwellings, and many other cities found similar short-term solutions to the shortage.[50] In Detroit, families shared apartments or found shelter in the Quonset huts erected for defense workers.[51] The housing problem received considerable media attention. Anticipating Fordist innovations in house building, *Fortune* magazine mounted a critique of the construction industry, arguing that houses should be manufactured in volume, like automobiles.[52]

The aftermath of the war brought other conditions conducive to mass suburbanization. The GI Bill introduced a new form of veterans' compensation. Instead of lump sum payments, money was awarded for specific purposes—principally for education and home ownership. Most veterans qualified, and education was funded for 7.8 million vets, more than half of those eligible. Also, the VA guaranteed or insured nearly $16.5 billion in loans for homes, farms, and businesses.[53] Both measures were obvious long-term stimulants to economic growth.

The construction industry was an immediate beneficiary of veterans' compensation: "The real estate boys read the Bill, looked at one another in happy amazement, and the dry, rasping noise they made rubbing their hands together could have been heard as far away as Tawi Tawi."[54] Single-family housing starts leapt from 114,000 in 1944 to 937,000 in 1946 to 1,183,000 in 1948 to 1,692,000 in 1950, the latter figure representing an all-time high.[55] Large building companies and large subdivisions began to dominate the market, so that by 1949, 70 percent of new homes were constructed by just 10 percent of the firms.[56]

The best-known suburban building firm of the period was that of Abraham Levitt and his two sons. The Levitts' career spans, and in many respects epitomizes, the period covered by this study. Throughout the 1930s, the Levitts constructed large houses for the upper-middle classes of Long Island. However, their methods were transformed by wartime experience. Throughout the war period, the firm received government contracts for war workers' homes near large military installations. The contracts called for temporary, mass-produced houses to be completed at short notice. The Levitts learned to lay several concrete foundations each day, and then to preassemble walls and roofs.[57]

After the war, the firm transferred mass production techniques to the private market. They continued to apply classic Fordist techniques to produce what essentially became the "Model T" of the postwar suburban house. Construction was divided into a twenty-seven stage process, which began with the foundations and ended with sweeping out the finished product. This "assembly line" approach enabled the Levitts to keep costs down not just by completing some thirty-five houses per day (the equivalent of a new house every fifteen minutes) but by employing mainly nonunionized, semiskilled labor.[58]

When the first Levittown houses came on the market in 1947, they could be rented at $60 per month, with an option to buy after one year. Nearly everyone bought, as the combined cost of mortgage, interest, and taxes was less than the rent. From 1949, renting was no longer an option, and sale prices ranged from $6,990 to $9,500.[59] The Levitts' financing and marketing procedures were ingenious. Using FHA/VA "production advances," the firm was able to offer cheap and simple mortgage arrangements. In two half-hour meetings with a Levitt agent, the buyer would have all legal, financial, and real estate details handled for $10.[60]

The first Levittown (located in Long Island) packaged more than the construction and home-financing processes. The suburb was planned as a "garden community," with winding streets zoned for housing only, as traffic and commercial properties were kept to peripheral strip roads. Pools, playgrounds, and baseball diamonds provided local recreational amenities that supplemented the small individual housing lots. Levittown was an unprecedented success as buyers sometimes queued for days to view their dream home and sign on the dotted line.

In the 1950s, the Levitts purchased 5,750 acres of farmland outside Philadelphia from more than 150 separate owners. There they built more than 17,000 houses, spread across 40 neighborhoods, each averaging about 400 homes.[61] Each neighborhood featured the same general type of house and same-size lots. Exact design and external color varied so that a house of the same shape and color occurred once in 28 houses. Each buyer had to conform to the Levittown regulations of no fences, no color changes, and weekly lawn mowing from April to November. In return, land was donated for churches, schools, and further recreational facilities.

By the time the New Jersey Levittown was built in the 1960s, Levitt executives had become sensitive to charges of homogeneity and began to mix house types, claiming, "Now Lewis Mumford can't criticize us any more."[62] But the overall packaging remained closer to Henry Ford's decree about the Model T: "Any color so long as it's black."[63] And as Herron points out, recent commentators have noted that the homogeneity of suburbia was indeed part of the attraction and that cultural anxieties about uniformity and sameness diminished following the initial wave of postwar critiques.[64] Herron remarks that it is possible to read the "affordable similitude of suburbia" as "liberating" and a signal of the "end to, and seeing through of, the historic discipline and distinctions of culture."[65] The representational success of Levittown lay in the notion that "democracy was achievable" in and through suburban sameness itself.[66]

Following the success of the early Levittowns, large builders in every large metropolitan area produced local versions of the Levitt system.[67] As Lefebvre points out, capital succeeded in achieving growth in the postwar period "*by occupying space, by producing a space.*"[68] Subdividers were confident that there existed a mass market for their houses, and suburban building provided the industrial and geographical component of the postwar reconsolidation of capital.

The need to educate, employ, and house veterans was part of the larger attempt to recover national political and economic stability following fifteen years of Depression and war. Whereas O'Neill celebrates the GI Bill as "one of the brightest things Congress ever did," Woodiwiss sees the Bill and related measures as belonging to "the economy's management of the state."[69] Citing changes in Federal Reserve lending practices, Woodiwiss contends that "although the state had become an integral part of the economy, the government had virtually no control over the economy, which consequently developed more or less just as capital desired."[70]

The Best Years of Our Lives presented GI Loans as evidence of America discovering the need to be generous to traumatized veterans. But in the more prosaic terms of capital stability, the VA/FHA mortgage arrangements for buyers and the financial breaks for builders put *new* housing construction firmly on the recovery agenda. David Harvey has noted the "cultural passion for newness," which had the immediate effect of stimulating both suburban building and suburban transience.[71] Increasingly for suburbanites, an "old house" might refer to any house that had a previous owner. For the transient middle classes, moving from one subdivision to another might now mean choosing from a limited range of designs and buying a newly built house with no ghosts, no memories, and no traces of previous occupation. In Harvey's account, this amounts to a planned obsolescence not unlike the annual model change institutionalized by the car manufacturers.

New houses meant new land deals on the fringes, peripheral commercial developments, increased car sales, and massive road building. The powerful postwar "highway lobby" was dominated by the auto industry and was the "driving" force behind the 1956 Highway Revenue Act, which procured $4.1 billion of federal monies for an interstate highway system.[72] Leading away from the Algiers Motel and its surrounding neighborhoods, these roads were the most tangible act of urban disinvestment and represented a statement that, in the vision of white expansionist America, the future was suburban.

The Postwar Suburban Ethos

All of the processes described earlier belonged to a complex set of political and economic developments that gave suburbia an important role in the postwar reconsolidation of order. In addition, the prioritization of housing and education under the terms of the GI Bill fostered a cultural ethos compatible with the suburban solution. A large number of veterans enrolled in college, married, and began having children all at once. Across the country, universities assembled parks of trailers, huts, or plywood houses for the student families. These campus communities became known as "vetsvilles" or "fertile acres"—the latter recognizing the rising birth rate.

The campus vetsvilles were formative elements in the suburban boom. They were helping to create a class of university-educated men, with wives and children already gaining experience of life in self-contained communities with relatively homogenous populations. Predominantly young, white, and conservative, these veterans were the prototypical "organization men" and "other-directeds" later decried by William Whyte and David Riesman.[73] The war itself was a divide that had been crossed and was now left behind in pursuit of a family and career life marked by success and affluence. The ethos was captured by Sloan Wilson in his popular novel *The Man in the Gray Flannel Suit:*

> The trick is to learn to believe that it's a disconnected world, where what is true now was not true then. . . . Now is the time to raise legitimate children, and make money, and dress properly, and be kind to one's wife, and admire one's boss and learn not to worry.[74]

The corporate liberal settlement depended on the urge to consume and advance in a meritocratic work culture. Leaving the past behind involved a renunciation of progress as *historical:* postwar consumption promised the "progress of products."[75] Success was a matter of individual effort within the organization; consumption of the suburban lifestyle was visible proof of that success. Once adopted, this was a lifestyle that needed defending and maintaining. William Levitt was frank about the political capital to be gained from this process: "No man who owns his own house and lot can be a Communist. He has too much to do."[76]

Of course, mass suburbanization would have been impossible without the staggering increase in credit financing that accompanied the postwar recovery. Americans went from being debt-free individuals at the end of the war to buying 69 percent of their consumer durables on installment credit by 1950.[77] In his 1957 account of the advertising industry, Vance Packard noted the effects of overproduction and credit extension:

> In the early fifties, with over-production threatening on many fronts, a fundamental shift occurred in the preoccupation of people

> in executive suites. Production now became a relatively secondary concern. Executive planners changed from being maker-minded to market-minded. The president of the National Sales Executives in fact exclaimed: "Capitalism is dead—consumerism is king!"[78]

Home ownership increasingly represented both status and real wealth, thus making it a prime focus for the growing credit industry and the ad men. At the same time, it was marketed and sold with the increasingly blasé attitude that was usually attached to smaller commodities. Buying a house was an "everyday activity." Packard cites a study that found (even to the ad men's surprise) that, on average, people looked at less than half a dozen houses before making a purchase, and their home shopping was "lethargic and casual."[79]

Suburbanization proceeded according to market forces, and as Harvey has argued, became the sine qua non of the postwar settlement of late capitalism. It is in these conditions that real suburban growth and suburbia as an imagined place became increasingly mystified; both began to appear natural, predestined, and without historical explanation. Herron argues that the "suburban utopia sited itself just at the vanishing point of history and described a state of social grace beyond which further change would not be required."[80] Indeed suburban space strategically "disappeared" historical reference, thereby (almost) emptying itself of critical possibility. Moreover, the trend toward homogeneity was seen, not as complex and ambiguous, but in terms of enterprise, opportunity, consensus, and other postwar topoi.

Although the surface homogeneity of suburbia may have represented part of its attraction, there were also distinct attempts by builders and home occupiers to create expressions of difference within what was essentially a foreclosed organization of space. Prospective residents selected first the suburb, then a house plan, both from within a fixed range of choices. In order to market new subdivisions and their houses, developers often included a decorated and furnished model among the real houses inhabited by real families. In an exercise equivalent to that of the department store fitting room, you could "try on" houses. Here, difference is a paradox in which you are encouraged to "express yourself" within your very containment. In Joyce Carol Oates's *Expensive People* (1969), subdivisions are theme parks. One subdivision differentiates itself through a range of "Distinctive Modern Colonials," but when one character moves to a similar suburb in another state, her confusion is such that she keeps mistaking her new neighbors for the old ones.

Increasingly suburban growth reflected both the haphazardness of market forces in the image of suburban sprawl and the commodification of living space in the packaged "bedroom communities." Suburban houses were detached, surrounded by yards, and set back from the quiet, noncommercial streets. By its own spatial organization, suburbia masked the postwar political economy within which it flourished. It is in this respect that suburbia was a secret and mystified geography. To suburban residents, whether they inhabited sprawl or thematized subdivision, this was a spatial world in which white WASPish privilege was naturalized and aestheticized.[81] "Difference" centered around house design and size, yard size, the number of feet separating house from pavement, and the number of miles from the city center. In *Expensive People*, Oates's characters identify themselves less in relation to the city than to the other suburban rings, as they drive away from the "miracle mile" to the "proletarian and proudly white Oak Woods," to "Bornwell Pass" with its huge shopping malls, and finally to the leafy subdivisions of the outer rings:[82] "We swung round and drove back home, seeing for ourselves how handsomely Fernwood emerged out of the anonymous miles of suburban wasteland that lay between it and the city."[83]

Suburbia held out the possibility of sustaining social divisions based on the consumption and distribution of space. As already noted, distinctions within suburbia rested on house size and style, yard size, and distance from the city; thus suburbia might mean anything from fringe, tract house sprawl to insular, country club–like subdivisions. Suburban space was being increasingly consumed by a cross-class segment of white Americans. Social divisions within suburbia were based on complex geographical expressions of class position, ethnicity, and consumer status. But regardless of their social position, all suburbanites could differentiate themselves from inner-city dwellers. And questions of race figured increasingly in this division.

Suburbia and the City

While the demography and culture of the campus communities were carrying over into the new packaged suburbs, the cities were also experiencing dramatic demographic and cultural changes, particularly in the North. Rapid industrialization of the South after 1940 had all but ended the dominance of the cotton culture. Mechanization pushed African Americans out of the rural South toward the northern cities. More than a million people left in the 1940s, and another 1.5 million in the 1950s.[84] The Motor City was regarded as a land of promise, as its black population doubled between 1940 and 1950.[85]

These population changes were accompanied by wartime activism. The segregation of the armed services began to come under attack, if only because it impeded the war effort and brought the United States into disrepute abroad. The need for domestic war workers resulted in two million African Americans gaining employment in defense industries and a further two hundred thousand entering federal government jobs. Black union membership had doubled by 1945. Membership in the National Association for the Advancement of Colored People (NAACP) multiplied almost ten times, to reach a half million. In 1942, the Congress for Racial Equality was established and began to experiment with the nonviolent direct action that would become so important during the civil rights movement.[86]

According to Harvard Sitkoff, the mass migration northward gave race an unprecedented national dimension. Moreover it fundamentally altered black experience and culture: "Freed from the confines of a rigid caste system, subject to urban formative experiences, and congregated in numbers large enough to foster group consciousness and solidarity, African Americans developed new norms and beliefs."[87]

Black urban arts, which had an important precedent in the Harlem Renaissance of the 1920s, received new impetus, and black descriptions of northern city life were not long in coming. Already, in 1940, Richard Wright's *Native Son* had appeared, and its portrayal of a brutalized central character, Bigger Thomas, provoked a controversy in black literary circles that lasted well into the 1960s.[88]

The novel gives a representation of a northern slum dweller (Bigger Thomas) by a writer who, like thousands of others, had spent his boyhood in the South, then migrated North. Bigger Thomas was, according to Wright, a composite of many people, all of whom in some way challenged the system under which they lived: "The Bigger Thomases were the only Negroes I know of who consistently violated the Jim Crow laws of the South and got away with it, at least for a sweet brief spell."[89] And by Wright's own account, it was his move to Chicago that enabled him to develop the Bigger Thomas character and commit him to paper:

> The urban environment of Chicago, affording a more stimulating life, made the Negro Bigger Thomases react more violently than even in the South. . . . It was not that Chicago segregated Negroes more than the South, but that Chicago had more to offer, that Chicago's physical aspect—noisy, crowded, filled with the sense of power and fulfillment—did so much more to dazzle the mind with a taunting sense of possible achievement that the segregation it did impose brought forth from Bigger a reaction more obstreperous than in the South.[90]

The impact of this changing urban demography on the postwar politics of space should not be underestimated. In terms of suburbia, American living spaces were returning to trends that had really begun in the 1920s. But the combined effects of New Deal legislation, the GI Bill, southern industrialization, and northward black migration brought a radical acceleration in metropolitan demographic change.

Increasingly, metropolitan politics would produce, and be produced by, the uneven social and economic development of city and suburb.[91] Tax, service, and boundary squabbles were commonplace as more and more suburbs incorporated in order to escape urban municipal power. By 1959, Robert Wood was reporting a proliferation of local, suburban (and actively anti-urban) governmental units—all working confidently to overturn the old adage "You can't fight city hall."[92] Conflicts developed out of the inequalities of tax resources and service needs throughout the new metropolitan areas. The city's tax base dwindled with the exodus of high earners to incorporated bedroom communities. Yet urban service demands remained high as many of these earners continued to commute downtown on a daily basis.

As it was whites who were moving out, it was clear that disinvestment in the city connected to American racism to "produce the ghetto as a Third World Colony in the heart of the American city."[93] In this respect, suburbanization was a spatial expression of racism. White southerners seized upon this as a defense of Jim Crow. For example, one southern white journalist expressed surprise that northerners could believe "that segregation in the South means literally that: *segregation*, the races stiffly apart, never touching. . . . In Charleston and New Orleans, among many other cities, residential segregation does not exist, for example, as it exists in Detroit or Chicago."[94]

The ironies of the situation were not lost on black writers. In "Fifth Avenue, Uptown: A Letter From Harlem" (1960), James Baldwin described the northern version of Jim Crow, some ten years after Richard Wright's remarks about Chicago:

> I once tried to describe to a very well-known American intellectual the conditions among Negroes in the South. My recital disturbed him and made him indignant; and he asked me in perfect innocence, 'Why don't all the Negroes in the South move North?' I tried to explain what *has* happened, unfailingly, whenever a significant body of Negroes move North. They do not escape Jim Crow: they merely encounter another, not-less deadly variety. They do not move to Chicago, they move to the South side; they do not move to New York, they move to Harlem.[95]

In Sugrue's view, residential segregation was "the most visible and intractable manifestation of racial inequality" in Motown.[96] His study of postwar Detroit leaves us with a tangible sense of the "races stiffly apart." And increasingly suburbia is identified with whiteness, the city with blackness. Urban and suburban identities are in part constituted out of these processes. The relationship between social identity and space is a dialectical one. Space is always the historical outcome of social relations. Social relations are reproduced in and through the organization of space.

There is less and less physical contact across divisions of race. We no longer know what might happen should contact occur.

In the Joyce Carol Oates story "How I Contemplated the World from the Detroit House of Correction and Began My Life over Again" (1970), we are given a rebellion against wealthy suburbia that throws its central character into proximity with urban Detroit. An adolescent suburban girl is caught shoplifting and sent to the house of correction. There she meets Princess, a black girl who works breakfast detail and "serves" the suburban girl. As she does so, she mockingly plays the "negro maid": "*Honey you sure you ate enough?*"[97] But at night, Princess gives "suburbia" a beating: "Princess vents all the hatred of a thousand silent Detroit winters . . . she rides across the Midwestern plains on this girl's body . . . revenge on Bloomfield Hills!"[98]

Being of Detroit is to be rendered invisible in the suburban field of vision. For Princess, both the theatricality of the "negro maid" and the beatings are claims to be seen. On her release, the suburban girl retreats in fear and confusion. Contact with Princess leaves her dimly aware of the social distance and violence upon which her space is built. But in the end, she can only long for the luxury of Bloomfield Hills and replace the image of Princess with the signs of safe suburban "having": "I weep for all the money here, for God in gold and beige carpeting . . . and the miracle of a clean polished gleaming toaster and faucets that run both hot and cold water, and I tell them, I will never leave home, this is my home. . . . I am in love with everything here."[99]

This chapter has provided an account of the material and historical processes that underpinned the postwar suburban boom, and I have begun to identify the political and cultural economy of American suburbia in this period In the next chapter, I turn more specifically to selected film, television, and popular novels of postwar culture in order to examine the ideological project of suburbanization. I will argue that, as for Oates's suburban girl, the collective longing for suburbia rested precisely on its action as an instrumental space: safe, mystified, and emptied of historical reference. Specifically, the suburban success story was dependent on a recasting of the American dream as essentially suburban.

3 Spaces of Detachment

Dreaming Ourselves to Be Suburban

> The sides of the bus became transparent. He saw out into the street, the sidewalk and stores. . . . No other seats. Only a strip, a length of planking, on which upright featureless shapes like scarecrows had been propped. They were not alive. The scarecrows lolled forward, back, forward, back. Ahead of him he saw the driver; the driver had not changed. . . . Driving a hollow bus . . . He was the only person on the bus, outside of the driver. The bus actually moved. It moved through town, from the business section to the residential section. The driver was driving him home. When he opened his eyes wide again, all the nodding people had returned. The shoppers. The clerks. The school children.[1]

Philip K. Dick's 1959 novel *Time Out of Joint* is set in the 1950s. Or is it? In the scene described here, Ragle Gumm is having a strange vision in which his safe suburban world can no longer be trusted. "I think we're living in some other world than what we see."[2] We only discover halfway through the novel that Ragle Gumm is not living in a 1950s suburb, but in a war-torn future-scape set in 1998. The "One Happy World" government survives only because Ragle has a gift for plotting missile intercepts. But Ragle has gone mad. He has retreated into a suburban wonderland concocted from his own memories. He sees himself watching Captain Kangaroo on the television while his father lounges on the sofa reminiscing about World War II and his mother does the dishes. So the "One Happy World" government simply follows him there, indulging his fantasy with a stage-managed 1950s suburb. There is a cast of 1,600 brainwashed "lunatics" (the government term for dissidents) to people Ragle's world, to act as family and neighbors. In "Old Town," Ragle is a local celebrity because he wins the daily newspaper puzzle at every attempt.

> Sixteen hundred people, standing in the center of a stage. Surrounded by props, by furniture to sit in, kitchens to cook in, cars to drive, food to fix. And then, behind the props, the flat, painted scenery. Painted houses set farther back. Painted people . . . Sammy (Ragle's son) sitting alone in a classroom, the only pupil.[3]

The purpose of this elaborate spectacle is to keep Ragle happily at its center, filling out the daily puzzle, which is how the government has disguised his missile plotting. Ragle gradually discovers that his world is a sham; he believes something is being done to him. And in a very real sense, something is being done to him. But Ragle's crucial discovery is not that such a world can be constructed but that he has *willed* its construction through his own dreams and memories: "You see . . . they didn't do anything to you, to your mind. You slipped back yourself. You've slipped back now. . . . You keep wanting to go back."[4]

The brilliance of the chimerical suburb is that it is the result of a convenient marriage between Ragle's dreams and the needs of his government. Ragle's everyday living space exists to shelter him from his collaboration in the violence that sustains that same living space. Old Town is a spatial orchestration in which everybody's happy. A brutal regime gets its missile codes, and action against the rebels can continue indefinitely. Ragle remains blissfully ignorant of his *real* time and place and of his part in the war effort. It is only when Ragle glimpses the connection that he begins to experience Old Town as a nightmarish locked ward from which he must escape: "So you recognize that they built for you—and placed you in—a safe, controlled environment in which you could do your job without doubt or distractions. Or the realization that you were on the wrong side."[5]

In *Time Out of Joint* it is the 1950s, and the author's own life world, that become the subjects of science fiction. Positioned from a possible future, Dick reconstructs his present and in so doing places the 1950s suburb under a scrutiny usually reserved for Mars or Oceania. By separating his Old Town from its violent underpinning—that is, by removing that violence to the future—Dick is able to examine suburbia as one flips a coin: heads, it's paradise; tails, it's an extravagant plot hatched against the entire population, with devastating implications for suburban residents and nonresidents alike. Dick critiques the suburb as abstract space, in the Lefebvrian sense of the term. This is mystified and instrumental space, produced and consumed according to the needs of the One Happy World government. And as in Lefebvre, it is space orchestrated to "reduce possibilities and cloak conflicts."[6] But the science fiction genre allows Dick to use *time* to show us the "violence intrinsic to abstraction"[7]—to coax it out of hiding. The utopian suburb and the dystopian civil war are seen at first to exist as opposing entities, seemingly separated by time. But the device of splitting them by the illusion of time travel only serves to reinforce their interdependence.

Dick's storytelling develops the notion of cultural dreaming as suburbia's keeper. In other words, the vitality of suburbia rests in part on the suburban "state of mind" of its inhabitants and aspirants. The willful desire to be there, to erase any knowledge of the social divisions that must be upheld in order to produce suburban space, to somehow forget that one's actions have implications for the city—these are the dream materials of the suburban subject. In *Time Out of Joint*, the suggestion is that one must be mad or dreaming to experience the 1950s suburb as utopian. As soon as Ragle awakes, his world is revealed to be full of contradiction, even dystopian. Dick's fictional unmasking of Old Town is not unlike Bunge's creative study of metropolitan Detroit in *Fitzgerald.* The latter acts as a provocative disturbance of suburban dreaming in its detailed exposure of an "American tradition of geographic ruthlessness [that] contradicts the school boy myths of free settlement in a free land."[8] Bunge even casts himself, the "third person," in his own story. He is the geographer:

> an intellectual with an international reputation . . . [who] harbors a peculiar disrespect for academic life. He considers it both too organized and too conformist. Yet, in the end, he is an intellectual in the humanist tradition. He is calculating, not an emotional personality . . . a fighter against the "ins" for the "outs," a fighter who hopes for eventual personal and social peace.[9]

Whereas Bunge's character is that of the —fighter-intellectual, the fictional Ragle becomes a civil warrior. Once he has understood that his 1950s suburb is a spatial fantasy created by, for, and within a dystopian future, Ragle has lost his political innocence: being at the "center" of utopia means being "on the wrong side." In an act of bittersweet renunciation, Ragle determines to leave Old Town and enter the struggle against those who built it: "That is what civil war means. In a sense it's the most idealistic kind of war. The most heroic. It means the most sacrifices, the fewest practical advantages. . . . I wonder if they'll keep up Old Town . . . without me in the center."[10] A valid consideration indeed, for with Ragle's loss of innocence, Old Town loses its raison d'être.

In *Time Out of Joint,* Ragle has dreamed himself to be suburban, much as Stuart Hall's postmodern world "dreams itself to be 'American.'"[11] In the introduction to this book, I proposed that the postwar period might be seen as a particular kind of precursor to postmodernity—as the last moment strongly marked by a domestic American dreaming, in which *Americans* dreamed themselves to be American. Which Americans? What dream? Suburbanization was part of the immediate postwar recovery, but it also helped to secure the long-term interests of capital. At the same time, suburbia provided the material and figurative location for a particularly spatialized negotiation of American identities and racial exclusion, anti-urbanism, and the American dream.

We dreamed ourselves to be American; we dreamed ourselves to be suburban. Like Ragle, we experienced strange and disconcerting gaps. But let us first examine the space of the dream to which Ragle returned with such deluded dedication. As in Ragle's world, the social divisions that underpinned the changing geography of postwar America were effectively hidden. The material and figurative space of the suburban dream was one in which social detachment, separation, and exclusion might be reframed as attachment, consensus, and inclusion.

Spaces of Detachment

A social critic, in a burst of facetiousness, once referred to the suburbs as "the manicured wilderness." The indifferent generation,

> more than any other generation in American history, has felt a longing for the green spaces. . . . [T]he overriding consideration for the indifferent generation was that of the desire for comfort, for space, for community identity, and for green and growing things.[12]

So writes "Professor Miles Minton," whose untitled manuscript haunts Arthur Douglas's move to suburbia in David Karp's 1957 novel *Leave Me Alone*. Arthur is a Manhattan publisher who gathers his young family to "Oakstown," a New York suburb. Professor Minton's rantings against the "indifferent" postwar generation lend academic credence to Arthur's subsequent resistance to the new lifestyle. But our interest here is in Professor Minton's articulation of the suburban dream. Its components are space, tamed greenery, and a sense of community. These are the qualities of a domain mapped out for a generation that, in the professor's opinion, is characterized by a desire for safety and isolation, a fear of individualism and controversy. Suburban space suits a postwar generation "grimly determined to be happy at any cost" and whose overriding cry is "Leave us alone."[13]

As in Professor Minton's vision, suburbia is the irresistible spatial arrangement in a culture of avoidance. The suburban conception of *lebensraum* is first and foremost a detached one. Specifically, suburbia maps three important spaces of detachment. First, the community itself is detached from the city, from the outward signs of capitalist production and urban life, and from various groupings of nonsuburbanites. Spaces of consumption are accessible, but confined to increasingly large shopping plazas and malls along the suburban strip roads. Then within the suburb itself there is another level of detached spaces. Lawns, driveways, and curvilinear streets make up the important spaces *between* houses. In the suburban imaginary, the desire for detached houses surrounded by large yards has to be inscribed as a longing for consensus, neighborhood, and community. And within the house, the idealized settlement of gender and generational relations was projected onto a vision of room arrangements that afforded both detachment and supervision. Children were afforded a degree of privacy through bedrooms and play spaces, while the garage, tool shed, and study were male preserves. As we shall see, women had a different experience of interior space.

In the postwar period, these were the general "space specifics" of the middle class, suburban production of a range of subjects and locations: husband, wife, children, family, neighbor, community, stranger, other, city. Here were positions, relations, and identities that had to be fashioned out of the detached spaces of suburbia. But for suburbia to work, the whole notion of detachment had to be reframed. In Karp's novel, Professor Minton's complaint is counterpoised by Barney Steel, the realtor who sells Arthur the house in Oakstown. When Arthur is ostracized by the Library Committee following an outburst of "leftish-liberal" sentiment, Barney assumes the role of suburban mentor:

> You see, people don't come out to the suburbs to start fights. They come out looking for friends, for a chance to belong, to get into things. They do it for themselves and they do it for their children. They want to know how they ought to behave so they watch their neighbors and they behave the way they do. . . . You still have the right to be different from your neighbor—provided you keep the difference to yourself.[14]

This is detachment reworked as a healthy avoidance of conflict. The privatized spaces of suburbia might contain the indulgence of minor eccentricities and harmless displays of individualism. But the public spaces of suburbia demand at least the illusion of like-mindedness, camaraderie, and consensus. Border spaces, such as the yard, allow for the safe negotiation of varying degrees of detachment/connection. The yard occupies a curious position in suburban space, and indeed Barney Steel compares his job to the planting of a lawn:

> You put down seeds and if you've put them in the right place at the right time they take and something comes up and it's a good thing to see—a family that's taken hold in a place and is happy there. They're like a tree. They begin to spread out a little. Their kids make friends, they make friends and before you know it, they're part of the landscape.[15]

If Barney Steel's horticultural metaphor was to have any sense to it, then the triadic spaces of *detachment from city, from neighbors, and from family members* had to work in harmony to produce dream suburbanites in dream suburbs. The suburban subject had to move in a world in which detachment and avoidance could be reflected back as attachment or connection.

Detachment and the City

A complex relation of city-suburb has always formed part of our cultural understanding of suburbia and the social order to which it belongs. In the pre- and early industrial "walking city," suburbia already functioned as a spatial expression of social division. For example, the growth of the "living out" system for urban slaves in the antebellum period resulted in many black people seeking to live outside city centers, well away from the masters. In New Orleans, such black districts were termed "suburb sheds."[16]

In northern cities, the suburbs were usually peopled by artisans and laborers, whereas the middle and upper-middle classes sought addresses in the center. As late as 1849, one observer remarked of Philadelphia that "nine-tenths of those whose rascalities have made Philadelphia so unjustly notorious live in the dens and shanties of the suburbs."[17] Twenty years later another commentator, talking about the same city, turned this image on its head: "Drive me . . . out into the suburbs of Philadelphia, and introduce me to the people who own their own homes with gardens and flowers . . . and I will introduce you to the very best people in character as well as in enterprise in our city."[18]

Considered together, these two statements provide a stark example of the changing currency of city-suburb. In both cases, the cultural status of the city-suburb is the result of an inscription of white, middle-class entrepreneurial values on both spaces. Simply put, they give a cultural representation of suburbia as "bad space" becoming "good space"—this in a period when the treble impact of industrial growth, mass immigration, and transportation developments were undermining the status of cities. The postwar suburban dream derived from this historical construct and its corollary that the city was increasingly a "bad space." Postwar anti-urbanism was a determining factor in the suburbanization process and in the success or failure of the suburban dream. Even in its most positive portrayals, the move to suburbia was always tinged with anxiety about the city.

In 1940s Hollywood cinema, crime films and film noir had already established the city as the locus of crime and corruption and a generalized cultural unease. The urban docu-thriller *The Naked City* (1948) had its 1950s incarnations in such films as *Chicago Syndicate* (1955), *Inside Detroit* (1955), and *The Case against Brooklyn* (1958). A racist subtext began to surface with the simultaneous run of "jungle" titles: *Asphalt Jungle* (1950), *Blackboard Jungle* (1955), and *Juvenile Jungle* (1958). In *Blackboard Jungle*'s Manual High School, it was the delinquency of black youth, as well as working-class whites, that was pitted against the values of the white middle-class teacher.

But for the most part, race questions were resisted with telltale vehemence—this at a time when black inner-city populations were growing, and whites were moving outward. Race was a powerful subtext, despite the fact that Hollywood avoided treating it as an overt and decisive issue, just as it avoided the casting of black actors in central roles. Indeed, Sidney Poitier's casting as Miller in *Blackboard Jungle* was unusual. Those films that did take race as the central issue appeared as an aftermath of the war and as American responses to wartime racist ideologies. *Crossfire* (1947) and *Home of the Brave* (1949) treated the issue of racism in the armed forces. Elia Kazan's *Gentleman's Agreement* (1947) sought to expose anti-Semitism through the story of a gentile reporter posing as Jewish. *Pinky* and *Lost Boundaries* (1949) explored the theme of race passing. However, film texts rarely addressed the changing race demography of cities as an issue. Under the rubric (descended from 1930s gangster films) of what came to be known as "Warner Brothers environmentalism," overtly expressed anxieties about the city focused on crime and delinquency, both of which were attributed to urban life.[19]

Blackboard Jungle was first and foremost a juvenile delinquency film, the first of a whole run of 1950s films dealing with youth and urban crime.[20] If anything, the presence of a black delinquent serves to underline white control, for it is Poitier's character who is most easily manipulated by the teacher into becoming a good and highly supervised teenager. Vic Morrow's white, working-class delinquent proves much more intransigent. In *Blackboard Jungle*, it is the space and not the race that proves crucial. Manual High School, with its obvious reference to labor, is an inner-city school. In a contrasting scene, the teacher is shown standing in front of an affluent suburban high school: "For every school like (North Manual), there are thousands like this one." The strains of the national anthem can be heard in the background.[21]

In Sidney Lumet's *Twelve Angry Men* (1957), the unspeakability of race cries out very loudly indeed. We know the defendant is probably Latino but his specific identity is withheld, and the film's preoccupation is with his urban environment. The jurors are confined to a room in the middle of New York; the sounds of the city drift in; the summer heat is stifling. The atmosphere is so unbearable that both characters and spectators are immediately pressed to deal with the city rather than with the case. The jurors who opt for a quick guilty verdict do so because they want to get out of the hot room. The most adamant of the lynching jurors sidesteps the racism implicit in his vote by blaming the New York tenements: "Children from slum backgrounds are potential menaces to society." The defendant is automatically guilty not because he is Latino, but because he lives in a ghetto. The juror's bigotry is spotted by Henry Fonda's liberal architect, who nonetheless also declines to name race in his arguments. Fonda attempts to delay the guilty verdict by citing what *he* sees as the defendant's disadvantage: growing up in a "broken home" in a "filthy neighborhood."

In an earlier film, *City across the River* (1949), delinquency is even more starkly synonymous with urban life, and suburbia is the posited alternative:

> For most of us, the city where juvenile crime flourishes always seems to be "the city across the river." But don't kid yourself. . . . Although this story happens in Brooklyn, it could just as well have happened in any other large city where slum conditions undermine personal security and take their toll in juvenile delinquency. . . . You may be lucky. You may be living where such conditions don't exist.[22]

The message is simple: the city corrupts its youthful inhabitants and, as such, poses a menace to the order of middle America. Even *City*'s Frankie, looking distinctly Latino and played by Peter Fernandez, attempts (but fails) to move to suburbia. In one scene, Frankie shows his gang around the house his parents are trying to buy. Senator Estes Kefauver (the first politician to spot the electoral potential of television) validated Frankie's suburban impulses in his investigation into juvenile crime: "Somehow we must get at the causes, must clean up the conditions, which breed criminals. We will find them, I think, in the slums, where the kids don't have a place to play."[23]

In the previously mentioned texts, there is a clear anxiety about the city, accompanied by an undeniable racist subtext. The source of this anxiety may be traced in part to the particular configuration of American racism in the postwar period. As discussed in chapter 1, black northward migration preceded and accompanied the suburban boom. Under southern Jim Crow laws, segregation was achieved through the institutionalized separation of public facilities—schools, restaurants, transportation, drinking fountains, theaters. In the absence of Jim Crow laws, segregation in the North took on a different spatiality. Less able to formally inscribe white power onto everyday urban spaces, complete separation became a standard white defense. "White flight" from the cities may be seen, at least in part, as a northern response to the absence of organized apartheid.

Zoning, redlining, restrictive covenants, and disreputable real estate practices were all accompanied by the expressly stated wishes of prospective suburban residents to "be with their own kind." The identification of one's own kind took on myriad forms and was influenced by a complex working of race, ethnicity, class, religious background, and place history. For example, in Levittown, New Jersey, Herbert Gans found a community that was predominantly American born, lower-middle class, and religiously and ethnically mixed. Of course, Gans's findings were influenced by his own and contemporary understandings of what all these categories meant. According to his definitions, 75 percent of Levittown was lower-middle class, "culturally speaking;" 37 percent of residents were of Northern European origin; 17 percent Eastern European; 10 percent Irish; and 9 percent Southern European (Italian). Roman Catholics made up 37 percent of the community, Protestants 47 percent, and Jews 14 percent.[24] But in Levittown, as elsewhere, black residence was nonexistent. Levitt defended his policy of black exclusion by stating that "economic realities" forced him to recognize that "most whites prefer not to live in mixed communities."[25] Indeed, 20 percent of Gans's interviewees gave "urban racial change" as one of the reasons for moving to Levittown.[26]

When *City across the River*'s Latino family fails to save their son from delinquency *because* they fail to move to suburbia, the suburban dream is itself upheld. The racist subtext is momentarily rendered in stark simplicity. At the same time, the more acceptable terms of anti-urbanism are upheld. Suburbia is confirmed as safe, clean, and spacious, in contrast to the dirty, dense, and crime-ridden city. Blaming the city contains a kind of displacement or denial of the social divisions underpinning the illusion of consensus. The space is to blame, not its inhabitants—and not the race and class divisions that are lived across the city-suburb divide.

Moreover, in the baby boom period, this version of anti-urbanism had a particular resonance. The physical and mental well-being of children demanded that they have greater access to green and supervised play spaces. Gans's Levittown interviewees listed similar concerns. Former city dwellers (who made up one-third of Levittown's inhabitants) indicated that they were "pushed" rather than "pulled" to suburbia because of worsening "urban conditions": "We just wanted to get out of the city." "The neighborhood is poor for raising children." And urban "dirt, noise and traffic" were often cited.[27] If there is any truth to the notion that we "live through our children," then the suburban dream in the baby boom era provides a case in point. In *Leave Me Alone*, the Douglas family's move to suburban New York is motivated by fears for the children:

> Jimmy and Edwina have a right to rooms of their own, a backyard in which to play, friends in the neighborhood suitable for them to play with, and good schools. You know how disgraceful New York schools are, how badly run down they are, how *unsafe* it is for children in New York streets.[28]

It is under the postwar emphasis of "concern for the children" that anti-urbanism might be reframed as pro-suburbanism. Jimmy and Edwina, apparently having no social life worthy of mention in Manhattan, leap at the chance to live in Oakstown, pressuring the parents to bring forward the moving date. Both children make dozens of friends from the first day; Edwina reverts to calling everyone "pal," "buddy," or "neighbor." Jimmy gets lost but is returned safely by caring neighbors, and Edwina replies to her parents' concern with, "But Mother . . . we're free—we're in the suburbs. What can happen to us?"[29] The Douglas children are soon pronounced to be "well-adjusted" by Mr. Foster, the Oakstown superintendent of schools. Foster extols the virtues of progressive education, which "places stress upon good citizenship, upon social adjustment." Moreover, "progressive education is here to stay . . . because it suits the temper and tastes and the values of the people who pay the taxes and send the children."[30]

What did "adjustment" mean? In Park Forest, Illinois, William Whyte found the defining cultural keywords to be "sociability," "well-roundedness," and "positive thinking." Self-improvement books advocated, "Adjust to the situation rather than change it." Schools taught courses in "family group living" under the "life adjustment" curriculum. One Park Forest wife summed up the ethos: "The best adjusted people are the ones who are constantly adjusting."[31] What critics like Whyte and David Riesman saw as suburban conformity and homogeneity was, in the eyes of the dream, consensus, cooperation, and neighborliness. The avoidance of conflict and of difference resulted in a sense of group purpose and containment that many suburbanites believed was revolutionary in its way—"a Russia, only with money."[32] The cohesiveness of the dream would work its magic on anyone having trouble adjusting. Of a potentially deviant family, a Park Forest devotee states, "I knew they were shy beneath it all. . . . They're part of the gang now. . . . [Y]ou wouldn't know they were the same people."[33]

Whyte is right to point out that the suburbs were a "mecca for thousands of young people moving up and out of the city wards" and at the same time "an education in middle class values."[34] But not all the new residents were from the city. Many war veterans were small-towners unable to reinsert themselves back home. Corporate jobs were metropolitan; the move to the suburbs was an attempt to move toward the opportunities of the city without actually having to live there.

The new subdivisions in no way resembled the small towns left behind. Suburban trees were young and pathetic, no ivy climbed round the door; picket fences were usually forbidden. Yet if small-towners brought an anti-urbanism to the suburban dream, it was one driven by the imagery of idylls left behind. As seen in chapter 2, Hollywood had already mapped out the ethos with a series of small-town films in the 1930s and 1940s. The quintessential provincial hero was Jimmy Stewart, whose lanky awkwardness and country cadence personified the American belief in the safety and innocence of small-town life.

But in William Wellman's *Magic Town* (1947), Stewart plays Rip, a corrupt and cynical city pollster who finds salvation in small-town Grandview. Rip goes to Grandview in the belief that it is mathematically perfect: it has a cross-section of opinion that exactly replicates that of the whole nation. Rip's project is to get accurate poll results quicker than the large opinion poll companies, thereby making himself a fortune. But Grandview works its magic on him, and in the end he rescues the town from the damaging results of his own schemes. In the process we discover that Rip's wickedness is the result of an impoverished urban background. A Grandview friend reminds him of a wartime conversation:

> Once in Italy during the war, a bunch of us got to talkin'. Funny place to be talkin' 'bout home and Ma. The Pipsqueak started it. Then the other fellas got goin'. Turned out they were all from small towns. You were the only city slicker there. You let your guard down that night Rip. You envied those guys. You never knew what it was to have neighbors . . . to have a sense of belonging.

The flight from the city to the suburb may have been fueled in part by the small-town imaginary. Many of the packaged suburbs worked from a limited range of pseudocolonial styles for houses, community sites, and commercial buildings. These were direct borrowings from the New England small town. Other postwar suburbs had actually started out as small towns located near to, but seemingly independent of, the metropolis. The Oakstown of *Leave Me Alone* is one such community, a fact that provides Barney Steel with his main sales pitch:

> It doesn't look like it's going to change in character much. . . . It is middle middle class. . . . At the moment there are a couple thousand

> more new-comers than old-timers there. Back in the thirties, about eight hundred people lived there—now there are, perhaps, three thousand, but don't let the three hundred per cent increase upset you. It has been fairly gradual and there has been room for them all. The town is developing but not quickly—the whole Main Street is perhaps two blocks long. I think it is an attractive little town with pretty nice people . . . and it's still small town enough to have charm. Most of the people there commute, so you'll have all the company you can want.[35]

Here are all the attributes of America's most cherished object of desire—the small town. Oakstown has a Main Street and friendly inhabitants; change is gradual—all this despite its obvious transformation into a commuter belt suburb. Yet the fact that a great many Americans continue to cite the small town as the most desirable living space may testify to the ultimate failure of suburbia to refashion postwar anti-urbanism into a convincing simulation of "Bedford Falls."[36]

Whether or not it finds its origins in the cultural power of the small-town imaginary, anti-urbanism is a crucial component of the suburban state of mind. Detachment from the city and from urban dwellers might be experienced not as exclusion, but as *inclusion* of those "good" Americans prepared to exercise firm but good-natured initiative in pursuit of the American dream. The pioneers of the American way would blaze trails of ex-urban miracle miles, parking lots, and shopping malls—thereby fashioning their identities around the central trope of consumption as the economic, political, and cultural settlement of the postwar capitalist life world. Thus production becomes "the kind of guilt people are freed from if they are able not to remember the work that went into their toys and furnishings."[37] Thereafter they might live in a world open to all, but accessed only through private effort in a meritocracy that denied the very existence of labor and power. The last reminders of the city disappeared in the great suburban denial. The *spatial* removal of the "urban wards," as the locus of class and race conflict, was so effective as to become *temporal.* For if we accept that the past is continually rewritten to address the needs of the present, then suburbia's grossly expressed message to the city was "You're history!" In other words the city was relegated to a newly invented "past."

Detached Houses and the Spaces Between

The most successful postwar dream suburb is one in which the memory of the city has almost disappeared, and the project of simulating the small self-contained community is underway. The focal point of this process is the *neighborhood.* In *Leave Me Alone*, Barney Steel tells Arthur that this should be his most important consideration in moving. For Barney, the flight from the city and even the house itself are secondary. It is the spaces between houses that make or break the suburban lifestyle:

> I believe that people should choose a neighborhood before they choose a house. People go about this business of buying a house ass-backward, if you'll excuse the expression. After all, you don't stay in a house twenty-four hours a day. You have to come out of it, you have to look out of the windows, you have neighbors, schools, shopping—what surrounds your house is just as important as what surrounds you inside.[38]

The suburban dreamscape is one in which single family houses are set back from the street, surrounded by well-kept lawns, but within sight of similar lawns and houses. The demand is for a series of detached spaces, which are nonetheless in contact with each other. Like-mindedness and community cooperation are the physical and emotional comforts of the subdivision.

Barney finds Arthur a long, rambling ranch house surrounded by large and irregular shaped grounds. Within the first week, every member of the family has several neighborly encounters. The children are playing in each other's yards, under a kind of "sisterhood of supervision" provided by the neighborhood mothers. Eleanor is visited by the Welcome Wagon—neighboring women bearing promotional gifts and discount cards. Eleanor is not offended by their commercial affiliations because the visitors are "charming women with no sense of being under pressure to rush off. They were perfectly willing to stop and chat and have tea."[39] During his "weekend chores," Arthur is helped by a neighbor when he has to carry an old rug to the rubbish bin. The neighbor tips him to the value of saving old rugs as lining for the car trunk:

> When you sell a car watch the salesman. . . . He checks the trunk. If the trunk is clean, chances are he'll think you've taken care of your car. You'll get a better price for it. I always average a hundred bucks more in trade-in for my car than my brother-in-law—even on identical models. I change the carpeting in my trunk—he doesn't.[40]

For both Arthur and Eleanor, these initial contacts underline their new positioning as suburban consumers. Detached from the world of production, they are now living in the domain par excellence of postwar consumption. They are the "landed consumers"[41] for whom the commodification of living spaces and suburban lifestyles masks the divisive social geography that underpins those lifestyles. Relationships of exclusion are replaced by the "imaginary social relations" created and maintained by consumer culture.[42] The salient feature of suburbia as produced space was that it created a spatial world in which middle-class privilege was naturalized and aestheticized.

Some ethnic and working-class groups made it into suburbia or created their own suburbs. Their presence was interpreted by the WASPish majority as both a form of social enfranchisement and proof of dream suburbia's "melting pot democracy." Where unable to exclude or openly express a desire to exclude, WASP suburbanites might reinscribe difference as so many "little differences" or eccentricities. For example, in Bernard Malamud's *A New Life*, Levin's new neighbors attempt to hide their anti-Semitism behind remarks about his "urbanity," his having a beard in a "beardless town." The significance attributed to "small differences" serves to reframe the narrow and essential WASPishness of the dream subject of suburbia. In Park Forest, working-class residents were renamed as "people who work with their hands more than with their heads."[43] One of Whyte's interviewees tells him that every block has someone who "has not had all the advantages some people have had."[44] And residents noted with pride their ability to socialize "marginal" types into the white-collar, Republican-voting ethos of the community. Whyte reports that many urban Democrats switched party upon arrival in the suburb.

The existence of blue-collar and ethnic suburbs and the presence of some ethnic groups in suburbia encouraged the suburbanite belief that residence in suburbia was open to all. Frank

Capra's *Bailey Park* was a working-class subdivision built for what the villainous Potter called a "discontented lazy rabble" of "garlic eaters." George Bailey defends his housing scheme in corporate liberal terms:

> You're all businessmen here. Doesn't it make them better citizens? Doesn't it make them better customers? You said . . . they had to wait and save their money before they even thought of a decent home. Wait, wait for what? . . . You know how long it takes a working man to save $5000? Just remember this Mr. Potter—that this rabble you're talking about—they do most of the working and paying and living and dying in this community. Well is it too much to have them work and pay and live and die in a couple of rooms and a bathroom?

Anticipating the more liberal Park Foresters, Capra's hero believes suburbia should be opened to the working classes because it will make them more like the middle classes. This is a reformulation of "melting pot" ideals alongside a "meritocracy" of suburbia. It was the spaces between houses that gave inhabitants the assurance that suburbia was an *everyday* manifestation of democracy—and as such, the quintessential space of American identity in the postwar world. The yards and streets were for barbecues, sharing household tools, trick-or-treating on Halloween, shoveling snow, and sitting on the front porch. These rites were the great levelers: "Every man, no matter his rank, was every man's assumed equal, very relaxing. . . . Lawn mowing went on and on. . . . Let the sun shine a minute and Ed Purtzer . . . rolled the mower out of the garage . . . then shaved his lawn . . . until it resembled his own stiff haircut."[45]

Suburban unity was upheld by the simple acts of planting flowers on a court's communal grass island or by holding "beatnik parties," where everyone wore black and invented an agreed suburban image of Greenwich Village. When suburbanites went home after these gatherings, they disappeared behind picture windows like every other picture window. They might look out and imagine that every family in its deepest privacy was like their own. Family life was rendered less lonely.

The yards and sidewalks and adjoining windows formed an important network of lifelines out of the detached household. In its interior spaces, the family was all-important and rested on the idealized subjects of wife and mother, benevolent and hard-working father, and "well-adjusted" children. The "freedom" of suburban privacy meant that suburban subjects had to be self-scrutinizing and self-monitoring. If discomfited by loneliness, or by fears of deviance and inadequacy (i.e., failing to be a dream subject in a dream suburb), family members might seek comfort and joy in those same spaces between houses that released them to find their counterparts in the neighbors.

Women sat in each other's kitchens; men rode the commuter train together and exchanged gardening tips at the borders of their property. Vaguely felt worries and resistances relating to the subject positions on offer—wife, mother, husband, father—might be defused by these collective meetings in the spaces that contained and created those positions. The group tagging of a few problem wives or husbands on the street might bolster the security of everyone else. When Liz Bonner commits adultery in Philip K. Dick's *Puttering about in a Small Land* (a non–science fiction novel written in the late 1950s to late 1960s), she tries to defuse a frightening sense of deviance and sudden isolation by looking out of her living room window and conjuring images of her neighbors.

> In the next house the living room lights were on, and so were other lights in other living rooms, in the houses across the street. A porch light shone more brightly than the others; she saw, on that family's front walk, a tricycle and a toy wagon. Lying there, she listened to radios and voices. They're sitting around the living room . . . watching TV and darning socks. . . . Mrs. Felton is saying that Tide soap is on sale at fifty-nine cents for the giant size. . . . What time is it? Nine o'clock? What's on TV?[46]

TV had a great capacity to bind the subdivision's detached spaces. Knowing your neighbors might be watching the same program at any given time was a suburban comfort particular to the 1950s and 1960s, the era of network television. As Dick's novel progresses, both Liz and Roger succumb to what Whyte termed the "misery of the deviate."[47] They make mistakes, they fragment, and they project their psychic state onto the neighborhood. Liz imagines the houses decaying and cracking; her neighbors turn to stone statues. She sees that the rose bushes grow over the houses, "weigh them down, cause them to collapse. And the stone statues gaped. 'We have got old watching,' the statues said. 'We could not look away.'"[48] This is suburban watching. We all watch each other. One person's mistake brings about the decay of everyone else. There is a moral obligation for each individual to keep the suburban dream alive. This is how we bridge the spaces of detachment.

Spaces of Femininity: Detachment and the Family

When suburbanites closed their door at night, they turned to face an interior space that must be the expression of the close-knit and well-adjusted family of the postwar world. Whereas living rooms and family rooms designated communal spaces, bedrooms, dens, and studies reinforced cherished notions of privacy and circumscribed roles. The orchestration of interior space was such that a negotiation of togetherness and detachment helped to delineate the various working parts that constituted the well-oiled family machine. Fixed and stable gender relations—the sine qua non of middle-class patriarchal order—found its spatial projection in suburban house design. Here women alone were denied private spaces. Living rooms, kitchens, and the "open plan" designs underlined woman's simultaneous and essential centrality and marginality. Communal spaces fixed woman's position and ensured the cohesiveness of the family unit, which surrounded that position. In their individual roles and as part of the whole, members of the dream family might know nothing of the intimate workings of power in their midst.

For women, the demography of suburbia was markedly different from the national picture. Nationally, there was a brief decline in women's employment at the end of the war. Then the numbers of working women began to rise and continued to do so throughout our period. Moreover married women and women with children featured prominently in the increase. Yet in suburbia, "there was a higher fertility rate than in the cities; and 9 percent of suburban women worked, as compared to 27 percent in the population as a whole."[49] Postwar representations of idealized femininity began to attach to suburban spaces. Following wartime upheavals in gender relations, there was, not surprisingly, a renewed emphasis on the notion of separate spheres for men and women. If the ideal 1950s woman was a stay-at-home wife and mother, then suburbia provided a perfect location.

The notion of suburbia as a "space of femininity" was one that carried two conflicting articulations of a feminine dream subject. In images reminiscent of the Victorian period, women were the angels of the suburban haven—subservient, selfless, and family oriented. At the same time, suburban women were a sisterhood, creating a daytime culture that validated women's ability to shape a space that reflected their strong presence within it.

The suburban sisterhood belied a demography that can only be seen as an idealized adaptation of the patriarchal order to the postwar context. The essentialist identification of women as homemakers was indispensable to the wider social and political economy. In this respect, the material and figurative spaces of suburbia served as a hothouse in which the postwar renegotiation of classed gender positions was mobilized. As Mary Beth Haralovich has pointed out, the suburban homemaker was "marginal in that she was positioned within the home, constituting the value of her labor outside of the means of production. Yet she was also central to the economy in that her function as homemaker was the subject of consumer product design and marketing, the basis of an industry."[50]

For suburban women, detachment from the city was total. Existing outside paid employment, trips downtown were rare and typically organized by men. A show, an anniversary dinner,—these were the carefully circumscribed urban pleasures offered to women. Even shopping, that last ticket to downtown spaces, gradually shifted to suburbia with the commercial development of shopping malls. In the postwar dreamscape, women were being asked to make a tradeoff. They would be the keepers of suburban space, in return for renouncing the world of production and embracing that of consumption.

However, *within* suburbia, the articulation of feminine space was less than straightforward. Here, the negotiation of detachment-connection became more complex and confusing than at any other point. Many postwar suburban households were organized around the "open-floor plan." In this spatial arrangement, women could remain in constant visibility to husband and children while fulfilling the roles of wife, mother, cook, cleaner, and consumer of a vast array of household products: "The northern two-thirds of the house was one large arena comprising kitchen, den, dining room and living room. There were no true divisions or doors, and the effect was one of a carpeted stadium enclosed in glass, yellow-stone, grass-clothed walls."[51]

In these carpeted stadia, ideal middle-class housewives must move with grace and authority. They should never be seen engaged in the drudgery of housework, yet these wide-open spaces were immaculate and peopled by neat and well-dressed families. The kitchen, a central location of women's labor, was nonetheless a space made available to other family members. The father of the family might separate his functions as breadwinner and man about the house by having access to the partitioned spaces of the study, the garage, or the tool room. Children could create secret spaces away from adult supervision in their bedrooms or in the far corners of the yard and street. But the wife and mother must fulfill all her roles at once, in wide-open spaces of display. To catch a glimpse of woman in her domain is to see someone who is simultaneously in one continuous space, an object of desire, a domestic servant, and a caregiver. The task of the house designer was "to provide houses that helped his clients to indulge in status-conscious consumption . . . to display the housewife as a sexual being."[52]

Given the radical simultaneity of all her functions, it is not surprising that the ideal suburban wife is rarely imagined as sloppy or out of sorts. Nowhere does the suburban woman look smarter than in the numerous TV sitcoms of the period. For example, in *The Adventures of Ozzie and Harriet* (1952–56), *Father Knows Best* (1954–62), *The Donna Reed Show* (1958–66), *Leave It to Beaver* (1957–63), and *The Dick Van Dyke Show* (1961–66), the female leads are stylishly dressed, typically in tight-waisted, full-skirted styles. One episode of *Father Knows Best* shows Margaret running to change out of her cleaning clothes before her husband gets home. Her daughter shouts out the warning, "You can't let Father see you like this!"[53] In our own period, the 1950s sitcom moms (played by the original actresses) meet their 1990s counterpart in an episode of *Roseanne*. The moms are at first offended by Roseanne's incarnation of sitcom motherhood until she tells them she earns $1 million per episode. At this point, the moms redirect their anger at the producers of the original suburban sitcoms, who they claim undervalued them as actresses *and* as the characters they played.

The postwar exception in sitcom representations of women was Mary Tyler Moore as Laura in *The Dick Van Dyke Show.* She appeared later than many of the previously mentioned shows, and her looks and style bore a striking resemblance to Jackie Kennedy, who was at that time showing the nation how to look good *and* redecorate the White House. Jackie Kennedy's televised tour of the refurbished mansion was a *grand theatre* validation of the unsung efforts of the nation's homemakers. At the same time, the program was an indication of the power of television, not only as a source of influential texts in the postwar settlement but as the "hearth" of suburbia: "Something had happened—perhaps something as simple as television . . . to remove the pain and sting of absence from the center, from the metropolis."[54]

Alongside Jackie (and in humble style more closely aligned with the tradition of American "homesteading"), the sitcom moms invited the entire nation to dream of a life in suburbia. Their interiors were cool on hot days, cozy when the snow fell, clean and simply furnished. These images, presided over by high-profile, yet unthreatening women encouraged the belief that a family-centered prosperity was open to all in the affluent 1950s. Indeed the underlying suggestion was that there *was* no other lifestyle in America. In the sitcom suburbs, the city is never named, never seen.

Most of the action centers on home and family. Although the opening credits often show the father leaving for work, the stories seem to unfold during evenings and weekends. This ensures the father's continual presence: he is relaxed, unfettered by work worries, and appears as a wise and benevolent ruler. Minor squabbles and childhood rites of passage are presided over by the father and supported by his deferential wife. When more serious problems arise, the parenting is done exclusively by the father, who talks to the children in their bedroom or summons them to his study. Mom waits anxiously in the kitchen and is then given patient guidance and reassurance by her husband.

Action outside the house is limited to comical misadventures involving neighbors, shops, or school. The most threatening character to appear in these sitcoms is teenager Eddie Haskell,

Wally's greaser-coiffed buddy in *Leave It to Beaver*. Eddie's smart-talking prankishness is easily contained by Wally and Beaver, whose healthy family environment is too solid to be undone by the soft delinquency of suburbia. Eddie Haskell resembles Grady Metcalf, the delinquent in *Rally Round the Flag, Boys!* who was "not the lean, hard, Sal Mineo type. He was more on the well-fed, spongy side. The tenement that spawned him was a $40,000 ranch house."[55]

As we have seen, detachment existed for men through the careful delineation of masculine spaces. The paterfamilias had the study, the garage, the tool room, the barbecue pit, the yard, and the meeting rooms of whatever civic organization he chose to join. For women, a degree of independence, privacy, and access to other women had to be negotiated within communal or public areas. Indeed a certain "field of negotiation" was opened by the very tradeoff that took women out of the city and work and made her "queen for the day" in suburbia. What the TV sitcoms failed to show was how the positioning of women as consumers, and the real technology of household appliances, gave women time and created an unexpected suburban dream space: that of a daytime sisterhood.

While men commuted their hours away, the "fabric of the community" might be woven by collectivities of women and their children. Shared childcare might be reinforced by coffee-klatch groups, baby showers, and Tupperware parties. Suburbia was by day a women's community; it was a "sorority house with kids," a "womb with a view."[56] "You don't find as many frustrated women in a place like this. . . . We gals have each other"; "the man who enters suburbia during the day can make the female group feel that here comes trouble."[57]

This introduces a troubling contradiction in the construction of suburban femininity. The woman who spends too much of her newly won free time with friends or engaged in community activities may be forsaking her part of the bargain. There are numerous texts in which women (to the dismay of their husbands and the marketing men) find a new lease on life in public activities. Eleanor Douglas in *Leave Me Alone*, Betsy Rath in *Man in the Gray Flannel Suit*, and Grace Bannerman in *Rally Round the Flag, Boys!* all join church groups, school committees, and a host of related charitable and civic organizations.

Arthur Douglas fears that Eleanor's conversion to suburban "participation" has undermined her fundamental positioning as wife and mother: "Eleanor and the children had already been woven into the fabric of community life so completely that they lost a little of their identity—even to Arthur."[58] Grace Bannerman fills her schedule with meetings, lectures, doorstep campaigns, fund-raising, amateur theatricals, and parties. Husband Harry rarely sees her and laments the bygone days in their Greenwich Village apartment when the two young lovers sat up late drinking wine and listening to Rodgers and Hart records. In other words, Grace is no longer fulfilling her sexual duties:

> For Grace and Putnam's Landing, it was love at first sight. Almost before she was unpacked, she had another baby, bought a large brown dog, joined the PTA, the League of Women Voters, the Women's Club, the Red Cross, the Nurses Aids, the Mental Health Society, and the Town Planning Commission. "How wonderful," she would cry . . . "to live in a town with real community spirit."[59]

When Grace begins to wonder if she should cut down on her activities and create more time for her husband, her mother tells her: "NO! . . . Don't you cut down one tiny bit! Just remember that we women have to make a life of our own, because men are only interested in ONE THING!"[60]

But for every Grace Bannerman, there is a Betsy Rath, who is exhausted by the social demands of neighborhood and community: "It's tense and frantic. . . . Tom and I are tense and frantic . . . and I wish to heaven I knew why."[61] Betsy gradually retreats further into interior spaces, foregoing female friendships with neighbors. Her first decisive act is to get rid of the television: "Bad for the kids . . . instead of shooing them off to the television set, we're going to sit in a family group and read aloud. . . . We've been having too much passive entertainment. . . . No more homogenized milk. . . . We're going to save two cents and shake the bottle ourselves."[62]

Betsy's "shakeup" of the home front (aided by an inheritance of valuable property) entices Tom away from the executive lifestyle and back to the domestic fold, where he will spend more time being a male role model to his son. Tom tells his workaholic boss that family comes first and is rewarded with the directorship of the company "mental health committee." The post is highly paid, but without the commute and long hours. This releases Tom and Betsy to develop their land into a profitable packaged suburb. Betsy's success is dependent upon keeping to her "space" and making it more attractive to Tom. Suburbia itself has been improved by Betsy's acceptance of her role within it. This has a civilizing effect on the people around her.

The civilizing role of women in suburbia is an oft-repeated message in 1950s popular culture. Two extreme examples are the films *I Married a Monster from Outer Space* (1958) and *The Next Voice You Hear* (1950). In the former, it is the wife who humanizes the instincts of the alien invader, thereby restoring civilized manhood to her husband and rescuing the rest of the human race. In *Next Voice*, God contacts humanity through the radio and speaks to suburbia first. Nancy Davis is the suburban wife married to a depressive, potentially violent working-class man who has not yet learned to appreciate the good life. Nancy tunes him into God and the benefits of family and suburbia.

The marketing men were quick to play on the dilemma of the suburban housewife with too much leisure time: "If you tell the housewife that by using your washing machine, drier, or dishwasher she can be free to play bridge, you're dead! . . . You are just rubbing her the wrong way when you offer her more freedom. Instead you should emphasize that the appliances free her to have more time with her children and to be a better mother."[63] A 1957 article in *Industrial Design* magazine cited by Haralovich betrays a more obvious male anxiety about suburban woman's free time. The *Design* writer suggests that women will use their leisure time badly by playing bridge, watching TV, or indulging in the "lonely togetherness of telephone gossip." He urges designers to "fill leisure hours . . . with objects that are esthetically pleasing."[64]

Eleanor Douglas, Grace Bannerman, and Betsy Rath all attempt to shape their identities across the two contradictory spaces of femininity: the ideal wife and mother in the home *and* the active member of a suburban sisterhood. In a sense the dream subject of suburban woman is a resolution of these two positions—one that contains both, but privileges the former. In other words, suburban woman might care about her friends and participate in her community, as long as she knows that husband, children, and home set the true parameters of her field of action and thus of her very identity.

This point is made more forcibly when a central female character steps beyond the more acceptable bounds of community involvement. In *The Thrill of It All* (1963), it is her position as dutiful housewife/consumer that leads Beverly Boyer (Doris Day) into the absolutely forbidden territories of a highly paid job, the city, and television broadcasting. Upon meeting the director of the "Happy Soap" company, Beverly unwittingly displays all the attributes of a perfect advertising mannequin. Her remark that Happy Soap "saved my life today" earns her a $1,500 per week job *because* she is a dedicated housewife and caring mother. She becomes the new "Happy Girl," replacing "Spot Checker," a Jayne Mansfield wanna-be, who is deemed not wholesome enough to sell a family soap. Beverly's claims that "I'm not an actress—I'm a housewife" are met with an increase in pay and the remark "it's so refreshing to hear someone speak so naturally and so honestly about a product." Beverly promises husband Gerald that her new life won't interfere with her "wifely duties," a promise that of course she is unable to maintain. The film ends with Beverly completely renouncing her career and opting for another baby. She succumbs to Gerald's assertion that "I'm the kind of husband who likes to *see* his wife. . . . I wanna see her and I wanna see her in person, and often!" But along the way, Beverly demands to know what happened to her "rights as a woman" and tells Gerald that "the PTA and home-bottled ketchup are not very fulfilling."

In her numerous incarnations as suburban housewife, Doris Day frequently subverts the gender order she is ostensibly trying to defend.[65] Although the plot is invariably resolved in favor of patriarchal order, Day's performances fueled an alternative dream of woman as power broker demanding a voice and greater access to public spaces. As we have seen, suburban spaces of femininity were complex and contradictory. Domestic interiors reinforced idealized notions of gender and family, with woman as the civilizing heart of the suburban household. But for the dream suburb to work, the public space of suburban sisterhood constituted an area of negotiation that had to be tolerated and defused.

We Can Build You

I have outlined a triad of detached spaces that, in their material and figurative workings, sought to define the dream subject of suburbia. Detachment from city, from neighbors, from family members—these were the features of Ragle Gumm's mad longings in *Time Out of Joint.* However, and with particular reference to the neighborhood and the family, the notion of detachment works by summoning its opposites—connection and unity. The varied workings of detachment and connection ensured that suburbia was never simple: it was complex and misleading. The difficulty of the suburban dream was to navigate white, middle America across the three levels of detachment and to make suburbia look simple, omnipresent, and incontestably *American.*

The space of Ragle Gumm's dream was one in which detachment, separation, and exclusion might be reframed as attachment, connection, and inclusion. The illusion of unity and consensus permeated the farthest reaches of the suburban dream garden. The social divisions that underpinned the produced space of suburbia were thus normalized, mystified, and ultimately made to disappear. But the success of suburbia rested upon this collective cultural dreaming. The ideal suburban subject is either mad or asleep. Should sanity or wakefulness return, the dreamscape reveals its profound irony, its inescapable contradiction, its necessary violence.

In *Time Out of Joint,* the production of space is, for a time, sufficient to produce a willing subject. But in *We Can Build You,* written less than two decades later, Philip K. Dick is unable to sustain the imagined power of produced space in and of itself. The suburban dream is on shakier ground, in this case, the moon. People are refusing to colonize the moon, despite the promise of climate-controlled subdivisions and reassuring tract houses. In an ominous progression from Ragle Gumm's story, the first inhabitants of the moon suburb must be simulacra. No "real" human being is fool enough to settle there:

> Can you produce simulacra that are friendly-like? . . . I could use a number of them designed to look exactly like the family next door

> . . . . Colonization has to begin. . . . The Moon is barren and desolate. . . . It's difficult, we've found, to get anyone to go first. . . . You'd give them (the simulacra) names. . . . Good old homey American names . . . They're going to the Moon; they're not afraid of the cold and the lack of air and the empty, barren wastes. . . . And as more and more people got hooked . . . you could quietly begin to pull the simulacra back out. The Edwards family and the Jones family and the rest—they'd sell their houses and move on. Until finally your subdivisions, your tract houses, would be populated by authentic people. And no one would ever know.[66]

In *Time Out of Joint*, the suburban subject carries the dream and longs to return to the space that he believes exists. The 1950s suburb is then constructed as a hoax, one that keeps Ragle in his real place, as servant to a dystopian future. In *We Can Build You*, there is no such dream, no such collective cultural longing. In order to colonize the moon as Earth's suburb, it is Ragle Gumm himself who must be invented. As the dreaming subject/the subject who believes in the dream can no longer be found, simulacra must be used. Taken together, the two novels signal a failure of the suburban dream and a gradual fragmentation of the suburban dream subject.

4 Critiques of Suburban Conformity

> Even while you read this, whole square miles of identical boxes are spreading like gangrene.
>
> Keats, *The Crack in the Picture Window*, quoted in Jackson, *Crabgrass Frontier*, 3

> Suburbs encircled the city's boundaries like an enemy and we thought of them as a loss of privacy, a cesspool of conformity and a life of indescribable dreariness in some split-level village where the place name appeared in the *New York Times* only when some bored housewife blew off her head with a shotgun.
>
> Cheever, quoted in O'Neill, *American High*, 23

Just as John Cheever's suburban short stories were originally published in *The New Yorker*, the first stones cast at the suburban picture window came from the urban intelligentsia. Suburbia's material and figurative detachment from the city made it an easy target for cosmopolitan critics. In this chapter I argue that in the context of the mass culture debates of the 1950s suburbia provided the spatial imaginary for the culture critics' assault on American conformity. Moreover the tendency to draw on an image bank of tract houses and subdivisions in discussions of conformity produced a critical cul-de-sac for *both* the detractors and the defenders of suburbia. These debates gained some complexity with the publication, in 1963, of Betty Friedan's *The Feminine Mystique*. Friedan delivered an important, early feminist critique of suburbia that began to add individual women's accounts to the language of the mass culture debates. Finally, this chapter examines a selection of popular cultural texts for their representations of deviance and dysfunctional families. I argue that these texts signaled not just cold war anxieties, but *domestic* fears about cultural difference that began to disturb the problematic of suburban conformity.

Cultural Criticism and Suburban Conformity

An early and influential articulation of the problem of conformity can be found in the realm of cultural criticism. In 1952, the *Partisan Review* held a symposium titled "Our Country and Our Culture." Attended by twenty-five "intellectuals" (primarily literary critics and sociologists), the symposium put forward the following proposition: "American intellectuals now regard America and its institutions in a new way. Until little more than a decade ago, America was commonly thought to be hostile to art and culture. Since then, however, the tide has begun to turn, and many writers and intellectuals now feel closer to their country and its culture."[1]

In their opening statement, the *Review* editors include a series of quotations to illustrate the arrival of this new optimism. A 1937 quote from Dos Passos's *The Big Money* states grimly that the American preoccupation with property and profits precludes a lively culture. But this is followed by a 1947 quote from Edmund Wilson proclaiming America to be the most politically advanced country in the world, a fact that had led to a "revival of democratic creativeness."[2] The origins of this sea change were political, economic, even military in nature. America was no longer dependent on Europe; Europe was dependent on America. Indeed America was now the "protector of Western civilization": the "intrinsic and positive value" of American democracy was pitted against "Russian totalitarianism."[3] As a result, writers and artists no longer saw themselves as rebels or exiles—"on the contrary, they want very much to be a part of American life."[4] The statement's flow of cold war nationalism is disturbed by only one central concern: the impact of mass culture. The threat of the culture industry is that it "removes the mass of people from the kind of art which might express their human and aesthetic needs."[5]

With few exceptions, conference delegates agreed with the editorial statement, and their responses echoed the statement's reconsideration of the virtues of American democracy.[6] Effectively, the corporate liberal settlement received the intellectuals' stamp of approval. The result was a renewed appreciation of a national culture that was, as Andrew Ross states, "defensively constructed against foreign threats and influences, and internally strengthened by the declaration of a consensus, posed in the form of a common and spontaneous agreement about fundamentals."[7]

Although the Institute for Social Research had moved back to Germany in 1949, the preoccupations of the Frankfurt School are visible in these debates. But where the Frankfurt School held to a critique of capitalism in order to mark the connection between mass culture and the de-politicization of the people, the *Partisan Review* debates focused on the American "excess of democracy" and the consequent threat to the social authority of the urban, academic intelligentsia. Indeed, Ross sees the intellectuals' position as belonging to a hegemonic moment in which a liberal-pluralist model was posited against the "broad class analysis of the thirties and the radical elitism of the left (Frankfurt School) analysis of mass society."[8] Perhaps this was a system to be cherished after all. Sidney Hook argued that "the democratic West will require the critical support, the dedicated energy and above all, the intelligence, of its intellectuals if it is to survive as a free culture."[9]

However, the cultural authority of the intellectuals was diminished by the workings of mass culture and its corollary of domestic conformity. Conformity was cited as a disturbing side effect of a generally beneficent American democracy. Only Mills and Howe eschewed the symposium contributors' preoccupation with "excessive democracy" and named capitalism as the source of American conformity: "I would of course impute the leveling and the frenzy effects of mass culture in this country not to 'democracy' but to capitalist commercialism which manipulates people into standardized tastes and then exploits these tastes and 'personal touches' as marketable brands."[10]

The *Partisan Review* symposium put the issue of mass culture and the threat of conformity squarely on the cultural and literary map, and these debates were to exercise the urban and academic intelligentsia throughout the decade. The same questions and anxieties were rehearsed again and again: Was "hyperdemocracy" producing a "populace of dopes"?[11] Could American intellectuals retain their critical authority over cultural products in an era of mass and popular entertainment? Was mass conformity the inevitable product of the democratization of culture? Ultimately, the corporate liberal solution was to posit pluralism and consensus as the saving topoi of the postwar settlement. As Ross states, the best way to "contain potential antagonisms in society and legitimize the maintenance of existing inequalities is to construct or create differences, in order to *signify* pluralism, and thereby advertise social diversity."[12] Thus was the American cultural apparatus kept firmly aligned with the postwar *pax capitalistica.*

It was in the context of these debates that critical attention turned to suburbia. A landscape of mass-produced, uniform tract housing and low-brow packaged subdivisions was not conducive to a culture committed to containing and concealing difference through the creation of "diversity." If mass culture encouraged conformity, suburbia appeared to provide the necessary geography. Already in the *Partisan Review* symposium, one contributor made the connection: "In today's American democracy the flow of taste, manners and ideas seems to circle rather idly and shallowly at the suburban level."[13]

Many contributors cited television, the hearth of suburbia, as the most worrying aspect of mass culture. Suburbia provided the "Great Audience"[14] of privatized viewers whose identical homes were "strung together like Christmas tree lights on a tract with one central switch."[15] Television provided the "window on the world": simulated outings that only reinforced the suburban culture of sameness and avoidance.[16] Although suburban viewers may have enjoyed a sense of spectatorship that was simultaneously private and collective, intellectuals lamented the lost opportunity to direct middle and low-brow spectators to those urban box offices sanctioned by the cultural elite.

As the decade progressed and the debates heated up, critics poked their telescopes out of Manhattan high-rise blocks and leaded Ivy League windows and looked for the signs of conformity in distant suburbs. Together with the first novelists of suburbia, they produced a critique from *without* and set the terms of an argument that persists to this day.[17] Focusing on the spatial, architectural, and demographic uniformity of the mass-produced suburbs, critics posited that such uniformity must inevitably create conformity.

With its rows of tract houses, its army of commuting men, and its daytime "femininity," suburbia was the breeding ground of David Riesman's "other-directed" Americans, of William Whyte's "organization men."[18] In Riesman's view, the move to suburbia is a search for new "frontiers of consumption." The cultural longing for "nice" neighbors in "nice" neighborhoods with "good" schools and shopping facilities betrays the importance of social contacts to suburbanites.[19] In other words, the goal is to achieve a sense of self and belonging by surrounding oneself with demographically similar and like-minded people. The living spaces thus created are ones in which people systematically lose their sense of "inner-direction" by constantly orienting to the expectations of others and by seeking to make themselves indistinguishable from their neighbors. The end result is that suburban spaces foster the American illusion that "men are created free and equal"—but, Riesman counters, "men are created different; they lose their social freedom and their individual autonomy in seeking to become like each other."[20] Although *The Lonely Crowd* is not intended to be an explicit attack on suburbia, it is a description of a postwar American "type" that would make its natural home in the subdivision. Elsewhere, Riesman makes plain his view that suburbia and inner-directedness are mutually exclusive and that cultural "progress" is a uniquely urban prerogative:

> There seems to me to be a tendency . . . to lose in the suburbs the human differentiations which have made great cities in the past the centers of rapid intellectual and cultural advance. The suburb is like a fraternity house at a small college . . . in which like-mindedness reverberates upon itself as the potentially various selves in each of us do not get evoked or recognized.[21]

William Whyte is even more explicit in his belief that suburbia is the breeding ground of the passive, conformist, postwar American. The "organization man" is he who sacrifices his individualism to the big corporation. He urgently "wants to belong"—to the corporation and to his packaged suburb, and is therefore a cautious, passive type with an urge to "work for somebody else."[22] The organization man follows the creed of Norman Vincent Peale and other self-improvement writers who advise him to "adjust to the situation rather than change it."[23] The adjusters are those "regular people" (i.e., white-collar, twenty-five to thirty-five years old, married, one to two children) who make their home in suburbia, but they are also transient. Ready to move at the corporation's request, the young white-collar worker and his family can "fit in anywhere. . . . The more people move about, the more similar the American environments become."[24] In other words, suburbia and the organization man create and sustain one another. Suburban neighbors mold a community out of transience itself: "The fact that they all left home can be more important in bonding them than the kind of home they left is in separating them."[25]

This was the suburbia that Whyte described following his study of Park Forest, Illinois. Set thirty miles south of Chicago, Park Forest opened in 1948 and offered housing for "young people with children, expectations of transfer, a taste for good living, not too much money."[26] Despite the constant threat of a transfer, Park Foresters made participation the central theme of suburban life. Whyte found sixty-six community organizations, all keenly supported. As one resident told Whyte, "The trick is to pretend to yourself that you're here for keeps and to join."[27]

For Whyte, suburbia is the second great melting pot. With its uniform house designs, its courts, its nondenominational churches, its "life adjustment" school curricula, its Tupperware parties, and the "hypnotic rhythm" of monthly credit and mortgage payments, life in suburbia is a quest for consensus and an expanded middle class: "People may leave the suburbs as middle-class. A great many who enter are not."[28] It is the suburban struggle to achieve middle-class status, to rework it as classlessness and equate it with America, that breeds the conformity so maligned in the mass culture debates.

By the end of the decade, the critique of suburban conformity was well established and summarized in a sweeping statement by Lewis Mumford, who bemoaned the

> multitude of uniform, unidentifiable houses, lined up inflexibly, at uniform distances, on uniform roads, in a treeless communal waste, inhabited by people of the same class, the same income, the same age group, witnessing the same television performances, eating the same tasteless pre-fabricated foods, from the same freezers, conforming in every outward and inward respect to a common mold . . . the ultimate effect of the suburban escape in our own time is, ironically, a low-grade uniform environment from which escape is impossible.[29]

Voices of dissent soon began to permeate the confident conclusions of the critics. However, and as we shall see, the arguments remained trapped within the frame of reference set by the mass culture debates. The most notable dissenters were Herbert Gans and Bennet Berger, whose commentaries followed the earlier accounts. When the Ford Motor Company transplanted a factory in Richmond, California, to a semirural spot north of San Jose, it moved many of its workers en masse to new tract suburbs near the plant. Following his observations and interviews in the new suburb, Berger declared war on the "myth of suburbia" created by the urban intelligentsia. The central tenets of the myth were that suburbia was a homogenous space peopled by armies of commuting, transient, hyperactive, Republican-voting conformists. Berger correctly pointed out that the critique of suburban conformity had been based almost exclusively on middle- to upper-middle-class suburbs and was therefore a critique of *bourgeois* America rather than *suburban* America. Rounding on the myth's originators, he asked: "Is the myth of suburbia one more example of the identification of the 'New York culture' with American culture?"[30]

Berger identified and defended the development of a "middle class working class" that aspired to suburban living, without all the trappings of bourgeois culture.[31] His study of 100 "suburbanized" Ford workers and their families found most tenets of the myth overturned. The Democratic Party remained dominant, and residents evidenced an increased interest in politics. Berger found neither the self-denying other-directedness cited by Riesman nor the feverish religious and community participation noted by Whyte in Park Forest. The majority of residents continued to identify themselves as working class, but cited an improvement in their living environment as changing their perception of themselves as members of the working class. One interviewee remarked that "they are better people than they were in the government housing, but they're the same class of people; give a man opportunity and he'll be okay; keep him down and he'll be a bum."[32] Berger found no "organization men," but he remarked a "new feeling of well-being, of counting."[33] Indeed, he concluded that suburbia, far from being a hotbed of conformity, was testimony that "Americans are living better than ever before."[34]

Gans's two-year sojourn in Levittown lent a fly-on-the-wall credibility to his defense of the suburban lifestyle. Underlining the religious, regional, and ethnic differences that he found amongst his immediate neighbors, Gans claimed to find a "suburban heterogeneity."[35] At the same time, he defended the "consumer preference" for homogenous communities of "young families who are raising children."[36] He further argued that the success of Levittown derived in part from the fact that because residents were "sufficiently homogenous to trust each other, they could share the common pains of newness and the needs of a new community."[37] These rather confused semantics led Gans to advocate homogenous blocks within heterogeneous communities as the ideal dispersal of suburban residents.

In a rare reference to black exclusion, Gans accepted (as the Levitts themselves were forced eventually to accept) the "inevitability of integration."[38] Gans approved of Levittown's gradual and carefully planned "desegregation"—which included screening out black families who were not considered middle class and scattering house sales so that no two black families were allowed to buy adjoining houses. As an apologist for suburban segregationists, Gans reminded the reader that most of Levittown's residents left the city because their urban blocks were "becoming black."[39] But in his view, "white anxieties about the predominantly nonwhite city are ultimately based on class rather than race"; the solution to such anxieties was for black people to become the "political majority of the city" and institute improved urban programs.[40]

The culture critics produced a wealth of quantitative and qualitative data taken in selected suburbs, but their findings were applied to a set of urban, academic anxieties revolving principally around the question of conformity. For Whyte and Riesman, suburbia was the landscape of white, middle America. As this was the section of American society considered most susceptible to the vagaries of mass culture, the popular sociological concepts of "other-directedness" and "organization man" entered the suburban imaginary. The implication was that urban culture was that of the elite literati; suburban culture was that of the white middle or lower-middle classes. These became the yardsticks against which the failings of mass culture might be measured. Moreover this was a "white" problematic: black culture did not figure in any of these discussions. For Riesman and Whyte, the perceived uniformities of suburban houses and neighborhoods provided the inevitable geography for the deadening impulses of conformity. In other words, suburbia was the perfect setting for stories told by culture critics.

For Berger and Gans, suburbia was an opportunity to extend the ranch house–owning franchise to a greater number of people within a certain continuum. In other words, the solution to the problem of suburban conformity was to give suburbia a greater (white) demographic diversity. Then suburbia might become the space, not of conformity, but of postwar pluralism. Significantly, both Berger and Gans underlined the real existence and agency of ethnic and working-class suburbanites. Berger's project was particularly clear in its validation of an indigenous working-class culture capable of molding suburban spaces to its own needs. But the overdue recognition of the real heterogeneity of suburban subjects and the more naïvely positive reappraisal of suburbia were conflated. The myriad absences, exclusions, and antagonisms necessary to create and sustain suburban space were obscured by a notion of heterogeneity that clung to the "age of consensus" notion of difference. At best, suburban heterogeneity might be extended to some working-class and ethnic groups, but no farther. Black workers do not feature in the suburb except as an absence. Berger notes that only one tract suburb accepted black residents. Most black employees had to commute from urban Richmond to the suburban factory.

For Berger, the opening of suburbia to white, working-class people would help to create a stronger, indigenous working-class culture. Suburbia itself would be enriched by an infusion of "working-class style." But Berger seems to want it both ways. Enthusiastic in his support of working-class consciousness, he nonetheless cites approvingly a blurring of class identities found in the Ford suburbanites as evidence of improved self-esteem brought about by the suburban environment. He quotes one resident who claims to be working class, but is quick to add that his neighbors were "good respectable people who could pass for anything."[41] Another resident responds, "Well, yeah, I guess we're middle class. Around here, the working class *is* the middle class."[42]

Although Berger's study provided a welcome corrective to the general perception that suburbs and suburban culture were middle to upper-middle class de rigueur, the book reads as an honest attempt at class analysis gone awry in the age of consensus. The contention that working-class residents do not metamorphose completely into conformist middle Americans risks sounding like yet another celebration of postwar diversity. The subtext is that if suburbia can be opened to white, working-class people, then suburbia itself will be host to the pluralism so essential to cold war America. (White) working-class and (white) middle-class people can swap style and identities and generally help make class antagonism obsolete.

The culture critics, whether for or against suburbia, were trapped by the logic of their own arguments. The economic class analyses of 1930s radicalism had increasingly given way to liberal-pluralist discussions of "cultural classes," "tolerated difference," and "status seekers." In a game in which the parameters were set by an anti-Stalinist defense of American democracy, the social divisions inherent in postwar capitalist formations were increasingly marginalized in intellectual debate. The peaceful coexistence of "interest groups," a harmonious consensus based on a celebration of defused diversity—these were the ideological trappings of postwar capitalism. While the editors of *Fortune* magazine "linked mass consumerism to the genius of American democracy," cold war liberals predicted a "convergence of social classes" in a new world characterized by pluralism, diversity, and affluence.[43] Increasingly for intellectuals, what needed to be defended was the idea of diversity itself.

Moving within a narrow continuum in which the social demography of suburbia matched the critics' target culture, the problem of disinvestment and the structuring absences and race exclusions of suburbia were barely considered. The disappearance of urban spaces, urban inhabitants, and spaces of production was the making of suburban identities. Yet that process of disappearance had itself disappeared in the critics' debates. In this respect, the critics dug an even deeper hole in which to bury the real and profound social divisions underpinning suburbanization. Just as the detached spaces of suburbia produced dream subjects, that same detachment produced a range of cultural criticism that was equally dreamlike. If the culture critics were searching for the underbelly of the dream, they never really found it. What they did find was a "dream critique"—one that belonged to the positioning of cosmopolitan intellectuals in the postwar corporate-liberal moment.

The Feminine Mystique

In 1963, a text appeared that employed the language of urban-academic critiques, but arose more directly from *women's* experiences of suburban life. In the late 1950s, Betty Friedan was herself a "suburban housewife . . . bringing up three children in Rockland County, New York."[44] Recounted as a disruptive moment in the everyday, here is Friedan's memory of how she stumbled upon "the problem that has no name":

> On an April morning in 1959, I heard a mother of four, having coffee with four other mothers in a suburban development fifteen miles from New York, say in a tone of quiet desperation, "the problem." And the others knew, without words, that she was not talking about a problem with her husband, or her children, or her home. Suddenly they realized they all shared the same problem, the problem that has no name. They began, hesitantly, to talk about it. Later, after they had picked up their children at nursery school and taken them home to nap, two of the women cried, in sheer relief, just to know they were not alone.[45]

The "problem" was an emptiness experienced by white, middle-class housewives, a "vague undefined wish for 'something more' than the trappings of the feminine mystique."[46] The problem was preventing middle-class women's smooth adjustment to the postwar settlement of gender roles: "I saw the same signs in suburban ranch houses and split-levels on Long Island and in New Jersey and Westchester County; in colonial houses in a small Massachusetts town; on patios in Memphis; in suburban and city apartments; in living rooms in the Midwest."[47]

As a graduate of Smith College and a working journalist, Friedan grabbed hold of the by now familiar language of the mass culture debates and peppered it with personal statements of hundreds of women living with "the problem." The result was an updated critique of the Victorian cult of domesticity. The postwar revalidation of separate spheres for men and women was made still more invidious by the "sexual sell" (the postwar emphasis on woman's role as consumer) and the popularization of Freudian theory. For Friedan, the uncritical application of Freudian doctrine "provided a convenient escape from the atom bomb, McCarthy, all the disconcerting problems that might spoil the taste of steaks, and cars and color television and backyard swimming pools."[48] Popularized Freudianism had its greatest antifeminist moment in the 1942 publication *Modern Woman: The Lost Sex* by Marynia Farnham and Ferdinand Lundberg. According to this work, feminism was "at its core a deep illness," while careers and higher education led to the "masculinization of women with enormously dangerous consequences to the home, the children dependent on it and to the ability of the woman, as well as her husband, to obtain sexual gratification. . . . [T]he psychosocial rule that begins to take form, then, is this: the more educated the woman is, the greater chance there is of sexual disorder."[49]

Suburban developers were well served by such pronouncements. Steaks, cars, and swimming pools were the status symbols of the suburban middle classes. Suburbia was where woman was invited to fulfill her sexual role in an idealized domestic sphere. In the logic of the feminine mystique, the suburban housewife was the "dream image of the young American women and the envy, it was said, of women all over the world."[50] In sum, suburbia was the geography par excellence of the "feminine mystique." Moreover, it was the *space* of suburbia that took away women's *time*. In a key chapter titled "Housewifery Expands to Fill the Time Available," Friedan argued that modern appliances had not released women from domestic labor:

> The house takes longer to clean, the shopping and gardening and chauffeuring and do-it-yourself routines are so time-consuming that, for a while, the emptiness seems solved. But when the house is furnished, and the children are in school and the family's place in the community has jelled, there is "nothing to look forward to," as one woman I interviewed put it. The empty feeling returns, and so she must redecorate the living-room, or wax the kitchen floor more often than necessary—or have another baby.[51]

In terms of gender politics, therefore, suburban space had an important role to play: it filled women's time—ensuring the endless repetition of domestic tasks and the containment of women. When

Friedan stated that "men re-created their own childhood in suburbia, and made mothers of their wives," she spoke quite literally of the way in which social relations were reproduced in suburbia.[52]

In her account of 1950s girlhood, Susan Douglas recalls that "thousands of [our mothers] ran out to buy [the book]. . . . In 1964, while teenagers were discovering the Beatles, older women made *The Feminine Mystique* the number one best-selling paperback in the country."[53] The success of *The Feminine Mystique* must have depended in part on women talking to each other—a factor relatively unexplored by Friedan. Most of the study is based on individual interviews with suburban women and the various professionals studying and treating them. Like the sitcom moms, many of Friedan's interviewees seemed to exist only in the house interiors, alone, at the center of the family. It would be another decade before female friendship in suburbia was openly explored. Moreover some feminist scholars now critique Friedan's portrayal of suburban woman as a "de-skilled and trivialized victim" isolated within the culture of consumption, arguing that in their role as consumers, women exercised a greater degree of self-determination and sisterhood than historians have allowed.[54] The theme of a "suburban sisterhood" is developed in chapter 5.

Suburbia and Postwar Popular Culture

While Friedan and other culture critics indicted suburbia and mass culture as belonging to the same plot to deaden the American psyche, they ignored the fact that critiques of suburbia were already appearing in popular cultural representations. In a number of films and novels of the period, one may further trace the cracks in the picture window that appeared in popular representations of suburban life. If we look at the family, the paradigmatic unit of the suburban postwar settlement, we may see how the ideology-saturated subject positions of husband, wife, parent, and child might be disturbed by a gathering menace of cultural difference. Indeed, 1950s texts suggest that the seemingly wholesome cold war family was full of strangers.

In film, the horror and science fiction genres gave us husbands who were aliens, children who were psychopaths, and teenagers who were werewolves.[55] Often these are "danger lurks within" stories, in which evil hides behind familiar faces inhabiting white clapboard houses, bright schoolrooms, and leafy residential streets. Family members and neighbors wrestle with the creeping sensation that something is wrong with one of their own.

Andrew Ross has argued that horror and science fiction representations belonged to the cold war culture of containment in which the "health" of the social body was threatened by alien "bugs," which were both internal and external. Fears that the enemy might have infiltrated the most "inside" spaces of America (i.e., "reds under the beds") may be seen in the rumors that fluoridation of the water supply was a Communist plot.[56] The "enemy within" narratives were given further expression in the spy mania surrounding the trial (1951) and execution (1953) of the Rosenbergs. The cold war espionage formula was one in which the spy seemed ordinary: "Signs of normality and social conformity could now be regarded by alert neighbors as signs of treachery.[57]

Peter Biskind argues that, although the "pods and blobs" of 1950s Hollywood are usually seen to symbolize the Bomb or the Red Menace, they more specifically reflected domestic political struggles: "More often than not, the Communist connection was a red herring, allowing the center to attack extremists, extremists to attack the center, and both centrists and extremists to quarrel among themselves . . . all in the guise of respectable anti-communism. . . . Fifties sci-fi was more concerned with Main Street than monsters."[58]

The notions of "domestic" and "Main Street" drama may be still more literal than Biskind allowed. The terms may well refer us to national discourses concerning political and cultural definitions of "America." But they also refer us more immediately to Main Street, U.S.A., and to the intimacies of neighborhood and family life. The best known of the "pods and blobs" films, *Invasion of the Bodysnatchers*, appeared in 1956. *Invasion* was certainly a domestic drama in the sense intended by Biskind. But it was also an office intrigue, a "the family next door is strange" story, a kitchen sink drama. Pod conversions disrupt the private comforts of marriage, family, and community. Becky's Aunt Wilma describes the change in her husband: "There's something missing. . . . Always when he talked to me there was a certain look in his eyes. Now it's gone. There's no emotion. The words are the same, but there's no feeling."

Invasion of the Bodysnatchers was domestic in the closest possible sense, and therefore deeply troubling to the suburban consciousness. If it makes metaphorical reference to "Communist brainwashing," the film also plays with the very notion of conformity; it "brings conformity home." The pod proponents tell the as yet unconverted Dr. Bennell that he will inhabit an "untroubled world" in which "everyone is the same." But is this a vision of Communist or suburban society? Pod people are flat, mechanical, devoid of expression—like the "John and Mary Drones" of John Keats's "mass culture" scare account of suburban conformity, The *Crack in the Picture Window* (1956). For Keats, the suburbs are "inhabited by people whose age, income, number of children, problems, habits, conversation, dress, possessions and perhaps even blood type are also precisely like yours . . . developments conceived in error, nurtured by greed, corroding everything they touch."[59]

Like "organization men" in "gray flannel suits," pod people suggest not "Communists," but the armies of suburban commuters going about their daily routines with a distinct lack of inner direction. In a successful pod takeover, the film's sequel might surely have been set in the drabbest expanse of tract housing within striking distance of the film studios. More troublesome for suburban viewers, *Invasion* problematizes its own critique of conformity by suggesting that conformity "has its place." When Becky looks onto Main Street, she sees pod people going about their business in much the same way as before. She remarks longingly, "It's just like any other Saturday morning." On the surface, nothing has changed. Dr. Bennell's patients, in states of high anxiety prior to their own conversion, now report that they are "back to normal." The suggestion is that there is little outward difference to be found between pre-pod Santa Mira and its post-pod incarnation. Prior to the invasion, conformity existed in healthy proportions, in a positive guise. A little bit of American conformity is both safe and desirable; it protects the nation against deviants and extremists. But how does one identify the point at which it becomes a menace? Because the film proposes that there is a good conformity and a bad conformity—but that the two are indistinguishable from each other—danger lurks in both states. Therefore, the suburban sameness, so reassuring to prospective dream residents, is not to be trusted. The ideal house containing the ideal husband, wife, or child may prove to be an illusion, with terrifying consequences for the family and the wider community. Suburbanites are damned both ways.

Domestic strangers did not only announce themselves as monsters and mutants. There were sullen and aggressive or absent husbands, mad and manipulative wives, and delinquent teenagers. Absent husbands were usually middle-class commuting corporation men such as Jim Blandings in *Mr. Blandings Builds His Dream House* (1948) or Tom Rath in *The Man in the Grey Flannel Suit.* These husbands are more or less forgiven their absenteeism because they are working to maintain a suburban lifestyle for their family. Tom Rath is able to reject the corporate grind only through a fantastic turn of events. Occasionally commuting husbands prove to be guilty of actively avoiding suburban family life. In *Rally Round the Flag, Boys!* (1958), Harry Bannerman spends his train journey developing a finely honed diatribe against Putnam's Landing. In the end, Harry's real home is the train itself:

> You know who saved more marriages in Fairfield County than the church, the state and the psychiatrists all put together? . . . Pat McGinnis. . . . Oh I know he ran a godawful railroad. . . . But he did one thing that every wife in Fairfield County ought to get down on her knees and thank him for every night! . . . He put club cars in the commuter trains. . . . Do you think us poor slobs could face what's waiting for us at home if we had to get off this train sober?[60]

But Harry too is excused his absenteeism because he is providing a fictional version of the mass culture critique of suburbia and a masculine corrective to the apparent menace of the feminized spaces of suburbia. Like Arthur Douglas in *Leave Me Alone,* Harry Bannerman is the voice of urban, elite, male reason pitted against women who have dragged their husbands to the suburbs, then turned said suburbs into domestic spaces of "female manipulation."

Absent corporate husbands were either devoted family men or social critics, but they were never violent. Aggression was left to men of working-class and ethnic origins. In Martin Ritt's 1957 film of the John McPartland novel *No Down Payment,* tension in a smart Los Angeles suburb is exacerbated by a resident working-class couple. The husband is a sexual predator; his wife is a nymphomaniac.

When the husband rapes his upper-middle-class neighbor, the couple's final inadmissibility to suburbia is secured. He is accidentally killed under the wheels of his new Ford (which he clearly didn't deserve to own); his wife is forced to leave suburbia.

In *The Next Voice You Hear* (1950), the credits introduce us to "Mr. Joe Smith, American" and "Mrs. Joe Smith," his wife. The Smiths live in tract housing in greater Los Angeles; Joe works for a nearby plane manufacturer. He is portrayed as a hard-working proletarian who loves his family, but just can't seem to overcome his innate working-class propensity for aggression and loutishness. He argues with his neighbors, with his boss; he beats his car and drives like a maniac. He rules over wife and son through a regime of fear spliced with slobbery expressions of loyalty. Mrs. Joe Smith (played by Nancy Davis) and son Johnny have adjusted to suburban life. When God speaks through the radio, they are afraid, but they have no real sins to repent. Joe, however, proclaims the broadcasts to be a form of "mass suckerology" and proves more resistant to divine enlightenment. He simply is not ready for suburban "middle classlessness."

Joe's struggle culminates in a drunken barroom scene in which Joe's friend Mitch tells him, "You're blowing your life away. Up to the same old grind, the same old house, the same old room." Joe finally redeems himself, replying, "Same old house . . . it's *our* house, *our* room. I'm ashamed of myself . . . we should all be ashamed. . . . You're sinners, and I'm a sinner. . . . I'm going home." He has finally understood God's message: "He's teaching us to take it easy." He befriends his boss, his neighbors, the policeman who gave him traffic tickets; he stops shouting at his family. A crisis of "suburban strangeness" is here resolved in favor of the dream.

The strangeness of women in suburbia had its first representations as a male fear, in that the urban academic critique of suburban matriarchal conformity was primarily a male construct. I have already noted that Grace (and her mother) in *Rally Round the Flag, Boys!* and Eleanor (and her mother) in *Leave Me Alone* were portrayed as feminine plotters, emasculating their male betters and then dragging them into a life of suburban dullness.[61] In the opening pages of *Leave Me Alone*, the wife and mother-in-law mount their attack: "Arthur turned his eyes at his wife. The word 'suburbs' was one of those emotional words. . . . The two women looked so obviously guilty and never had he seen, more clearly, the physical resemblance—the same cool grey eyes, . . . the same short, straight nose, tending slightly to pointedness . . . 'Conspiracy again?' Arthur asked softly."[62]

After giving Arthur their arguments in favor of suburbia, there is a conspiratorial aside between the two women. Eleanor's mother confidently predicts Arthur's conversion to the suburban dream: "Leave him alone. Don't nag him, dear. Arthur has a good mind. He'll think it through sensibly. . . . Arthur is like every other man. He wants to be happy in the same way that everyone else is . . . . Call me tomorrow?"[63]

Herman Wouk's *Marjorie Morningstar* (1955) is an entire novel devoted to blaming women for suburbia. The central character is a middle-class aspiring but talentless actress. The novel is a sort of female "rake's progress" of Marjorie's long, slow descent from Manhattan's theatrical bohemia to affluent but dull suburban life. The men in the novel all have authority and membership in the New York artists' community. By focusing on a female character whose "descent into suburbia" is essentialist and unavoidable, Wouk overlays suburbia with a negative construct of femininity. Noel Airman tells Marjorie she is a "Shirley":

> I went out with Shirley after Shirley. . . . She was everywhere. I would hear about some new girl . . . the name didn't matter. I'd telephone her, make a date, go up to the apartment, she'd open the door—and there would stand Shirley. In a different dress, a different body, but with that one unchanging look, the look of Shirley. The respectable girl, the mother of the next generation, all tricked out to appear gay and girlish . . . but with a terrible threatening solid dullness jutting through, like the grey rocks under the spring grass in Central Park.[64]

Noel informs Marjorie that "Shirley's" final resting place is always suburbia, where she has dragged any man foolish enough to fall in love with her. Marjorie's denials that she will end in suburbia are presented as laughable; her professional efforts as petty, for ultimately she is "pure cat, sniffing nervously but surely, toward a house in Great Neck and a husband making a minimum of fifteen thousand a year."[65] In the novel's final scene, she is visited in her big white house near New Rochelle by an old admirer, now a successful playwright. The playwright has dreamed of flaunting his success in the face of this "suburban housewife gone to seed." But he finds Marjorie has not just faded, but completely disappeared—she has become a Shirley: "The person I wanted to triumph over is gone, that's the catch. I can't carry my achievements backward fifteen years and flaunt them in the face of Marjorie Morgenstern, the beautiful elusive girl I was so mad about. And what satisfaction is there in crowing over the sweet-natured placid grey mama she has turned into?"[66]

In these texts, the mass culture critique resurfaces in a new guise. American conformity exists; its heartland is suburbia, but *women* are the architects. It is not so much a surfeit of democracy that is deadening the populace; rather it is matriarchal power that is "emasculating" men. As the spatial manifestation of the cult of domesticity, suburbia becomes a kind of 1950s "herland" and therefore a convenient dumping ground for a range of male anxieties and hostilities.

Occasionally the positioning of woman as matriarchal suburban ruler emerges as a positive construct, validating the space and the woman at its center. In *Young at Heart* (1954), Doris Day plays Laurie Tuttle, one of three "marriageable" sisters in a musical middle-class family living in suburban Connecticut. When Laurie meets down-on-his-luck urban songwriter Barney Sloane (Frank Sinatra), she discovers that he has two serious flaws: he is Italian and he hates suburbia. Barney tells Laurie he has "Americanized" his Italian name, but still has not had a hit song. Laurie refuses to accept Barney's view that his lack of opportunity is connected to his working-class ethnic background: "Anybody can feel sorry for himself. . . . I happen to believe that a man decides his own destinies . . . if he has enough courage and enough ambition." Throughout the film, Barney stands on the edge of the family circle, which is always presented through the picture window, revealing lacy, affluent, pastel interiors. Laurie sets out to rescue Barney, feeding him, teaching him to laugh, sneaking into his rooming house to hang curtains and giving him a dress sense.

As an unmarried suburbanite with a music-professor father and an eccentric and outspoken aunt as female role model (her mother is dead), Laurie is self-possessed and assertive. She has greater access to public spaces than most suburban women, and even in those spaces she is usually the most powerful character. In the local piano bar, it is Laurie who prevents the intractable Barney from being fired. Indeed, Barney's ethnic, working-class positioning is there to increase the stock-in-trade of Laurie's white, middle-class confidence. She is a "strangely" strong woman, in part because Barney, with all his inadequacies, is the real stranger. Barney's strangerhood has its source in his working-class ethnicity. His hopes for success lie in how far he can simulate the look and lifestyle of suburban Connecticut. Without Laurie's interventions, he is completely clueless as to how this might be accomplished: "There's something you should know about the state of Connecticut—the crease in the pants is strictly constitutional. I think a pair of pressed pants would be just the right note for tonight's party."

Young at Heart is one of the first cultural representations of suburbia in which a member of an excluded group is allowed in without undergoing a total transformation. Barney's admittance is mediated through Laurie's powerful positioning within suburban space. When she rejects Gig Young's WASPish successful Broadway songwriter for the cynical Barney, she shocks everybody's expectations. The family and community are forced to accept Barney, who remains unsuccessful, even suicidal, until the final minutes of the film.

Not unlike Elizabeth Bennet in *Pride and Prejudice*, Laurie provides a glimpse of a powerfully positioned female subject *within* a marginalized space. As such, she dominates and valorizes that space, drawing outsiders into it. She even has access to town, to the barroom, to Barney's apartment—privileges not granted married suburban women. However, Laurie's independent excursions ultimately serve to reinforce her position within the domestic sphere. In other words, Laurie steps out of place because Barney is weak and lets her. Moreover she only steps out of place in order to more firmly draw Barney in and close the door behind her. Like Betsy Rath in *The Man in the Grey Flannel Suit*, ultimately she "gets her man" by "knowing her place."

Where suburban women did not keep to their space, they were much more likely to be punished. The best example of this occurs in *Mildred Pierce*, Michael Curtiz's 1945 film of the James M.

Cain novel (1941). Cain set his story in Depression-era California and therefore owes many of his themes to the specificities of the Los Angeles property boom and its 1930s aftermath. But the film finds a context in the postwar gender (and suburban) settlement, featuring Joan Crawford as a tract house wife and mother who becomes a divorced, successful businesswoman, but pays a heavy price along the way. The film opens with the murder of Mildred's lover and Mildred's interview by the police chief. Mildred's story is recounted in three lengthy flashbacks, two of which are delivered from Mildred's narrative viewpoint. She describes her suburb as one in which "all the houses look the same" and women are imprisoned: "I was always in the kitchen. I felt as though I'd been born in the kitchen and lived there all my life except for the few hours it took to get married. . . . I married Bert when I was seventeen. I never knew any other kind of life—just cooking and washing and having children."

Indeed, from the opening scene, Mildred's suburb is presented as no pastoral paradise, but as the drab setting for the futile machinations of no-hopers like her husband Bert. Mildred's dress and the house's interiors are neat, but decidedly "down market." We learn that Bert is a "poor breadwinner" when he comes home, flops on the sofa, and warns Mildred not to ask whether he has found another job. We also learn that Mildred is maniacally devoted to her two daughters. She bakes pies to earn money to give them the middle-class lifestyle she never had. In an argument over Mildred's "fixation" with her children, Bert leaves.

With Bert out of the way, Mildred climbs out of suburbia and, through her own business acumen, achieves wealth and independence as a restaurant owner. However, as the film progresses, Mildred's success is linked to "bad mothering" and she is punished accordingly. One daughter dies while Mildred is out having fun. The other daughter, Veda, is increasingly the object of Mildred's overzealous attentions, and increasingly difficult to please. She takes Mildred's money, but rejects Mildred for "getting her hands dirty" by working. When Veda murders Mildred's lover, both mother and daughter collude to conceal Veda's guilt.

The film links Mildred's public achievements to her rejection of husband and suburbia and to her pathological mothering. She is reprimanded for being simultaneously too much of a mother and not enough of one. When Veda's guilt is discovered, the chastened Mildred returns to Bert, who has hovered in the film's background, gaining authority with each of Mildred's setbacks. We are left with the impression that Mildred will return to a sanitized middle-class suburbia where Bert is now strong and successful and Mildred "doesn't need to work." Bert and Mildred have been restored to their proper "places," but not before we are shown the double bind of the feminized space of suburbia, and one woman's struggle against it. Five years later, Joan Crawford's character was punished for her coldly calculated *embrace* of domesticity in Vincent Sherman's *Harriet Craig.* The film explores the dangers of a domesticity that so engulfs its female protagonist as to disrupt her primal subordination to her husband.

If strange wives did not announce themselves as manipulative, overly dependent, or overly independent, only one path remained open to them: mental illness. Mrs. Rochester's legacy of domestic madness (in *Jane Eyre*) is a long one and includes, for our period, *Now Voyager* (1942), *Experiment Perilous* (1944), *Possessed* (1947), *The Snake Pit* (1948), *Dementia* (1953), *The Cobweb* (1955), *The Three Faces of Eve* (1957), *Interlude* (1958), *A Woman under the Influence* (1974), and *Sybil* (1977). In *The Cobweb,* the remark is made that "in all institutions, something of the individual gets lost." If the suburban household is *the* institution of the postwar domestic settlement, are women's identities sacrificed in order to ensure its maintenance? In the previously mentioned films, the ambivalence surrounding representations of female madness is explored to varying degrees. In other words, is she sick or are husband and the patriarchal order really trying to drive her crazy or even murder her?[67] In many of these texts, female madness is explored as a hysterical outburst against the patriarchal (or in the case of *Now Voyager,* matriarchal) household.

Whether the female protagonist's madness is real or imagined, cured or not, it is certainly subversive (on both sides of the screen) to the domestic order crucial to the suburban dream. For example, in *The Snake Pit,* the mad wife hears voices and has memory lapses. She is also coldly uninterested in love and marriage; she removes her wedding ring and uses her maiden name. When she is released from the Frances Farmer Memorial Sanitarium, she asks for her wedding ring to be replaced. She is cured, that is, reconciled to marriage and family life. Like Dr. Jacoby in *Now Voyager* and Dr. McIver in *The Cobweb*, *The Snake Pit*'s doctor features as a benevolent (and male) guardian of the postwar gender settlement.[68]

Film texts of domestic madness were accompanied by a real increase in the numbers of suburban women on the psychiatric case registers. The Gordons' 1950s case studies in Bergen County, New Jersey, found that women patients far outnumbered men: "In fact, young housewives (18 to 44) suffering not only childbirth depression, but all psychiatric and psychosomatic disorders with increasing severity, became during the fifties by far the predominant group of adult psychiatric patients. The number of disturbed young wives was more than half again as big as the number of young husbands, and three times as big as any other group. (Other surveys of both private and public patients in the suburbs have turned up similar findings)."[69] The Gordons' findings were of course subject to period definitions of mental illness and the postwar popularization and practice of Freudian theories. As Janet Walker points out, "The subject matter of psychoanalysis and femininity promised a pleasurable spectacle which could both bring up fascinating aberrant sexuality and unconscious processes, and also diffuse and regulate issues threatening to get out of hand."[70]

Moreover, if the fringe communities could be renamed "Disturbia," it was women who were seen as the source of the disturbance. But Disturbia was a geography. Indeed, Betty Friedan gave it the extreme name of "comfortable concentration camp."[71] As in the Victorian household and the First World War trenches, madness was here a sickness of space. It has been argued that the confinement of the trenches had similar effects on soldiers as did the confinement of the Victorian household: "the symptoms of shell shock were precisely the same as those of the most common hysterical disorders of peace-time."[72] The suburban women who found themselves on the psychiatric registers belonged to a particular history of madness that connected to the spatial confinement of particular groups. At the same time, constructions of the mad suburban housewife revealed a great deal about male anxieties during this period. As the manipulative architects of suburbia, women were luring men there; as mad suburban subjects, women were undermining the patriarchal suburban settlement.

It has been suggested that a cultural preoccupation with teenage deviance was inevitable in a suburban spatial order that had no "depressed minority of poor . . . people that rival or exceed adolescents as a focus of police attention."[73] In a yearlong study of one New York suburb, Baumgartner found that young people constituted one of three main areas of police work; the other two were traffic violations and the movement of "suspicious persons."[74] In 1955, James Dean brought juvenile delinquency to Hollywood's vision of suburbia when he appeared as Jim Stark, the angst-ridden son of an affluent family in Nicholas Ray's *Rebel without a Cause.* Moving to a new suburb every time Jim gets into trouble, the Starks are as transient as the worst of William Whyte's "organization men." Jim's neighborhood has a safe, ordered, wealthy appearance. But the facade slowly crumbles as family relationships are explored. Jim's father is weak and unable to support his son's search for a stable masculine identity. His mother is "domineering" and therefore stunting the emotional development of both husband and son. She complains that she nearly died giving birth to Jim, while the father is seen wearing an apron and crouching on all fours to pick up a spilled dinner. Jim's problems are firmly located in the inadequacies of his family and won't be resolved until his father reasserts patriarchal authority.

Suburban delinquents were not criminals like their urban counterparts. In keeping with the popularized Freudianism being applied to middle-class angst, suburban delinquents were victims of bad parenting. Indeed, it has been convincingly stated that as the decade's best-known delinquent, Jim Stark, is the most sane and moral character in the film: "[I]t is not Jim, Judy, or Plato who are the delinquents, but their parents. . . . With its trilogy of sick families, *Rebel* touches all the bases. Parents are criticized for being too strong and too weak, too authoritarian and too permissive, for being absent when the kids need them and smothering them with affection when they don't. . . . In *Rebel,* parents can't do anything right."[75]

In the "affluent society," suburban delinquency could not be explained in the language of "Warner Brothers environmentalism."[76] When a Senate subcommittee found affluent, suburban delinquency to be as big a problem as urban youth crime, it placed the blame squarely on Mom and Dad: "Better children can only come from better parents."[77] Suburban delinquents were not innately evil; nor were they the victims of poverty. They were sick and in need of professional help. Suburban delinquent films typically featured a police chief, teacher, or social worker who was well versed in pop Freudianism and could give the parents a good talking to. The gentle cop in *Rebel without a Cause* lets Jim hang on to the wind-up doll he carries and sympathetically asks Jim if his "folks don't understand." In *The Unguarded Moment* (1956), a teacher has been sexually assaulted by a delinquent high school student. But she defends him from the tough cop, arguing that he is "just a boy" who needs understanding, not punishment.[78]

In John Frankenheimer's *The Young Stranger* (1957), the delinquent is Hal Ditmar, the Beverly Hills son of a successful movie producer. Provoked by the local cinema manager, he lashes out and then can't get anyone to believe that he hit the manager in self-defense. Hal's real problem is his father, who talks to him only to tell him what clothes to wear, or to punish him. When he has to pick Hal up from the police station, Dad refuses to listen to the police chief's assertion that his son is troubled. He tells the chief that his son is not a "j.d." because "he comes from a good home." The chief replies angrily: "Look Ditmar, you're not talking to one of your studio cops. Some of you smug people out there in Beverly Hills seem to have the idea that delinquency just wouldn't dare happen to one of your kids."

Hal's mother is also a victim of Dad's career success. When Hal complains that he only sees his father when he does something wrong, she replies sadly, "He'd like to be with you more often. It's just . . . success takes an awful lot of time." Finally, she tells her husband that she has had enough of living in the fear invoked by his overbearing manner. Things go from bad to worse in the Ditmar household as the misery of life under Dad's regime is gradually uncovered. Mom admits that she's been thinking (for the previous five years) about leaving him. And Hal erupts during dinner, forcing his father to listen: "You wanna know something? I'm glad I hit that guy. . . . I'd do it again just to find out what you really think of me. I never did know. The only time I ever see you is at this crummy dinner table. And then all you do is make speeches. . . . I don't know why I ever expected you to believe me. You don't even know me!"

Hal storms from the room, but his mother supports him, telling a now remorseful Dad that Hal "is right. . . . You don't know him. He's a stranger to you." But it is the police chief, as the film's professional Freudian, who has the last word: "When a boy has to hit someone to get his father to believe him, there's something wrong." *The Young Stranger* also parodies the use of popularized Freud to treat delinquents. In a speech reminiscent of the Officer Krupke song from *West Side Story*, another j.d., sounding distinctly urban and streetwise, tells Hal his story:

> It's that psychiatrist ya know. . . . He's got me all mixed up. Yeah, I'm confused, I'm insecure and I don't relate no more. The cops keep bringin' me here, the chief send me down to the judge, the judge send me back to the psychiatrist. Talk, talk, talk, talk! I'm not responsible for my actions no more. You know if this keeps up much longer, they're gonna have to send that psychiatrist to jail.

Films like *City across the River*, *Blackboard Jungle*, and *Twelve Angry Men* treat delinquency as an urban crime problem. Urban j.d.s are either innately criminal and are victimizing society, or they are themselves the victims of urban life. Their families barely make an appearance; it would seem that city teenagers don't *have* a family life. In suburban texts, the family is regarded as the core unit of the community; explanations for delinquency can only be found there. Jim Stark and Hal Ditmar are estranged, but at the same time, they are sane, moral, and longing for parental love. They only *look* strange, because they are surrounded by dysfunctional families.

While the culture critics debated the merits of suburbia and popular films and novels registered domestic incarnations of cold war otherness in suburban spaces, another kind of critique emerged more directly out of the intersection of culture and everyday life. A range of cultural representations began to treat suburbia as a quite specific experience, as a space in which people *spend their time.* In these representations, homogeneity and conformity were themselves explored as both intimate and imaginary states of being. Chapter 5 discusses a selection of texts that locate a critique of suburbia in the themes of everyday life and estrangement.

5 Everyday Life and Suburban Estrangement

In this chapter we turn our attention to a series of fictional treatments of everyday life in suburbia. Representations of everyday life provided the most cogent references to the theme of suburban conformity, but at the same time illustrated the limits of the culture critics' debates. For if the homogeneity and sprawl of suburban spaces produced conformity, that conformity was itself an imaginary. Unaccountable differences in the form of joys, troubles, or subversions erupted from time to time out of the smooth dream surface. There were a number of cultural texts that explored these lifelines beneath the surface, suggesting a suburban estrangement manifest at the level of everyday life. These are representations of de-familiarization, of a feeling of being "out of place," of profound ambivalence, or even a heightened appreciation of suburbia. Estrangement is therefore a productive experience of *difference*, one that serves to disturb any easy assumptions about conformity, about suburban happiness or unhappiness. It is in the expression of estrangement that we might identify moments of critical knowledge and potential. It can be further argued that in relation to the city-suburb divide, estrangement is again productive; it is the tie that binds. In representations of estrangement, we might begin to track the profound inseparability of city and suburb.

Looking for Lifelines

The repetitions and ruptures of daily life and the storing of memories ensure that the critique of everyday life comes from within. Seemingly insignificant moments and encounters conceal the complex identities and relations that underpin them. Lefebvre cites the example of a woman buying a pound of sugar in order to disentangle the myriad conditions that might attach to that simple act. The woman's biography, family, class, race, and other determinants are all embedded in her daily routines enacted in space:

> Thus the simplest event—a woman buying a pound of sugar, for example—must be analyzed. Knowledge will grasp whatever is hidden within it. To understand this simple event, it is not enough merely to describe it; research will disclose a tangle of reasons and causes, of essences and "spheres." . . . And although what I grasp becomes more and more profound, it is contained from the start in the original little event. So now I see the humble event of everyday life as having two sides: a little, individual, chance event—and at the same time an infinitely complex social event, richer than the many "essences" it contains within itself. The social phenomenon may be defined as the unity of these two sides. It remains for us to explain why the infinite complexity of these events is hidden, and to discover why—and this too is part of their reality—they appear to be so humble.[1]

The spaces and moments of everyday life continually belie and produce the heterogeneity of the individual; it is in everyday life, therefore, that the politics of space resides. In abstract space, everyday life is the space of "programmed consumption" in which we all carry on buying our bags of sugar.[2] But as soon as we begin to look for the lifelines beneath the surface, we glimpse relations, histories, and sometimes the raised voices of local and accentuated difference. Opposed by the totalizing dreaminess of suburban space, there are everyday moments, tiny acts, and puzzled expressions that go "against the grain" of abstraction. In these we sense what Foucault termed the "increasing vulnerability to criticism of things, institutions, practices."[3] We become aware of "a certain fragility . . . in the very bedrock of existence . . . in those aspects of it that are most familiar."[4]

In Raymond Carver's short story "Menudo," the narrator is an estranged suburban husband having an affair with a woman who lives across the street. In a state of anxious, guilty insomnia, he begins to rake leaves. Turning to an everyday outdoor activity, he attempts to reestablish some sense of belonging to the neighborhood. Completing his own yard, he moves on to the adjoining lot, belonging to the Baxter family. As he rakes, he thinks about himself, his lover, his neighbors: "We're nice people, all of us, to a point."[5] He ends up on his knees in the middle of the Baxters' yard and looks up to see Mr. Baxter sitting in his car, ready to leave for work. To the sleepless, yard-raking adulterer, it is the seeming ordinariness of Mr. Baxter that makes him special—his night's sleep, his commuting routine, his wife's expectation of his return:

> Mr. Baxter is a decent, ordinary guy—a guy you wouldn't mistake for anyone special. But he is special. . . . For one thing he has a full night's sleep behind him, and he's just embraced his wife before leaving for work. But even before he goes, he's already expected home a set number of hours later. True, in the grander scheme of things, his return will be an event of small moment—but an event nonetheless.[6]

As Baxter drives off, he glances at the man kneeling in his yard with a rake, and lifts his hand from the steering wheel: "It could be a salute or a sign of dismissal. . . . And then he looks away toward the city."[7] A sense of mystery attaches to the brief glance between them. There is no attachment, nothing to affirm that the suburban dreamscape is safe, inclusive, and forever. Two neighbors are seen to exist worlds apart, as the narrator measures his sense of deviance and failure against a neighbor about whom he, in fact, knows nothing. When Baxter turns his gaze to the city, the deviant raker experiences himself as still further diminished. The manicured lawn becomes a place to do penance in the middle of the night—a place to be left behind in the cold light of another business day.

Most of Carver's stories map low-income suburban space, that of tract housing and trailer parks. This is rent-paying suburbia, and his characters are transient tenants who drift aimlessly in and out of a suburbia that resembles more a derelict sprawl than a subdivided utopia. Women work, but like men, are in dead-end jobs along the miracle mile. In this setting, residents are at pains to recognize one another—there is no basis for connection. In "Bicycles, Muscles, Cigarettes" (1963), a father tries to help his son resolve a dispute over a trashed bicycle. As he accompanies his son to the neighbor's house, he experiences a sense of estrangement from the suburban landscape and even from his son, whose daily movements are mysterious to a commuter father: "They turned down a dead-end street. He hadn't known of the existence of this street and was sure he would not recognize any of the people who lived here. He looked around him at the unfamiliar houses and was struck with the range of his son's personal life."[8]

In "What Do You Do in San Francisco?" (1963), a postman comments upon his town and upon the arrival of a "beatnik" family from San Francisco. Arcata (the town) is "not the end of the world," but "people here aren't used to seeing men wear beards—or men who don't work for that matter."[9] To the postman, San Francisco is where you go once or twice a year for a meal at Fisherman's Wharf or for a baseball game. If the beatnik family has come to suburbia, it must be "to get out of the unhealthy San Francisco environment."[10] Misunderstandings proceed to pile up. Rumors flow: the beatnik wife is a drug addict, the children have a different father. There are mysterious visits by a white sports car. The beatnik garden goes to seed despite offers of help from a neighbor. Sallie Wilson, the "Welcome Wagon" representative, has visited the family but says, "'No lie, there was something funny about them.' . . . But Sallie Wilson has been snooping and prying for years under cover of the Welcome Wagon."[11] This is a landscape inhabited by jagged puzzle pieces that do not fit together. Even longtime residents are unable to unite, if only in their fear and antagonism of the newcomers. There is too much distrust between them.

The more Carver moves into interior spaces, the greater the estrangement within and between people. In "Fat" (1963), a waitress tells a friend about her sexual relationship with her husband: "As soon as he turns off the light and gets into bed, Rudy begins. I turn on my back and relax some, though it is against my will. But here is the thing. When he acts on me, I suddenly feel I am fat. I feel I am terrifically fat, so that Rudy is a tiny thing and hardly there at all."[12]

Elsewhere, Carver has explored the "fear of fatness" as a stick used to exert male control and to diminish women's confidence. For example, In "They're Not Your Husband" (1963), a husband puts his wife on a diet, policing her food intake by hanging around the diner in which she works as a waitress and engaging other male customers in discussions about her size.[13] But in the previous passage from "Fat," we move from an initial feeling that a woman's sexual encounter with her husband reinforces a negative sense of her body to a subtle shift in which her own feeling of fatness is used as a weapon against his intrusion. She grows fat in order to diminish him.

Carver's frequent tactic is to describe and then disrupt an alienated suburban existence. In Carver's works, the detached spaces of suburbia really *are* detached, but his characters have a sense of, sometimes even a wisdom about, that detachment. The dualities of intimacy-estrangement, sleep-waking, and alienation-disalienation are treated as important and specific forms of suburban *knowledge*.[14] In "So Much Water So Close to Home" (1968), a wife describes her marriage with grim complacency:

> Nothing will change for Stuart and me. Really change, I mean. We will grow older, both of us, you can see it in our faces already, in the bathroom mirror, for instance, mornings when we use the bathroom at the same time. . . . We have made our decisions, our lives have been set in motion, and they will go on and on until they stop.[15]

But a surprising event affects her ability to live as before. When her husband returns from a fishing trip with his buddies, she learns that they discovered a woman's body floating in the river. Instead of reporting it straight away, the men finished their fishing, throwing out their lines and camping on the bank next to a murdered woman. The wife asks herself, what if

> something happens, that should change something, but then you see nothing is going to change after all. What then? Meanwhile, the people around you continue to talk and act as if you were the same person as yesterday, or last night, or five minutes before, but you are really undergoing a crisis, your heart feels damaged.[16]

In *The Critique of Everyday Life*, Lefebvre asks the reader to search texts for "evidence that a consciousness of alienation is being born, however indirectly, and that an effort toward disalienation, no matter how oblique and obscure, has begun."[17] "So Much Water So Close to Home" has Carver at his most Lefebvrian, using his characters to ask what constitutes change. The wife is brought to an estranged awakening; she rejects any further intimacy with her husband. She has not left the house or her daily existence, and therefore she feels no change has been effected. And yet her complacency has been irrevocably turned upside-down—her "heart feels damaged." In a later story, a woman has succeeded in leaving a violent man. She describes the single, powerful question that allowed her to effect change: "He beat me up one night. He dragged me around the living room by my ankles. He kept saying, 'I love you, I love you, you bitch.' He went on dragging me around the living room. My head kept knocking on things. . . . What do you do with love like that?"[18]

In Carver, radical change is rare. It is in everyday life that people experience their moments of deepest estrangement. These are moments of difference in which people may open their eyes, see their world as a puzzle, pose a question, and gaze upon possibilities. Sometimes they see one another, or at the very least realize that they belong to the same "social mystery," where "society . . . ceases to be comprehensible to the very people who participate in it."[19] Carver's characters share their detachment, even if it cannot be reframed as attachment. In "Boxes," a man stands at his window at night, looking at the lighted houses on his street. He sees a car turn in its driveway and a porch light go on:

> The door to the house opens and someone comes out on the porch and stands there waiting. . . . What's there to tell? The people over there embrace for a minute, and then they go inside the house together. They leave the light burning. Then they remember, and it goes out.[20]

The tract house dwellers of suburbia know the significance of the porch light. They stand on the inside of their picture windows and gaze out, looking for signs from the other houses. They watch for commuters to return to their respective homes and be welcomed there. They wonder who is at home, who is expecting company, whose house is dark. Who has left the porch light on because they are lonely, afraid, or waiting—or because they simply want to be noticed? They look for themselves by looking for each other in the identical windows across the way. The porch light is a way of saying, "Hey, I'm alive in here!" Indeed, at the height of the antiwar protests and campus rebellions, the Nixon administration called on the (suburban) "silent majority" to "speak up" by turning on its collective porch lights at the same moment.

If Carver maps the spaces of poor, white suburbia, John Cheever climbs the hill to those subdivisions built to exclude tract house tenants. These are the wealthy suburbs, far from the urban center. Apart from the coming and going of commuter trains, there is little notion of a nearby city. Most of Cheever's characters identify themselves by reference to their neighbors, or to other suburbs. Many of the stories are set in "Shady Hill," whose residents are periodically threatened by the tract house suburbs that surround them:

> So it wasn't over and done with, Mrs. Selfredge thought indignantly. They wouldn't rest until Shady Hill was nothing but developments from one end to the other. The colorless, hard-pressed people of the Carsen Park project, with their flocks of children, and their monthly interest payments, and their picture windows, and their view of identical houses and treeless, muddy, unpaved streets, seemed to threaten her most cherished concepts—her lawns, her pleasures, her property rights, even her self-esteem.[21]

Mrs. Selfredge's neighbors include "The Wrysons," whose civic activities are confined to "upzoning," as "they seemed to sense that there was a stranger at the gates—unwashed, foreign, the father of disorderly children . . . a man with a beard, a garlic breath, and a book."[22] But when we meet these characters behind their hedges, walls, and gates—we discover that they are threatened by internal disturbances to match any tract house intruder. Irene Wryson has a recurring dream about a hydrogen bomb exploding over Shady Hill. In the light of day, she is unable to relate this dream "to her garden, her interest in upzoning, or her comfortable way of life."[23] Donald Wryson has periodic depressions, which he can only alleviate by baking cakes in the middle of the night, as he had done in childhood with his mother after his father abandoned them both. Like Irene's dream, Donald's baking habit is a well-kept secret. Then one night, Irene has her dream and wakes to a sweet smokiness in the air. She believes the end of the world has come. But instead she discovers Donald, head in hands, lamenting a burnt cake. Irene runs to open the window, but hesitates,

> for what would the stranger at the gates—that intruder, with his beard and his book—have made of this couple, in their nightclothes, in the smoke-filled kitchen at half past four in the morning? Some comprehension—perhaps momentary—of the complexity of life must have come to them, but it was only momentary. . . . [T]hey turned out the lights and climbed the stairs, more mystified by life than ever, and more interested than ever in a good appearance.[24]

The Wrysons, like many of Cheever's characters, are threatened by a sense of vulnerability about their space; they distrust the apparent safety of their position within that space. In "A Vision of the World," a wife tells her husband that she feels she is a character in a television sitcom. Like the sitcom moms, she experiences herself as attractive and well-dressed, with nice children: "But I have this terrible feeling that I'm in black-and-white and that I can be turned off by anybody. I just have this terrible feeling that I can be turned *off*."[25]

For Cheever, it is the apparent success of suburbia that disturbs its inhabitants. The closer one gets to achieving the dream appearance, to resembling a TV family, the greater the fear of being "canceled" by unknown forces.[26] In "The Worm in the Apple," the very perfections of suburbia serve to indicate that there is something wrong. For example, the large picture windows suggest that only people with a "guilt complex would want so much light to pour into their rooms."[27] The wall-to-wall carpeting covers disturbing memories and loneliness. Gardening is pursued with "necrophilic ardor."[28] The classic features of dream suburbia are the very basis of a suburban malaise.[29]

In Joyce Carol Oates's *Expensive People*, the malaise is more dramatic and has disastrous results. The story is narrated by Richard, a disturbed young boy who describes Fernwood as a paradise:

> If God remakes Paradise it will be in the image of Fernwood, for Fernwood *is* Paradise constructed to answer all desires before they are even felt. . . . And if it occurs to you, my clever reader . . . that Richard Everett, miserable slob as he is, is being cute and praising

> Fernwood while (beneath it all) he despises Fernwood—you are wrong. . . . Fernwood is an angel's breath from heaven.[30]

But Fernwood is also the place, Richard claims, where his childhood troubles begin—the site of his disintegration. Richard has an obsessive love for Nada, his mother, who does not really "fit" in Fernwood, or in any of the other wealthy suburbs to which her business magnate husband moves the family. Nada is a published author; she receives mysterious phone calls from New York, declarations of love from unknown men; she occasionally runs away—only to reappear later, contrite and ready to try again in yet another suburb. In between Nada's disappearances, both boy and mother attempt to live a life of suburban perfection. But Richard gradually fragments under the daily grinding fear that Nada will leave. He fails to make friends; he fails at his exclusive, private boys' school. Richard's outward disintegration is matched by an inner lucidity:

> I can see that Fernwood itself was a dream, and everyone in it dreaming the dream; all in conjunction, happy, so long as no one woke up. If one sleeper wakened, everything would have been stretched and jerked out of focus, and so . . . the end of Fernwood, the end of Western civilization.[31]

Following another of Nada's absences, the family removes to Cedar Grove, which looks exactly like Fernwood. As if by magic, Nada is there waiting in the new suburb, claiming (yet again) that she has found the perfect house, the perfect life. But Richard now begins to wreak havoc on the dream spaces around him. He experiences moments of rage: he destroys the neat flower bed in front of the bank; he begins to play with a gun, taking aim on Cedar Grove from his bedroom window. Finally he shoots (to miss) a neighbor, bringing fear to the neighborhood and unleashing the deviance of another suburban resident, who engages in copycat shootings. But when he spots Nada emerging from the house with a suitcase, clearly intending to leave again, he shoots to kill. Unable to convince anyone that he is guilty—that a dream son in a dream suburb could murder his dream mother, he departs to live in the anonymous spaces of "downtown."

Oates's novel reads like a suburban *Notes from the Underground*. Richard narrates himself as a dysfunctional blot on an otherwise perfect landscape. Indeed the perfection of suburbia serves to throw the flaws of all its inhabitants into relief. They wander arcadia telling lies, committing petty and sometimes violent deeds, and ultimately damaging themselves and others. Yet nothing they say, think, or do dents the smooth surface they inhabit. When Nada's death is reported in the local paper, the accompanying photograph is not of the murdered woman, but her house, "described as a $95,000 home in the heart of Cedar Grove."[32] Indeed, the main characters in *Expensive People* are not Nada and Richard, but Fernwood and Cedar Grove. And that is precisely what drives Richard mad. His explorations of the contradictions of suburban space are contained and defused by the space itself. In his creeping madness, he is estranged in a paradise that refuses to exclude him. Ultimately, self-exile is Richard's only option.

For the reader looking in on Oates's worlds, a population of partial strangers is now seen to inhabit suburbia. In the postwar suburb, everybody is someone who "comes today and stays tomorrow."[33] The condition of membership is in this *coming*, in suburban transience itself, and in the embrace of the postwar culture of forgetting. The space is marked by newness: new houses, new streets and trees, new subdivisions and shopping centers, new people. In Richard Yates's *Revolutionary Road* (1961), Frank and April Wheeler express the profound ambivalence invoked by the suburban space economy. They recoil at the idea of buying a house with a picture window. Yet Frank hopefully suggests that one picture window might not necessarily "destroy our personalities."[34] The Wheelers' story unfolds in rooms that are "too symmetrical" and yet "the very symmetry of the place was undeniably appealing":

> The gathering disorder of their lives might still be sorted out and made to fit these rooms, among these trees. . . . Who could be frightened in as wide and bright, as clean and quiet a house as this?[35]

The Wheelers' failure to "sort out their lives" results directly from a profound doubt about the suburban life choice and from an ultimate inability to deny questions of "what might have been" in favor of "this strange little dream world" in which the whole idea was "to keep reality at bay."[36] When April dies following an attempt to abort her pregnancy, Frank notes that the little dream world persists, undisturbed by his sudden and violent loss:

> The Revolutionary Hill estates had not been designed to accommodate a tragedy. Even at night, as if on purpose, the development held no looming shadows and no gaunt silhouettes. It was invincibly cheerful, a toyland of white and pastel houses whose bright, uncurtained windows winked blandly through a dappling of green and yellow leaves. . . . A man running down these streets in desperate grief was indecently out of place.[37]

As with Nada's murder by her son, April's death by her own hand is diminished by the very perfection of its setting. But our longing for that perfection is now marked by a heightened awareness of lifelines beneath the surface, by an undeniable expression of suburban knowledge. With Yates, Oates, Cheever, and Carver, we have moved from the easy accusation of conformity to the disruptions of everyday life and the "damaged hearts" of estranged suburbanites. Conformity, it seems, is psychologically impossible.

Female Friendship and Suburbia

In Martin Scorsese's 1974 film *Alice Doesn't Live Here Anymore*, Alice lives in a tract house development in New Mexico. Here she talks to everyone *except* her bad-tempered husband, Donald. To her son she says, "How are we supposed to have a meaningful family relationship when he's on the verge of killing you half the time?" To the packer at the supermarket, she explains why she has bought an expensive lamb cut: "My husband hates me and I'm trying to get him to chase me around the bedroom." When Alice produces the special meal, her husband is unmoved and refuses to talk at dinner. Alice acts out both sides of the conversation, deepening her voice in imitation of the man of the house.

Yet Alice finds moments of real joy in the company of Bea, her next-door neighbor. When Donald dies, and Alice decides to move to Monterey and become a singer, the centrality of the two women's friendship and mutual support is disclosed. Alice's tears are less for the dead Donald or the loss of a home than for Bea. The women fantasize about Bea leaving her family in order to join Alice's adventure: "Wouldn't that be hysterical if you just got in the car now and drove off and they never saw you again? I can see their faces."

Later, Alice talks to Flo, her waitressing companion at Mel's Diner, about her loneliness. But it is not Donald she grieves for; it is Bea: "I miss my friend Bea. What time is it now, about 2:30? Bea is now watching *All My Children*." Alice's memory of tract-house life refers not to husband, children, or home, but to the everydayness of friendship and the regular repetition of soap operas that mark time for women in suburbia.

The dinner table scene in *Alice Doesn't Live Here Anymore*, is unrivaled in its brief, mundane critique of family tract-house life. As Alice swells her chest, takes on a husky voice, and bravely fills in her moodily silent husband's side of the conversation, her son looks on with an expression of alarm and amusement. Behind him, the dining room wallpaper shows a pastoral scene, a green lane leading to a nineteenth century suburban bungalow. For the female viewer, the family dinner provokes an embittered recognition of a quite specific space and form of emotional neglect, and in that moment we rage at suburbia. And yet when Alice and Bea hug and cry their good-bye outside Alice's car on that sad, safe suburban street, memories of longing and love for suburbia are undeniable. A critique of suburbia issues from this profound ambivalence within the text and at the level of spectatorship.

The intimacy of Alice and Bea was quickly followed by a text that used suburban sisterhood as its organizing theme. *The Women's Room* was published in 1977, casting a glance back over 1950s suburbia, uncovering configurations that came as no surprise to the thousands of women who had lived there: "It is often noticed that women in suburbia, much like the women in ancient Greece, are locked into the home and see no one but children all day. . . . But suburban women have each other."[38] Marilyn French described a highly integrated space in which the law of detachment between houses was transgressed by the women placed at the center of those houses: "There was a kind of cell network. . . . [T]hey spent most of their free time in each other's kitchens and yards. . . . The houses were close enough together that they could even risk leaving napping children alone: with the windows open, you could hear anything loud that happened in another house."[39]

In French's account, suburbia is a closed world of drudgery and painful isolation. Over and over again, her female characters live out "the problem with no name" as described by Friedan. But suburbia is also a spatial arrangement frustrated by its daytime inhabitants. With the commuting men away, doors and windows are opened, lawns are crossed, babies handed over fences, everyday tasks shared, secrets given away:

> There were two cultures—the world, which had men in it, and their own, which had only women and children. Within their own world they were there for each other physically and emotionally. They gave, through good humor and silent understanding, support and affection and legitimacy to each other and to the concerns they shared. Mira thought that they were more important to each other than their husbands were to them. She wondered if they could have survived without each other. She loved them.[40]

Feminist consciousness raising (CR) groups were in existence by the late 1960s. Recognizing the importance of personal testimonies and exchanges and using the term "bitch session," such groups drew directly from the suburban coffee-klatch model. Male hostility to the coffee klatch featured in the classic critiques of suburbia: "Left to themselves during the day, the neighborhood ladies get in the habit of sitting around drinking coffee and exchanging lies."[41] The often spontaneous formation of CR groups that typically met in the kitchens and living rooms of members emphasizes the legacy of suburbia's "herland" to 1960s and 1970s feminism. At the same time, there were rigid constraints placed on women's friendships in suburbia. Relations in *The Women's Room* are strained by domestic exhaustion, jealousies over men, and a fundamental inability to stretch intimacy beyond a certain point:

> No one ever suggested that the situation could be changed; no one ever challenged the men's right to demand and control. . . . The women had intimations, but no one said anything about causes when Samantha developed a rash all over her hands, or Natalie was seen to start drinking in the afternoon. . . . No one seemed to hear the day Bliss went tearing out of her house screaming for Cheryl to get her bike out of the street, and Bliss's voice went out of control and

> sounded like hysterical shrieking. All of them heard their own voices do the same thing on occasion.[42]

In the suburban-set parts of her novel, French proposes a joyful and important engagement between suburban women, but at the same time, a *containment* of female dissatisfaction. For French, the suburban sisterhood is a culture of mutual aid and consolation rather than one of open questioning or active feminist resistance.[43]

Other texts explored the disorientation of postwar suburban women unable to use the women's movement as a vehicle for change. In Alison Lurie's *The War between the Tates*, Erica is torn between a feminist awakening and a longing for 1950s certainties:

> Nineteen-sixty nine—it doesn't sound right, it's a year I don't belong in. It doesn't even feel real. Reality was when the children were small. . . . [W]e knew all the rules for that world . . . where to shop, what to read and talk about and wear, whom to have for dinner and what to serve, what kind of sandwiches to make for each lunchbox, everything. But now . . . the A & P has burned down. . . . [E]verybody's children have got big and awful. Everything's changed, and I'm too tired to learn the new rules.[44]

Erica occupies an uncomfortable position, one she must have shared with thousands of suburban women who read *The Feminine Mystique* and witnessed the subsequent burst of feminist activism. For if the women's movement borrowed some of its energy and organization from the suburban "herland," it took even more from the campus and youth rebellions and antiwar protests. Like many other suburban women, Erica can only be a marginal player in the explosive intersection of gender and generation. Therefore she struggles to inscribe her new awareness onto everyday spaces and routines: "I don't care about rock festivals or black power or student revolutions or going to the moon. . . . All these new developments they have, maybe they're interesting or depressing or amazing, but they have nothing to do with real life."[45]

In Lurie's account, the Tate family comes apart and then rebuilds itself in light of the learning brought about by rapid social change. In *The Women's Room*, the central character Mira only begins to recover her identity when she divorces her husband, gets out of suburbia, and heads for Boston and Harvard. Mira appears to be following Friedan's advice to move to the city where education and jobs await.

> In the city, of course, there are more and better jobs for educated women; more universities. . . . A sociologist's study of upper income suburban wives who married young and woke, after fifteen years of child-living, P.T.A., . . . garden and barbecue, to the realization that they wanted to do some real work themselves, found that the ones who did something about this often moved back to the city.[46]

In Lurie's *Nowhere City*, Katherine is an easterner who initially despises her new home in the tract-house sprawl of Los Angeles. But gradually she begins to use *downtown* spaces to create anonymity and, finally, a release from a dull, suburban marriage. "Nobody was watching her; she was in Los Angeles, she reminded herself again, where nobody saw or cared what she did. And at this thought, as always recently, came a little burst of giddy euphoria."[47]

When women forsake suburbia for the city, they disrupt the gendered order of postwar settlement and its spatial manifestation in white, suburban detachment. In addition, the suburban denial of urban life is called into question. In chapter 2, I argued that the most successful dream suburb was one in which the memory of the city had almost disappeared. But inevitably, any attempt to seal off our space gives energy to that which is excluded.

Estrangement and the City

In his short story "The Commuter" (1952), Philip K. Dick suggests the impossibility of disappearing the city in the suburban settlement. A passenger tries to buy a ticket for a destination that the rail worker has never heard of, for a suburb no one knew existed. Macon Heights was a proposed suburban tract development that had never been approved. Voted down by the county board of supervisors seven years before, Macon Heights has somehow crept into existence through an "instability" in the past: "Maybe that particular period, seven years ago, had been critical. Maybe it had never completely 'jelled.' An odd thought: the past changing, after it had already happened."[48] Again, Dick uses tricks of time to alter his character's (and the reader's) perception of a spatialized present. The rail worker, Bob Paine, is an urban dweller who gradually uncovers the real threat of Macon Heights, with its population of five thousand drawn from his own city:

> Stabbing realization chilled him. Suddenly he understood. It was spreading. Beyond Macon Heights. Into the city. The city was changing, too. . . . Macon Heights couldn't exist without warping the city. They interlocked. The five thousand people came from the city. Their jobs. Their lives. The city was involved.[49]

Bob Paine rushes home to the city to find his life more or less intact. But a fear has been seeded along with the young trees of Macon Heights. Suburbia does violence to the city, to its inhabitants. If you go to suburbia, you are part of that violence.

A nagging awareness of the city is the foundation of suburban fragmentation. Nowhere is this more thoroughly explored than in John Updike's *Rabbit* novels. In the first of these novels, *Rabbit, Run* (1960), we learn that Rabbit (Harry Angstrom) lives in Mt. Judge, a suburb of the fictional city of Brewer—"fifth largest city in Pennsylvania."[50] Mt. Judge is built into the side of a mountain and therefore has an elevated view of Brewer. In the opening pages of the book, Rabbit makes a furtive attempt to run away not only from his suburb but from all the nearby cities whose presence haunts his daily treks around Mt. Judge:

> He doesn't intend ever to see Brewer again. . . . He accelerates. The growing complexity of lights threatens him. He is being drawn into Philadelphia . . . the worst direction . . . a smothering hole where you can't move without killing somebody. . . . The further he drives the more he feels some great confused system, Baltimore now instead of Philadelphia, reaching for him.[51]

As he drives southward, Rabbit is forced to turn off the car radio because it "speaks with the voice of cities."[52] Throughout the book, Rabbit experiences the city as smoky, seedy, and a landscape of lowlife. He regards the city with distaste, and yet he can't stop thinking about it. Therefore, he is continually pulled to Brewer. He feels guilty for not living there; he experiences moments of liberation there. He meets Ruth downtown, and their affair unfolds in the neon bars, Chinese restaurants, and bedsits of Brewer. When Rabbit sneaks home to get his clothes, we are struck by the proximity and similarities between Mt. Judge and Brewer. Mt. Judge is not the suburbia described by Whyte or Riesman, nor does it resemble the suburbs studied by Gans and Berger. It is white, lower-class suburbia. Rabbit lives in a cramped apartment; it is cheaply furnished and cluttered:

> The living room has the feel of dust. The shades are still drawn. Janice drew them in the afternoons to keep glare off the television screen. Someone has made gestures of cleaning up; her ashtrays and her empty glass have been taken away. Rabbit puts the door key and the car keys on top of the television case, metal painted brown in imitation of wood grain. As he opens the closet door the knob bumps against the edge of the set.[53]

Here we are told that Rabbit's wife Janice is an alcoholic who spends hours enclosed in a darkened suburban apartment. The fake wood television is no "window on the world." In fact it is at the center of a depressive retreat *from* the world. As a former high school basketball star, Rabbit experiences his young marriage and first jobs as a slow decline from the heights of the American dream. He deserts Janice (who is pregnant with their second child) and his job as a five-and-dime demonstrator of "Magipeeler." When he hits the pavement outside Ruth's apartment in Brewer, the city street sparkles and his stomach sings: "Funny, the world just can't touch you."[54] Rabbit's sense of guilty loathing of Brewer is here transformed into exhilarating, unstoppable escape. He now relishes urban density and anonymity. Finally, Brewer represents a return to safety. The city becomes "mother of a hundred thousand, shelter of love, ingenious and luminous artifact."[55]

Walking the streets of Brewer, Rabbit notes the "warping" of city by suburb. Spotting a corner grocery store glowing in the dark, he realizes that its owners are now forced to stay open late in order to compete with the large supermarket chains. In the city park, there are no baby boom families—only old men on benches and "a few toughs, fourteen or younger. . . . The ornamental pool in front of the band-shell is drained and scum-stained."[56] The tennis courts have no nets; the lines are unpainted. In other words, the city as a family recreation space has been forsaken for the suburban Arcadia.

But at the same time, suburbia has none of the monumental grandeur or sad fading of the city. Passing a fringe housing development, Rabbit finds it pathetic with its "half-wood half-brick one-and-a-half stories in little flat bulldozed yards with tricycles and spindly three-year-old trees, the un-grandest landscape in the world."[57] Returning home to Mt. Judge after Janice has their second child, Rabbit is again struck by the cheap, failed project of suburbia:

> The flat tin-and-tar roofs of their neighbors . . . glitter with mysterious twists of rubble, candy-bar wrappers . . . (are) planted with television aerials and hooded chimneys the size of fire hydrants . . . three broad dirty steps leading to a brink below which the better homes begin, the stucco and brick forts, rugged with porches and dormer windows . . . guarded by conifers, protected by treaties with banks and firms of lawyers. . . . Wilbur Street was paved for a block past Rabbit's door, and then became a street of mud and gravel between two short rows of ranch-houses of alternating color erected in 1953 on scraped red earth that even now is unsteadily pinned by the blades of grass that speckle it.[58]

So Rabbit lives in down-market suburbia, constantly reminded of his low status by the security-wrapped upper-income houses just three steps from his front door. The successful suburbanites live close by; but the erstwhile basketball star lives on a street not considered worth paving to the end. Rabbit's adult life unfolds in an environment of suburban dereliction even grimmer than the dereliction of forsaken cities. It is only on outings with his son Nelson that Rabbit recalls some sense of home in suburbia. Together they go to the playground and to the high school baseball field, where Rabbit remembers the smells and textures of his own childhood:

> It floods Rabbit with an ancient, papery warmth, the oblique sun on his cheeks, the sparse inattentive crowd, the snarled pepper chatter, the spurts of dust on the yellow infield, the girls in shorts strolling past with chocolate popsicles. . . . He feels the truth: the thing that

> has left his life has left irrevocably; no search would recover it. No flight would reach it. It was here, beneath the town, in these smells and these voices, forever behind him.[59]

In Updike's imaginary, the suburban dream works only in childhood and thereafter at the level of childhood memory. To grow up is to fail, and your space reflects back loss and disappointment. When Rabbit makes another flight to Brewer, abandoning Janice with a new baby, the story takes a tragic turn. In a state of upset drunkenness, Janice accidentally drowns the baby in the bath. Rabbit returns, having presided over a total shattering of his world. Walking along the streets of Mt. Judge, he experiences self and space as conflated into one bleak unknown.

> The houses, many of them no longer lived in by the people whose faces he all knew, are like the houses in a town you see from the train, their brick faces blank in posing the riddle, Why does anyone live here? Why was he set down here, why is this town, a dull suburb of a third-rate city, for him the center and index of a universe that contains immense prairies, mountains, deserts, forests, cities, seas? This childish mystery—the mystery of "any place," prelude to the ultimate "Why am I me?"—ignites panic in his heart. . . . The details of the street . . . no longer speak to him. He is no one.[60]

Perhaps more than any other, this passage confirms the preoccupation with space and place that runs through all the Rabbit novels. Mt. Judge is an absolutely crucial factor in Rabbit's journey. The star basketball player is a small-town hero, playing out the American dream for all the other inhabitants. But the reader never meets Rabbit in his high school days; they are the past, from the very first page of a saga that covers more than a thousand pages. From the beginning, Rabbit's heroism is a memory inscribed across the spaces of Mt. Judge. What follows is a kind of prolonged and mutual estrangement of space and subject. Rabbit's failures always refer us back to Mt. Judge's failures and vice versa.

In *Rabbit Redux*, published a decade later, Rabbit's fear of Brewer has become almost entirely focused on race. Here Rabbit is living in the immediate aftermath of the civil rights movement and the black urban rebellions of the mid-to-late 1960s. In the opening pages Rabbit takes the bus from Brewer, where he now works as a printer, to "Penn Villas," a new ranch-house development south of the city:

> The bus has too many Negroes. Rabbit notices them more and more. They've been here all along, as a tiny kid he remembers streets in Brewer you held your breath walking through, though they never hurt you, just looked; but now they're noisier. Instead of bald-looking heads they're bushy. That's O.K., it's more Nature, Nature is what we're running out of.[61]

As with the city itself, Rabbit is simultaneously drawn to and repelled by Brewer's black community. He has a nagging awareness that, as a suburbanite, it is *he* who has killed nature. Afro styles, as emblematic of an emergent and more militant black urban culture, seem to refer more directly to nature than does suburbia with its green spaces:

> It's as if, all these Afro hair bushes and gold earrings and hoopy noise on buses, seeds of some tropical plant sneaked in by the birds were taking over the garden. His garden. Rabbit knows it's his garden and that's why he's put a flag decal on the back window of the Falcon even though Janice says it's corny and fascist.[62]

Rabbit is beleaguered. A suburbia he never fully believed in is now more fragile than ever. The black city is "noisy"; even his wife employs the language of campus militants and feminist CR groups. She tells Rabbit she is looking into herself—"searching for a valid identity."[63] Moreover she calls her husband "silent majority . . . but he keeps making noise."[64] For Rabbit can't stop thinking and ranting about all the things that are destroying his garden: thieves from downtown who "come out to the suburbs," campus radicals, antiwar protesters, and most particularly black activists:

> I don't follow this racist rap. You can't turn on television now without some black face spitting at you. Everybody from Nixon down is sitting up nights trying to figure out how to make 'em all rich without putting 'em to the trouble of doing any work.[65]

While Rabbit passes his days in a permanent state of confused rage, Janice has an affair with Charlie Stavros, a Greek car dealer who works for her father. When Janice moves out, Rabbit is approached by August Buchanan, a black coworker who appears to know all about the separation. Buchanan invites Rabbit to Jimbo's, a black club in Brewer. Again, Rabbit's guilty, angry ambivalence leads him to pursue an experience of difference that allows him to explore his dwindling sense of self. At Jimbo's, he meets Skeeter and Jill, who move into Rabbit's house and proceed to tear away the last remnants of his safe, suburban existence.

Jill is a white teenage runaway from the wealthy Connecticut suburbs, who has been living in Brewer's black neighborhood. Skeeter is a black Vietnam vet, who has jumped bail on a drugs charge and turns up in Rabbit's front room shortly after Jill's arrival. Rabbit advises Skeeter to turn himself in, predicting the police will be lenient because "this isn't the South." Skeeter laughs: "The news is, the South is everywhere. We are fifty miles from the Mason-Dixon line where we sit, but way up in Detroit they are shooting nigger boys like catfish in a barrel."[66]

Thus commences Rabbit's long education at the hands of Jill and Skeeter, who he fears and resents, loves and protects, even as he threatens to turn them out in the street. When Rabbit returns home from work along with the other commuters, he sees that his house is "intact, and all around it the unpopulated stretches of similar houses hold unbroken the intensity of duplication. That the blot of black inside his house is unmirrored fools him into hoping it isn't there."[67] But Jill and Skeeter form a surrogate family for Rabbit and his lonely son, Nelson—a family that subverts the spatial settlement of suburbia. Jill, a suburbanite herself, tells Rabbit, "I ran away from it, I reject it, I shit on it . . . where you're still loving it, you're eating it, you're eating my shit. . . . Don't you see how you're used?"[68] They eat health food, smoke dope, and argue about American history. Skeeter taps into Rabbit's perseverative interest in the race exclusions of suburbia: "We fascinate you, white man. We are in your dreams. . . . We are all the good satisfied nature you put down in yourselves when you took that mucky greedy turn."[69]

When his father asks what his neighbors think about having a black man on the street, Rabbit replies that he doesn't know the neighbors. His family and neighbors now against him, Rabbit finds that with Skeeter there he sleeps better. When he is approached by two local men who complain that their children have seen Jill and Skeeter "screwing right on the downstairs rug," Rabbit replies, "That's the kind of thing you see, when you look in other people's windows."[70] The two neighbors insist he "move the black out," but Rabbit refuses to throw out his "guest."[71]

Finally the house is firebombed, leaving Jill dead and Skeeter back on the run. Rabbit helps Skeeter get away. Instead of looking for the arsonists, the police concentrate their efforts on the black fugitive. Rabbit wanders away; the sound of the police radio calling out an "APB" on Skeeter rings in his ears. But for Rabbit, neither the arsonists nor Skeeter are the real fugitives: "Again in his life the net of the law has slipped from him. He knows he is criminal, yet is never caught."[72] Returning with Janice to the half-burned house, Rabbit tells her he has been offered a considerable sum of money for the house and lot, because Penn Villas is becoming a fashionable area. Janice is surprised: "I thought Brewer was dying," she says. "Only in the middle," replies Rabbit.[73]

As in the first novel, Rabbit is a suburbanite who compulsively runs his finger along the cracks in the picture window, draws back a bloody finger, and tastes it. However much he fears and loathes his own fragmentation and its mirror image in his space, he cannot stop exploring it. That, perhaps, is Rabbit's only redemption.

Suburban Estrangement: The Tie That Binds

In *them* (1971), Joyce Carol Oates's novel of 1960s Detroit, Jules is a working-class young man who lives in the city, but whose work as a driver takes him to Grosse Pointe, Bloomfield Hills, and other wealthy Detroit suburbs. Traversing the boundaries of city and suburb inflicts upon him an acute consciousness of his positioning in relation to those spaces:

> Set back on a larger lawn . . . it had a raw, expensive look, a look of newness totally impersonal. Jules drove up the oval driveway and parked in front of the door. . . . He saw himself sharply from a distance, a character in a photograph or in a film. An X hovered over

> him, near him, pointing him out. As he took the keys out of the car's ignition he felt a strange sickness rise in him, the dread of a foreigner in a neatly cultivated land.[74]

Jules's story is that of a painful struggle to reclaim a sense of place in a social order that holds him in impoverished entrapment. When Jules escapes with Nadine (a young woman from Grosse Pointe), they hide in an empty downtown Detroit apartment. He tells Nadine that they are people in a painting: "thinking of a nameless painting he'd seen once in the art museum. . . . It had seemed then, to hold a secret for him—the way out of Detroit. Now, standing with Nadine in this empty apartment . . . he felt . . . he had gone beyond himself. He was being in a painting, embracing a woman in a painting."[75]

Jules's escape from Detroit is thus enacted as a spatial imagining—less a "breaking out" than a breaking inward. But the cost to Nadine is the way in which Jules presses her into an assignment of passive femininity, which is already part of her suburban identity and from which she is herself estranged. She tells Jules: "I know what the edge is just as you do . . . but you don't believe that I'm real. . . . I'm something you made up, even my body is something you made up. . . . You came right into my father's house. . . . I can't escape."[76]

Like the Cheever character in "A Vision of the World," who fears she is the creation of a TV sitcom, Nadine is a suburban daughter who has a sense of being "made up," which bumps against Jules's sense of being a misfit, a foreigner. All his attempts to break out of his own "place" have a violence that dooms their relationship; violence results when the chasm between two people is such that they can only approach one another as fictions. Jules is urban, Nadine suburban: the connection between them derives from this opposition and from their separate experiences of spatial estrangement.

In the spatialities of the postwar period, estrangement was perhaps the only experience that bound city and suburb together. Estrangement derived in part from a mutual awareness, a sense of inseparability hanging across the spaces of suburbia. This was a social order founded on racist segregation and exclusion. Therefore the boundaries and social divisions were bound to assume a heightened importance for black and white identities. As early as 1940, Richard Wright was mapping the potentially explosive relations of city and suburb. Thus Bigger Thomas questions his friend Gus:

> "You know where the white folks live?"
>
> "Yeah," Gus said, pointing eastward. "Over across the 'line.'"
>
> "Naw; they don't," Bigger said.
>
> "What do you mean?" Gus asked, puzzled. "Then where do they live?"
>
> Bigger doubled his fist and struck his solar plexus.
>
> "Right down here in my stomach," he said.
>
> Gus looked at Bigger searchingly, then away, as though ashamed.
>
> "Yeah; I know what you mean," he whispered.
>
> "Everytime I think of 'em, I *feel* 'em," Bigger said.[77]

Twelve years later, Ralph Ellison mapped the subversive uses of black urban America's enforced invisibility. Ellison's *Invisible Man* takes up residence in the basement of a white apartment building—and nobody notices. Invisibility here creates for its character first, depression, and then a freedom of movement and possibility for action:

> That was all anyone wanted of us, that we should be heard and not seen, and then heard only in one big optimistic chorus of yassuh, yassuh, yassuh! All right, I'd yea, yea . . . and I'd walk around in their guts with hobnailed boots. . . . Oh, I'd serve them well and I'd make invisibility felt if not seen, and they'd learn that it could be as polluting as a decaying body.[78]

In the aftermath of the 1967 riot, suburban Detroit housewives were seen on television practicing pistol shooting. The leader of "Breakthrough," a suburban defense organization, warned that an armed response and bloodshed would meet any perceived attack on white property. But Carl Cooper had experienced and internalized the divisions of space before any of these events took place, before his own death at the Algiers Motel. At the age of thirteen, the police began to pick up Carl on a regular basis:

> They'd take him to the police station and keep him overnight or maybe two days, there was never any charge, just suspicion, they never put a finger on anything he actually did, you know. . . . One time he come home and said they grabbed his arm and bent it up his back, and they're saying, "Come on, now, where you been? What you been up to?"[79]

The implication in the police questions is that Carl had committed a spatial transgression; he had ventured "out there" into white Detroit.

> When he began to get into trouble, going in people's houses and like that, I'd ask him, "What you doing out there where white peoples live?" And he'd say, "They the ones got the nice things, Momma." I'd be crying and he'd say, "Don't you cry, no use to cry, I did this to myself."[80]

In comforting his mother, Carl Cooper evokes the critical ambivalence, the personal estrangement that issue from the everyday experience of a segregated spatial order. He goes "out there" for the "nice things" *and* he goes out there because of something unnamed in himself. Here we see estrangement finally as the internalization of the "wounds of geography" and at the same time, a reinscription in space of the subjective effects of those wounds.[81] A small remark from an unknown Detroit teenager contains all the complexity of Marx's most famous statement about history and all the mystery of Lefebvre's woman buying a pound of sugar.[82]

6 The City That Would Not Go Away

> An awareness of social space . . . always entails an encounter with history—or better, a choice of histories.
>
> Kristin Ross, cited in Gregory, *Geographical Imaginations*, 348

Ford Detroit: A Choice of Histories

To dream suburbia was to inhabit a series of stories and histories about space that, taken together, constituted a specific sense of postwar America. In particular, suburbia was implicated in a problematic attempt to relegate the city to the past, to narrate the city as historical artifact, to make the city "history." In this chapter, we return to Detroit in order to examine local evidence of processes of disinvestment in the postwar production of space and culture. As a city in which industrial development had a close and early link with suburbanization, it was the long-term effects and traces of Detroit's industrial past that tangled the plot lines of 1950s suburban storytelling.

In Detroit, even the earliest spatial practices tended to underline the relation between city and suburb. Henry Ford invented (his)stories with the same facility with which he invented cars. For our purposes, Ford's stories can be seen as historical markers in which the long-term space specifics of suburban Detroit might be discerned. This chapter begins with a discussion of series of those stories in order to track the cultural logic attached to Detroit as a space of uneven development and to note the increasing importance of race as the axis upon which city-suburb relations turned.

That five dollars a day . . .

. . . paid to good, clean American workmen

who didn't drink or smoke cigarettes or read or think,
and who didn't commit adultery
and whose wives didn't take in boarders,
made America once more the Yukon of the sweated
workers of the world;
made all the tin lizzies and the automotive age.[1]

On January 5, 1914, Henry Ford announced a new pay plan that he described as "the greatest revolution in the matter of rewards for its workers ever known to the industrial world."[2] Delivered in the flivver king's characteristic homespun rhetoric of "social improvement," the "five dollar a day" offer met with derision in some quarters, admiration in others. The *New York Times* called it "distinctly Utopian and dead against all experience"; several industrialists echoed the sentiments of the president of the Pittsburgh Plate Glass Company, when he declared the pay offer "would mean the ruin of all business in this country."[3] But some editorialists treated the announcement with reverential praise, describing it as "a magnificent act of generosity" by "one of God's noblemen."[4] Unemployed workers from across the country and beyond voted with their feet and headed for Detroit.

The "five dollar a day" offer was a hoax, in more ways than one. Between the lines of Ford's "revolutionary" declaration of employer progressivism, the demands of increasing "Taylorization" could be discerned. The purpose of the pay plan was to adjust working patterns to the recently installed moving assembly line in the Highland Park factory and to reduce the chronic problem of employee turnover. Since the introduction of the moving assembly line, labor turnover had increased dramatically, reaching 380 percent by December 1913. Consequently, one condition of the pay offer was that only workers who had been with Ford for at least six months could apply.[5] The "five dollar a day" story provided a means of mass hiring into the newly introduced three-shift operation at the plant. Moreover, Highland Park had more machines than workers, and mechanization was blurring the distinction between skilled and unskilled jobs. The new pay plan was part of an attempt to hurry the process whereby an increasingly homogenous workforce of machine operators, fitting into a rotation of three eight-hour shifts per day, could be brought into "line" and kept there.

Ford was seeking to recruit about five thousand workers, but by dawn the day after the announcement, some ten thousand men stood in freezing temperatures outside the Highland Park plant. Out-of-towners began arriving the following day, and by mid-January an average of fifteen thousand men gathered each morning only to gaze through swirling snow at the "No Hiring" signs in English, German, and Polish that were posted on the factory gate. Shocked by the press of desperate job seekers, the Ford management backpedaled by adding another qualification to the offer. Just three days after the original statement, it was announced that only men who had lived in Detroit for at least six months would be hired. Ford agents went undercover in the crowd, quietly slipping hiring papers to handpicked recruits. This sent waves of rumors and panic through the crowd, and attempts were made to bribe or intimidate the agents. Older men applied boot polish to their hair and stuffed newspapers in their shirts to pad thin shoulders. Fights broke out, bricks were thrown, and hired workers were attacked. Eventually the police turned fire hoses on the crowd, causing their clothes to ice up in the freezing winter air.

Those who made it past the factory gate soon tripped over the strings attached to the "five dollar a day" announcement. The "wage increase" turned out to be a profit-sharing bonus, which could only be earned by meeting certain conditions. The Ford worker was paid $2.34 for a day's work; the additional $2.66 might be granted if the worker lived in a style approved by Henry Ford. The worker in search of the full amount had to do more than turn out cars; he had to remake *himself* according to a mold as fixed as the Model T body parts. Or as Ford stated, "We want to make men in this factory as well as automobiles."[6]

So in addition to the pressures of speedups on the moving assembly line, the line worker returned home to be met by the well-paid inspectors of Ford's notorious "Sociological Department." The inspector arrived in a new Model T, with a driver and a language interpreter appropriate to the neighborhood. Worker, family, and neighbors were questioned on marital status, religion, citizenship, savings, health, hobbies, and life insurance.[7] To navigate the dangers and temptations of Detroit's rooming houses, brothels, and "blind pigs," workers were given a Ford Motor

Company pamphlet titled *Helpful Hints and Advice to Employees.* Here the road to the five-dollar day was rolled out, complete with illustrations delineating the difference between "profit-sharing" and "non profit-sharing" dining rooms.[8]

A contemporary cartoonist depicted his idea of the five-dollar-a-day Ford worker as fur-coated and chauffeur driven: "Hawkins, will you step over to the pay window and get my wages: I quite overlooked the matter last week."[9] Doubtless, some workers did benefit from the scheme. However the reality for the *average* Ford worker was that life at Highland Park began with an invasive physical examination, followed by a probationary period under the eye of the Sociological Department and the ever-present threat of exclusion from the profit-sharing scheme. Ford's 1916 financial statement showed that 30 percent of the company's payroll were receiving five dollars a day.[10]

The stresses associated with working for Ford were well-known in Detroit: "Ford stomach" referred to a set of physical ailments related to the tension of working on the assembly line.[11] One worker returned to his three-dollar day at the Dodge plant, following a short stay at Ford's, which he later described as: "a rancorous memory—a form of hell on earth that turned human beings into driven robots. I resented the thought that Ford publicists had made the company seem beneficent and imaginative when in fact the firm exploited its employees more ruthlessly than any of the other automobile firms, dominating their lives in ways that deprived them of privacy and individuality."[12]

Despite the less than utopian realities of the five-dollar-a-day scheme in action, the number of autoworkers in Michigan increased dramatically in the years following Ford's announcement.[13] At the end of 1914, there were more than fifty nationalities working at the Highland Park plant, including Polish and Russian Jews, Greeks, Armenians, Syrians, Lebanese, Bulgarians, and Macedonians. By the 1920s, Detroit had a range of spatially delineated ethnic communities. For example, the Jewish neighborhood could be found around Hastings Street; Hamtramck was the Polish area; Italians lived on the east side. But the ethnic clusters began to fragment, and ethnic groups mixed increasingly in all-white neighborhoods. Although Thomas Sugrue notes particular exceptions such as Polish Hamtramck and Hungarian Delray, he finds that in the period between 1920 and 1940, "Residents of Detroit's white neighborhoods abandoned their ethnic affiliations and found a new identity in their whiteness."[14]

For foreign-born workers, Ford added "Americanization" and English language classes as prerequisites to the five-dollar day. Wandering past Highland Park on warm days, Detroiters might observe Ford's English students (outside their work hours) seated at long rows of tables placed on the grass lawn outside the plant. Each table was supplied with a blackboard and an unpaid language instructor drawn from the ranks of English-speaking workers. And as a part of their reeducation, workers were pressed to take out citizenship papers.

Mr. Ford's Melting Pot

To the elaborate fiction of the five-dollar day, Ford added his own version of the American melting pot myth. At the end of the employee "Americanization" course, successful students underwent Ford's "melting pot" ceremony. Robert Lacey's history contains the following account:

> "Across the back of the stage was shown the hull and deck of an ocean steamship at Ellis Island," described on eyewitness to the graduation ceremony. A gangway led down from this ship and, in the dim light, a "picturesque figure" appeared at the top of the gangway, dressed in foreign costume and carrying his possessions wrapped, Dick Whittington-like, in a bundle tied to a stick over his shoulder. It was the first graduate of the after-hours language classes, and one by one the other graduates followed him down the gangway into "an immense cauldron across which was painted the sign *Ford English School Melting Pot.*" Each successful graduate entered the Melting Pot in his foreign costume, carrying a sign indicating the country he had come from. But minutes later they all emerged from the great cauldron "dressed in American clothes, faces eager with the stimulus of new opportunities. . . . Each man carried a small American flag in his hand."[15]

Ironically, in light of Henry Ford's anti-Semitism, the Ford ceremony was inspired by Israel Zangwill's 1909 Broadway play *The*

Melting Pot. The play tells of a love affair between a Jewish boy orphaned in a Russian pogrom and a Russian aristocrat. Despite the obvious obstacles to such a match, it succeeds in its Manhattan setting because "the real American" is constituted by "the fusion of all races."[16]

The melting pot image postulates America as the utopia in which unity is fashioned out of diversity and an integrated society is forged out of multicultural groupings. Here is a social fiction in which America achieves its utopian harmony precisely *because* it works its totalizing magic on all manifestations of difference. When Ford sought to "make Americans" with the same magnificent repetition with which he produced Model Ts, he mapped the basic image of the American way as a reduction of difference. And if Ford promised any color Model T the customer wanted, as long as it was black, the promise of the melting pot was equally constrained by *whiteness.* The pride of Ford's melting pot derived from its work of simultaneous identity suppression and creation amongst foreign-born white workers.

In this sense, the melting pot is the "cooking up" of social identities, a fictional process that closes the circle by constant reference back to utopia, or rather to the myth of the American people as a "colorless" (i.e., white) blend of once-present, but now mercifully absent (albeit nostalgia-laden), manifestations of ethnic difference. But (to borrow from Lefebvre) "if someone smiles at this utopia, he is wrong."[17] Lefebvre is enthusiastic in his belief in the social usefulness of utopianism. But as he celebrates "Fourier, Marx and Engels, whose dreams and imaginings are as stimulating to theoretical thought as their concepts," he also warns against that utopianism that "does not utter its name, covers itself with positivism and on this basis imposes the harshest constraints."[18]

In the myth of the melting pot, the unutterable is race or, as Fanon explicitly states, the "racial epidermal schema" that replaces the "corporeal schema" in the "composition of my self as a (black) body in the middle of a spatial and temporal (white) world."[19] For Fanon, the "dialectic between (the) body and the world" is here disrupted by the "fact of blackness."[20] In this sense, the rules of entry to the melting pot have a stark naiveté, or to borrow again from Fanon, "Simple enough, one has only not to be a nigger."[21] The imagery of the melting pot is one of inclusion; but where difference cannot be made to disappear, it becomes subject to exclusion. It is that exclusion, or rather the material presence and fact of blackness that becomes unutterable in the white supremacist cultural expression of American-ness. If utopia is "no place," the melting pot is "no race."

At the same time, it is the crude theatricality of the melting pot ceremony that makes explicit the very failure of the melting pot myth. In making race unutterable, the ceremony speaks race everywhere. The five-dollar-a-day offer and the First World War had already sparked a northward migration of southern blacks and whites that continued throughout, and after, the war. Moreover, from the moment wartime labor shortages and production needs prized open the factory gates to large numbers of black workers, Fordist notions of the melting pot were redundant. A 1917 survey of twenty large-scale Detroit employers reported 2,874 black workers. Two years later, a survey of the same employers found 11,000 black workers, 6,000 of whom were employed at Ford.[22]

It was Henry Ford himself who, by fashioning himself as the friend and benefactor to Detroit's growing black community, inadvertently underlined the centrality of race to the history of industrial Detroit. In the 1920s and 1930s, Ford became the foremost employer of black labor in southeast Michigan, as well as the foremost antiunion employer. Black workers obtained jobs in every department of the Rouge plant, although as in other car companies, they remained disproportionately concentrated in the undesirable occupations (such as janitorial or foundry jobs) and received lower incomes than whites.[23] There can be no doubt however that in terms of job openings and wages, black workers fared better at Ford than anywhere else in Detroit. "He who worked for Ford in those days, even though they were almost slave-like conditions, economically, was looked up to."[24] Detroit activist James Boggs recalled that "Ford was the one where blacks worked, and they worked in the foundry. I used to have a cousin working at Ford. Even at that time, they was big shots. Big shots because they was always the ones who had a paycheck, getting about twenty-five . . . dollars a week. At that time it was lots of money."[25]

At the same time, Ford's hiring practices protected his antiunion stance by stoking the racist sentiments of white union organizers, their fear of being replaced by black workers, and black distrust of traditionally white unions. He cultivated the allegiance of several prominent black church leaders by only hiring black workers recommended through those churches. "These preachers had demonstrated complete agreement with Henry Ford in matters of politics and industrial relations. In other words, they were pro-Republican and anti-Union."[26] When one church stepped out of line by inviting black labor leader A. Philip Randolph to speak, Ford workers who belonged to that church were dismissed and told that Randolph's appearance was the reason.[27] This hiring system remained more or less intact until the late 1930s, when the unionization drives gained pace, and the divisive role of race in the auto industry achieved a greater transparency in the eyes of black and white activists. In 1938, a liberal black minister exposed the Ford system in an article titled "Who Owns the Black Churches?" causing hiring practices to come under severe scrutiny and eventually to be abandoned.[28]

Mr. Ford's Suburban Villages

> Take the people and point them. The problem is to point them. This is what Henry Ford has done.
>
> City architect, Robert Hastings speaking in the late 1960s about how to "recycle" American cities, quoted in Georgakas and Surkin, *Detroit*, 239

> When I came to Detroit, Ford Motor Company had an allegiance to the city. Ford no longer has any allegiance to Detroit.
>
> James Boggs, interviewed in Mast, *Detroit Lives*, 10

By sparking the beginning of a mass migration of job seekers to Detroit, the five-dollar-a-day episode can now be read as a historical moment in which the long-term demographic and space specificities of metropolitan Detroit might already be discerned. The new arrivals found an industrial city in which established locational advantages were about to be boosted by wartime production needs. By 1920, southeast Michigan was at the heart of the U.S. auto industry, and the auto industry was at the heart of the organization of living and working space for the whole area. Car factories were built near rail lines, followed by related machine plants and finally housing subdivisions. "So as the auto industry expanded, the Motor City sprawled, farther and farther out."[29] Such was the "leapfrog spatial logic" that greeted the thousands of workers and their families arriving in Detroit over the next decade.[30]

If Ford's employment practices contributed to the continued migration of southern black families to Detroit, his antiurbanism suggested the larger, future mappings of race and suburbanization in the Motor City. Stating that "the real United States lies outside the cities," Ford remained a steadfast suburbanite.[31] When he headed for his native Dearborn in the woods just outside Detroit, Ford removed more than house and family. He dragged a significant portion of the auto industry behind him. With the opening of the Rouge plant in 1920, the largest industrial complex in the world located itself in suburbia. The decentralization of production away from the urban center was an early factor in Detroit, one that underlined and complicated the relation between city and suburb and the role of race in metropolitan space. The Second World War would see another boom in factory construction, one almost entirely concentrated in the suburbs. This was aided by a national defense policy calling for the dispersal of war production away from urban centers, but the Rouge plant had already set a precedent for the sprawling industrial complex set in the periphery.[32]

Decentralization was also an effective way of weakening trade union power. Detroiters called the new suburban plants "runaway shops."[33] Moreover, by 1939, the Big Three (Ford, Chrysler, and General Motors) were all building plants in various sites around the United States.[34] Thus a spatialized view of the long-term, uneven development of automotive capital in Detroit looked something like a large stone tossed in a pond, dispersing waves in concentric rings away from the center. Capital moved from downtown to the industrial suburbs and wider areas of southeast Michigan, then out of state. The irony of this pattern was that many of Detroit's blue-collar suburban residents would eventually experience some of the devastation of disinvestment already long familiar to inner-city people.

With production transplanted to the Rouge plant, Dearborn—not Detroit—became the center of Ford operations. Many Ford workers who had arrived in Detroit in search of the automotive dream soon became part of the early localized dynamics of Motown's suburbanization. Buying up huge tracts of Dearborn land, Ford's storytelling began to take on a direct and tangible spatiality. The dream mansion at Fair Lane would eventually be followed by Greenfield Village, the Henry Ford Museum, the Ford Rotunda, the glass house (Ford World Headquarters), and that monument to corporate power, the Fairlane estate. By the 1970s, Fairlane had become a two-thousand-acre residential, business, and commercial park, "touted to be the largest contiguous, privately owned piece of urban real estate in the nation."[35] Many of the firms now based at Fairlane moved there from Detroit.

Nowhere were Ford's space fantasies made more manifest than in his two model suburban villages: one Dearborn based, the other just a few miles away. Both model villages derived from the particular combination of Detroit's early industrial and residential suburbanization; Ford's hiring practices; and relations with the black community, his anti-Semitism, and his fantasies about history and social design.

Although most of Detroit's industrial tycoons tended to occupy downtown offices by day and the wealthy residential waterfront suburbs along Lake St. Clair by night, Ford placed himself at the heart of a suburbanized space of production. And although white Ford workers might reside in Dearborn, the town was effectively closed to black residence. Yet the Rouge plant had its own steel and glassmaking operations, and therefore more of the hot, dirty, and basically undesirable jobs typically given to black workers. Some of Detroit's first black suburbanites settled in the town of Inkster during the 1920s, receiving practical help and encouragement from John Dancy, Detroit director of the Urban League.[36] Inkster's early development as a suburb with a sizeable black population was a direct response to the housing crisis caused by massive black migration and to the suburban apartheid practiced by Dearborn and other communities near the Rouge plant. In 1921, a local property developer bought a twenty-acre tract of land in Inkster and built cottages at low cost for black Ford workers employed at the Rouge complex.[37] Along with Ecorse and River Rouge in the downriver corridor, Inkster became (and remained) one of the few Detroit suburbs with significant African American populations. By 1990, Inkster had a black population of about nineteen thousand.[38] However, residents in these towns did not follow the typical trajectory of blue-collar migration from downtown to the suburbs. Black suburbanites tended to arrive directly from the South in order to work in suburban plants. In other words, Inkster, like River Rouge and Ecorse, "evolved primarily as a satellite city in contrast to the evolution of (white) residential suburbs."[39]

As one of these satellite suburbs, Inkster was a shantytown hit by hard times during the Depression. Because black workers typically held unskilled jobs, they were the first to be made redundant. In Detroit, the Depression experience contributed to a growing network of radical labor organizations, but as an island surrounded by hostile white suburbs, Inkster residents had less hope than downtown workers of connecting to those networks. When Henry Ford shut down the Rouge plant for four months at the height of the Depression in 1931, disaster followed for Inkster families. For example,

> In his darkened house in Inkster, Odie Stallings despaired of the future. Even before the Ford shutdown, the community had been in critical straits. When the shutdown came, the town's meager resources were already exhausted. Like a bankrupt business, it ceased to operate. The people slid back toward the standard of living of the Dark Ages from which most had emerged. Not a police officer remained on duty. Children were not going to school. The doors of the bank were locked. Storekeepers who during the winter of 1929–30 had extended credit were bankrupt or on the verge of bankruptcy. People who had subsisted for two years on starches and water were dying of malnutrition. Odie's weight had dropped from 160 to 125 pounds.[40]

A survey of the southwest area of Inkster found that 500 out of the 700 jobless had been employees of Ford Motor Company.[41] In 1933, Inkster was one of a group of suburban townships to make a direct appeal to Henry Ford for assistance. From his residence at Fair Lane in white-only Dearborn, Ford sought to revive his role as benefactor to a local segregated black community. Inkster became for a time a new and highly spatialized social project: a suburban model village. With the reopening of the Rouge plant, black workers were hired back under a four-dollar-a-day pay scheme. However only one dollar was paid cash in hand; the remaining three dollars were channeled into the "rehabilitation" of the Inkster community. A public commissary was established, and the school was reopened. Men were given seeds and garden allotments; women were given sewing machines and taught to sew. But just as Ford's previous hiring practices in relation to black workers had stoked white racism and undermined pro-union organization, the Inkster project had its own subtext. In shaping himself into "the patriarch of Inkster," Ford stated that "the Negro had not yet developed a sufficient intellect to be able to be on his own (and) had to be guided and supervised" and thereby rescued from the Jewish "exploiters."[42]

Beginning in 1920 with the publication of a series of articles in the Ford-owned *Dearborn Independent*, Ford had already introduced the public to his version of the "international Jewish conspiracy" and announced his now well-documented anti-Semitism. Prominent among Jews hated by Ford were New York bankers and the publisher of the *New York Times*. Moreover, stated the *Dearborn Independent*, "the Jewish revolution in Russia was manned from New York. The present Jewish government of Russia was transported almost as a unit from the lower East Side . . . Bolshevism is Jewish."[43] Jewish financiers were ruining the American farming community and thus destroying rural values; the Jew was an urban "huckster . . . a trader, who doesn't want to produce, but to make something out of what somebody else produces."[44]

In these various pronouncements, Ford's anti-Semitism and his antiurbanism were mutually reinforcing. Dearborn was well on its way to establishing itself as the racist, xenophobic American suburb par excellence. Ford's paternalism in relation to his black employees was couched in the confused terms and localized expression of his vehement anti-Semitism, but there can be no doubt that Ford's hiring practices and the philanthropic activities in Inkster raised his stature in large sections of the local black population.

Ford's activities contributed to a quite specific configuration of Detroit's first and subsequent waves of suburbanization. Pitting himself against the fashionable suburbs epitomized by Grosse Pointe to the east of downtown, Ford reinvented his native Dearborn. In the Ford narrative, Dearborn was populist, steeped in farming history, and once again, a home for *producers.* The road to Dearborn was the road taken by blue- and white-collar whites; many of the suburbs that eventually sprawled around and beyond Dearborn maintained that demographic distinction. Yet situated in the middle of the all-white suburbs was Inkster, which can only be described as first an accident brought about by Ford's early industrial suburbanization, and then as a "model village"—spatial object of yet another Ford experiment. The rehabilitation of Inkster, despite the material benefits to its inhabitants, had the effect of throwing a noose around the town. Although Ford insisted that neighboring Garden City remove a race exclusion sign at its border, he seemed entirely at ease with the exclusionary practices of Dearborn. The reality was that no black Inkster family could easily cross the town line into the great white "out there" and risk forfeiting what safety and few benefits it had. At the same time, Inkster residents were effectively cut off from the growing black community in Detroit.

As already stated, Inkster can be described as a "satellite city"—one that evolved according to a different set of laws to those that governed suburbanization as a gradual, outward expansion of the central city. As such, it was relatively disconnected from the surrounding white suburbs *and* from Detroit. With the Rouge plant as "mother ship" and Henry Ford as navigator, Inkster had something in common with Greenfield Village—Ford's other suburban village. Surrounded by high brick walls and opened to the public in 1933, Greenfield Village was a historically and geographically jumbled collection of imported buildings including a stagecoach tavern, a gristmill, the Wright brothers' bicycle shop, a cider mill, a farm, the courthouse where Abraham Lincoln practiced law, and a Cotswold cottage.

Greenfield Village was originally intended as a campus for students of the Edison Institute, opened in 1929 and later renamed the Henry Ford Museum. It provided a laboratory for Ford's educational ideas, which took a "learning by doing" approach, in a setting that, according to the Village promotional booklet, combined the "homespun values of a pre-industrial American past, as well as the belief in technological progress."[45] The Village was also a spatial mobilization of Ford's historical storytelling. Although "history is bunk" may be the best-remembered phrase associated with Henry Ford, his disparate collection of historic buildings, objects used by "common folk," and the relics and workshops of famous inventors, including himself, perhaps constituted Ford's vision of "true history." Ford history was also a suburban dream, part of the relegation of the urban present to history. Moreover the historical and spatial "leaving behind" of the city was Ford's particular contribution through his own invention: the automobile. "Cars, he believed would allow people to move out of congested cities. . . . The village was as much his prescription for the present as it was his description of the past."[46]

Nowhere was the failure of the melting pot made more manifest than in the simultaneous space experiments of Greenfield Village and Inkster in the larger context of Dearborn. While Dearborn hardened its borders against any black access except to the Rouge plant foundries, Greenfield Village was an attempt to bypass the melting pot altogether and return to an assembled, fictional past or, as William Cameron publicized it, "that honest time . . . when America was in the making."[47] Not surprisingly, apart from the selected students of the Edison Institute and guides dressed in period costume, Greenfield Village had no inhabitants. It was an abstraction, a space apart, a heritage theme park, an antiurban fantasy and a precursor to Disneyland. Indeed, in the 1950s and 1960s, those Michigan suburban children who never got to California to meet Mickey Mouse spent their school outings at Greenfield Village. Like the small-town film, the Village provided a local dreamscape to accompany the real suburbanization of southeast Michigan.

Sharon Zukin maintains that the central difference between Greenfield Village and Disneyland is that, in Disneyland, the pretense of historical reconstruction is removed. "Disneyland . . . had no educational veneer. It merely told a story, offering the selective consumption of space and time as entertainment."[48] But Greenfield Village, like Disneyland, told stories about American space that bore little relation to the lived histories taking place just outside its walls: in, for example, the Rouge plant or Ford's other space experiment—Inkster. And like Disneyland, no one could actually live in Greenfield Village, least of all the real-life black inhabitants of Mr. Ford's other model village. Indeed it is only in recent years, with the opening of Disney's Florida town, "Celebration," that the 1950s *inhabited* suburban theme park has been merged with the classic Disney theme park.[49]

Inkster had another connection to Greenfield Village, in the person of Edward Cutler, the man who supervised the movement and reassemblage of buildings imported to Greenfield Village. Ford asked Cutler to make the drawings for the school that would be built at Inkster. Cutler remembered Ford's project for Inkster in the following way:

> During the Depression, these people here at Inkster, Michigan (of course, they are all Negroes in that subdivision) were taken care of by him. . . . Of course, the men had to work or do something. They all got credit for working if they were cleaning up their yards and the subdivision. . . . They were all very fond of him. It was even more than that. There was a certain love for him, I would say. You take the Negro people down South. You could tell the plantation Negroes, because they were all clean and had clean overalls and shoes on. He cleaned them all up.[50]

Yet in their important history of the League of Revolutionary Black Workers, originally published in 1975, Georgakas and Surkin draw on the plantation memory to provide an alternative reading of the Inkster project and Ford's larger relations with the black community:

> Racism had always been used as a weapon against unions in the auto industry, and Henry Ford had systematized the practice. Beginning in the late 1920s, Ford made it a rule to employ blacks in his factory at every job level in the same percentage as that of the general population. Ford helped finance the all-black suburb of Inkster and always provided low-paying jobs to any unemployed residents. This new style "plant-ation" owner also cultivated a select group of black clergy and professionals, but his motives were strictly business ones. . . . Dearborn, the city which Ford built . . . the headquarters of the Ford empire, prohibited black residents.[51]

Trouble at the Dearborn "Plant-ation"

To black people living downtown, Inkster might seem an island stranded in the "out there" of Dearborn and the other white suburbs.[52] But as the last to be hired, first to be fired, Detroit's black workers and their families were equally devastated by the

Depression. At the worst point of the Depression, unemployment among Detroit's African Americans reached 80 percent.[53] Just a month before the Ford shutdown, Detroit's city council had ordered that welfare expenditure be cut in half. By 1931, forty-eight thousand families were on reduced relief moneys, this after one hundred fifty thousand people had left Detroit and gone back to their small hometowns.[54] When Henry Ford stated that the Depression was "good for the nation," he drew the wrath of the city's unemployed.[55] The opening of the Rouge Plant in 1920 and the shutdown of Model T production at Highland Park in 1927 graphically demonstrated that the suburbanization of Ford production had put a longer road between the average Detroit worker and a job at Ford. Not surprisingly, Detroit's radical groups chose Dearborn as the site for one of their biggest actions.

In 1932, the city's Communist-led Unemployed Councils organized a march through the city, across the city line into Dearborn, and up to the gates of the Rouge plant. The idea was to petition the Ford Motor Company for jobs and food. With a police escort on the Detroit side of the border, the three thousand demonstrators proceeded without incident. But at the Dearborn city line, a group of fifty police officers met the marchers. The Dearborn chief of police was a former Ford serviceman who ordered the marchers to retreat and backed the order with tear gas and fire hoses. Intense hand-to-hand fighting broke out between the police and Ford servicemen on one side and the marchers on the other. The police opened fire, leaving four dead and many more injured. The Ford Service Department, under the command of the notorious Harry Bennett, was well-known for its connections to the criminal underworld. The Service Department was effectively a hit squad, employing corrupt and violent tactics in defending Ford interests. Moreover, and as Robert Conot states, "The Ford and Dearborn police were, in actuality, interchangeable, and men moved back and forth freely."[56]

The Ford Hunger March was neither the first time nor the last that Ford's antiunionism and his antiurbanism found the ideal playing field in the suburb of Dearborn. When the United Auto Workers (UAW) tried to organize the Rouge workers in the late 1930s, both sides attempted to play the race card. Because of Ford's practice of hiring large numbers of black workers, union and management alike needed the allegiance of those workers. In spring 1937, the UAW gained permission from the Dearborn city council to pass out leaflets at the Rouge plant. Walter Reuther and his union colleagues climbed to the overpass leading across Miller Road to the plant:

> The overpass offered a panoramic view of the surroundings: the Rouge River . . . the huge Ford complex . . . the famed "rotunda" . . . the acres and acres of parking giving proof that the American worker was the world's most affluent. . . . From the direction of the plant came a group of men, their hats pulled down over their eyes. Among them were a professional wrestler, a boxer, an ex-convict with twenty-one arrests . . . a Ford foreman and the president of the Knights of Dearborn. . . . One had a cigarette dangling from the corner of his mouth. Another, coatless, exhibited a colorful vest. . . . As Reuther . . . watched their approach, they so resembled the stereotype of the hoods in gangster movies that he smiled. . . . In the next instant, he was cracked across the back of the head, and went down.[57]

The Dearborn police stood by and watched as Reuther and the others sustained severe injuries in the "Battle of the Overpass." And in the aftermath of the battle, the Dearborn city council passed an ordinance forbidding the distribution of handbills at congested areas, that is, the Rouge approaches.

With union activism at Ford intensifying in 1940, the company tapped into black ambivalence about white unions, hiring some two thousand unemployed black men for strikebreaking and in some cases for use in the Service Department.[58] After a spontaneous strike action occurred in the Rouge plant in 1941, the union's victory there was only secured when the combined efforts of local black leaders and UAW organizers convinced black workers to leave the plant and join the picket lines.[59] Indeed columnist Horace Cayton noted the increasing importance of black community support for the union against the "great white father of Dearborn."[60]

Later evidence does support the argument that Ford hiring practices and the cultivation of black loyalty throughout the 1930s had been motivated by the fear of unionization. Meier and Rudwick note that, after the union victory and as early as mid-1942, there was an emerging "pattern of discrimination in the employment of black males" at Ford, with white workers being actively recruited from "other Michigan cities, while turning away black applicants in Detroit."[61] Also in 1942, "Ford unceremoniously ended all philanthropic interest in Inkster."[62] And one contemporary observer suggested that the closing of the Inkster Commissary appeared to be "a form of punishment."[63]

Despite the post-1941 shifts in hiring practices, the long-term legacy of Ford's hiring practices meant that with the unionization of the Rouge plant workforce, black UAW membership increased dramatically.[64] In this respect, the Ford Motor Company unwittingly provided a crucial space for black activism that, in time, would reach beyond the Rouge plant to impact Detroit's militant black community, this from right within the heart of white supremacist Dearborn. Events at "plant-ation" Dearborn only served to underline yet again the impossibility of the dream space of a detached suburbia. City and suburb were profoundly attached in a space of uneven development, deep interdependence, contradiction, and conflict. Even in death, and not for the last time, the body in space served as a politicized site, enabling an act of space appropriation. Although most accounts note four deaths in the Ford Hunger March, a black Rouge plant worker and UAW member remembered this about the incident:

> Five men were killed—four whites and one black. We were able to discover the graves of the four whites in later years. I was a catalyst behind that in that I got the union to mark the graves. The black fellow had been refused permission to be buried in the cemetery with his brothers, so his body lay in the undertaker's for several weeks, until finally a group got together and had it cremated. They flew the ashes over the Rouge plant and scattered them over the plant. That's one of those untold stories.[65]

The "vigilante and lynch" practices developed by Harry Bennett's Service Department, the city machine, and Dearborn residents themselves persisted long after the previously mentioned events described.[66] There can be no doubt that until the early 1940s, Ford owned the local political process. "Outside the plant, Bennett, liberally sprinkling money about, extended his tentacles into every facet of the area's life. . . . The mayor of Dearborn was a Ford concessionaire."[67] For the white, ethnic working class, the pact between the company and the company town penetrated the cracks and crannies of workaday life. A Polish resident of Dearborn remembers:

> They had in Dearborn . . . either small bars and restaurants, people who were selling jobs for the Ford Motor Company. The only thing you had to do was go there, leave your name, address and phone number; and in a few days you were called to work. You worked there for about three months, and then you were fired. How I discovered this, when I came there for the summer, I ran into . . . a lady who had a restaurant at that time that closed, and she told me that she had sold probably five hundred jobs.[68]

Such practices played on race conflicts among Ford workers first by giving an advantage to those white workers spatially situated (in all-white Dearborn) to access jobs by whatever means necessary, then firing them before any seniority could be established. The device was bound to divide the interests of black and white workers. With unionization, such practices went underground.[69] But white insecurity and race hostility remained and increasingly announced itself in a rigid defense of Dearborn—as a "for whites only" living space. The white rank-and-file of Local 600 typically supported Dearborn's segregation policy in defiance of union endorsements of black housing for Dearborn.[70]

The election of Orville Hubbard as mayor in 1941 was seen as a victory of local white, ethnic, working-class interests against the Bennett regime in Dearborn. It was also a victory for those white workers who, unable to keep African Americans out of the Rouge plant and the union, increasingly sought to defend white suburbia as the last bastion of northern Jim Crow. During his three decades in office, Hubbard came to personify the particularities of spatial organization in Dearborn. Ford could not have left a more transparent and outspoken legacy of his own space politics than in the texts and practices of the Hubbard machine.

In a series of housing-related contests, Hubbard crudely defended his best constituency, specifically the working-class Poles and Italians living close to the Detroit border and who he claimed had been "crowded out of Detroit by the colored people."[71] In 1944, the federal Public Housing Administration called for unrestricted housing projects for war workers. The Detroit mayor, whose own policy was "not to violate the racial characteristics of white neighborhoods" argued that "thousands of Negroes work in Dearborn; therefore, Dearborn ought to help some of them."[72] Hubbard replied, "When you remove garbage from your backyard, you don't dump it in your neighbor's."[73] Hubbard and his supporters successfully blocked the construction of any federal war housing in Dearborn. Four years later, the John Hancock Life Insurance Company planned the construction of a thousand-unit housing project on land bought from Ford Motor Company. There was never any evidence that any of the units were intended for black families, but rumors of the imminent arrival of "black hordes" quickly began to circulate. The Hubbard machine circulated handbills calling for Dearborn residents to vote against the project and "Keep Negroes Out of Dearborn."[74] Hubbard defended his actions: "If whites don't want to live with niggers . . . they sure as hell don't have to. Damn it, this is a free country. This is America."[75]

Hubbard was the loud American who threw open the picture window and shouted the realities of suburban detachment. And his neighbors were not offended; they did not huddle embarrassed around the backyard barbecue but kept him in power for more than thirty years. Indeed one Detroit journalist declared Hubbard to be one who "speaks his city's mind . . . and the mind of many northern white suburbs as well."[76] Sometimes Hubbard's inflammatory statements were backed by local mob actions. In 1963, a crowd of 250 angry white Dearborners attacked a house that they believed had been rented to a black family. For seven hours they hurled stones and racial insults at the white owner while the police stood and watched. Only when offered proof that the black man first spotted by neighbors was not a resident, but a man hired to move furniture, did the crowd disperse. In that same year, the NAACP made Dearborn the target of a sponsored march to highlight the problems of racist housing practices in suburbia. Bystanders shouted to the marchers "Go back to Detroit," and when one demonstrator reminded the crowd that African Americans worked in Dearborn without being able to live there, the response was "Then don't bother working in Dearborn."[77]

This last remark brings us full circle, back to the original decision by Ford to suburbanize together production and living space. Neither the early fantasies of melting pot utopia nor the model villages of Inkster and Greenfield could resolve the contradictions inherent in that original move. The orchestration of space in Dearborn rendered the race politics of uneven development permanently visible. Dearborn space involved the confinement of African Americans to employment at the Rouge plant and, at the same time, the often violent defense of its borders with Detroit and of its internal white living territories. Dearborn space also involved the construction of a corporate empire at Fairlane—an early expression of the vernacular of global capital. In all these arrangements, Dearborn was designed to wake the Ragle Gumms of this world from their suburban dreaming. But in Ragle's awakening, the suburban world is revealed to be full of contradiction and therefore a space to be resisted. In Dearborn, to wake from the suburban dream is to embrace and announce its violence and contradictions, to "speak your city's mind," and, finally, to borrow from Joyce Carol Oates, to make your suburb "as real as any dream, more real than a nightmare, terribly real, heavily real."[78]

North of the South

> I live in the North now. So the first question comes to mind is North of what? Why, north of the South. So North exists because South does. But does that mean North is different from South? No way! South is just south of North.[79]

> Much of Detroit was really a community that had been exported from the southern communities. . . . Whole communities, for example, came from Marian Junction, Alabama . . . and they all lived around here. . . . You could throw a stone in any direction in this area and hit a Chrysler worker and somebody who had come from Selma or Marian Junction.[80]

Detroit was "north of the South" in more ways than one. Those who migrated to Michigan in search of the automotive dream left family members behind and retained connections to southern towns. For many black Detroiters, an already politically charged sense of space derived first from the "Great Migration" itself, and then from having to navigate the southern *and* northern versions of Jim Crow. At least until the late 1950s or early 1960s, northern black travelers used "green books" when they drove south to visit family. The books were road maps indicating safe routes. William Lowell Hurt grew up in the Twelfth Street area of Detroit and recalled the painstaking preparation and anxiety attached to trips south:

> We never stopped at restrooms. My mother would always carry all the toiletries we needed, and we'd have to stop on the side of the road and go to the bathroom. We never thought anything of it. We just called it country. . . . I never realized how anxious my parents always were. . . . I never knew the fear they experienced, of how dangerous it was traveling, whether it was daytime or nighttime.[81]

Hurt also recounts his Alabama cousins' embarrassment when he walked in the front door of southern shops: "The storekeepers would say, 'Those are Burt's kids from Detroit . . . they don't know better.'"[82] This is reminiscent of Richard Wright's description of northern urban life as holding out a "taunting sense of possible achievement" that, when it failed to deliver, became the site of greater explosions of frustration and anger.[83] At the same time, there was more South in the North than anybody cared to admit. Southern whites had also moved north, carrying some of the same Jim Crow prejudices that had operated below the Mason-Dixon line.[84] In the 1920s the Ku Klux Klan had a high profile in Detroit, and white hoods and burning crosses were a fairly common sight. With a membership numbering in the thousands, the Klan held a public mass initiation ceremony and sponsored a write-in candidate for mayor in 1923. The Black Legion, a more violent wing of the Klan, was estimated to have murdered more than fifty black Detroiters in the early 1930s.[85]

With so many people migrating to Detroit in the same period, living space was contested from the start by various groups. With the Jewish and black populations least able to suburbanize, the black community tended to follow Jewish groups as they gradually pushed the boundaries of Detroit's ghetto areas. The changing shape of the ghetto was described by one Detroiter: "When the Jewish community moved north, the black community expanded behind it. When the Jewish community hit the Boulevard, that was it. They didn't cross the boulevard directly, and so they leapfrogged and went from the east side . . . to Dexter, 12th, and 14th."[86]

In any given period, African Americans had to map urban living and working spaces with the same heightened awareness that William Lowell Hurt's parents employed when they traveled south. If a black Ford worker had to get up in the early hours in order to reach the Rouge plant for the morning shift, he also had to know which roads were safe and which ones to avoid. Families looking for housing knew, street by street, where the ghetto boundaries were at any given time. For example, in the 1920s and 1930s,

> The black people were forced to live in the downtown area below Jefferson, below Vernor, down toward the river and east of Russell, east of Riopelle. . . . Before I came here, my family lived in that area too. But as the neighborhood spread as a consequence of the migration of blacks from the South, they advanced east of Beaubien, and as far north as Canfield, Garfield, and Willis.[87]

To live in a circumscribed ghetto space was to experience confinement and a limitation of life chances; at the same time it was a source of strongly defined local knowledge, identities, and subversions. In Morrison's *Song of Solomon*, the black residents of a turn-of-the-century northern urban street rename it Doctor Street as a way of identifying the location of the only local black doctor. Fifty years later, the city posts notices insisting that the street "had always been known as Mains Avenue and not Doctor Street." But for local black residents, this was a "genuinely clarifying public notice because it gave Southside residents a way to keep their memories alive and please city legislators as well. They called it Not Doctor Street, and were inclined to call the charity hospital (closed to black people) No Mercy Hospital."[88]

In Detroit, the first ghetto area, known as Black Bottom, was close to downtown, but one former resident remembers it as "very far removed in terms of being isolated economically and geographically."[89] At the same time "it was home to me; it was a safe place. . . . People trusted each other; people knew each other."[90] In Black Bottom, informal church and neighborhood networks frequently worked as northern outposts of "down home." The numerous churches functioned as aid centers, job agencies, cultural and recreational facilities, and political arenas. In this sense, Henry Ford's connection with some black ministers was an astute move, but one that depended on the agency of the black community. When Ford workers wore their employment badges to church on Sunday, they underlined the strength of the church as a bargaining tool used against the white establishment. When more militant ministers challenged the role of the church in Ford's employment practices, a lively and complex debate took place in the whole community.

At the same time, city life afforded a level of cultural experimentation denied in southern rural settings. Black Detroiters renamed the worst of the ghetto areas "Paradise Valley," and despite crowded and impoverished living conditions, a vibrant nightlife developed in that part of the city. There was a proliferation of black bars and theaters, jazz clubs, and chili parlors concentrated in the narrow confines of Paradise Valley. Louis Armstrong and Bojangles Robinson played there; local hero Joe Louis was a regular customer in various entertainment spots.

With cultural and street life focused on an area of a half-dozen streets, individual streets assumed a heightened significance for local residents and a reputation that reached African Americans in other parts of the country. For example, when Dorothy Lawson traveled to Illinois during the 1940s and told people she came from Detroit, "they would say, 'Where, on Hastings Street?' . . . Everybody thought everybody from Detroit was from Hastings Street or Black Bottom; and then it was changed to Paradise Valley."[91] Indeed, the name Hastings Street appears in numerous accounts of Black Detroit from the 1920s to the 1940s, signifying pride, regret, freedom, and confinement. Paul Shirley records the following memory:

> Hastings Street—there will never be another street like it, and it is known all over the world. Hastings Street in Detroit. I've felt pretty bad about it, because I've played up and down Hastings Street as a child, and it wasn't anything that could be done about it 'cause they were putting the freeway in anyway.[92]

Kermit Bailer recalls the limitations of the Hastings Street area:

> What I am talking about is living a very narrow life in a large, dynamic city with a host of opportunities but for "whites only." There's almost nothing you can ask me about . . . my life that was not controlled by matters of race. . . . For example, why would I tell you about being on the corner of Hastings and Adams. . . . It's only significant because if you go there today, you'll see it's an empty, ugly space. What was I doing there? I was there because I couldn't go downtown to more pleasant surroundings.[93]

When the freeways came in the 1950s, they erased an entire space on which the memories of segregated black Detroit were inscribed. With the construction of the east-west Edsel Ford freeway and the north-south John C. Lodge freeway, Paradise Valley disappeared and the beginnings of the Twelfth Street ghetto could be discerned. If Paul Shirley had cause to regret Hastings Street, Kermit Bailer might have noted that the destruction of Hastings Street may have "opened up" new areas of the city by displacing the ghetto, but it underlined a new geography of confinement—that between city and suburb.

If ghetto displacement occurred according to the patterns of industrial and white residential suburbanization, ghetto expansion was always resisted. Families moving to the ghetto boundaries were frequently harassed and stoned. When a black doctor named Ossian Sweet deviated from the prescribed route in 1925 and purchased a house in an all-white neighborhood, violence was inevitable. More than ten thousand people attended a Klan rally and cheered the proposal that "neighborhood improvement associations" be formed to protect white areas from black residence. On the night the Sweet family moved in, an angry mob surrounded the house. When Mr. Sweet's brother arrived and was threatened by the crowd, someone fired shots from the Sweet house and a white man was killed as he sat on his front porch across the street. All eleven people in the house were arrested and charged with murder. With help from the NAACP, the Sweets obtained Clarence Darrow as defense lawyer and after a long, acrimonious trial, an acquittal was returned.

The Sweet case gave early publicity to what would become a long history of local hostilities to integrated housing in Detroit.

With the Second World War bringing another wave of migration of war workers into Detroit, the housing shortage reached crisis point. In response to growing white hysteria over the mixing of black and white workers in war production, the Detroit Housing Commission declared its intention not to "change the racial characteristics of any neighborhood in Detroit" in the construction of housing for war workers.[94]

In 1941, the Sojourner Truth public housing project was financed by the federal government under contract to the Detroit Housing Commission. The project was located in northeast Detroit near a Polish neighborhood, but was intended as housing for black war workers and their families. After a concerted campaign by local white residents led by a Polish churchman and a local real estate agent, the project, retaining the name Sojourner Truth, was turned over to white occupancy. The NAACP and the Urban League fought the decision in what became a national cause celebre: similar situations were occurring in other cities, and the national office of the Urban League used the Sojourner Truth project to draw attention to black housing shortages around the country. Continuous picketing of city hall finally led the Detroit Housing Commission to request federal housing officials to return the project to the black community.

Once that decision was secured, the Ku Klux Klan became involved. A huge mob cheered as a cross was burned near the project on the night before families were to move in. By dawn, more than a thousand armed whites met the first moving vans, and hand-to-hand fighting followed. With blacks sustaining more injuries and being arrested in greater numbers than whites, news spread to black ghetto areas.[95] Hundreds of black youths arrived to support tenants, and fighting worsened. "Recruitment" handbills circulated in nearby white neighborhoods called on residents to "Help the white people to keep their district white. Men wanted to keep our line solid."[96] The Sojourner Truth housing project remained closed for three weeks while a coalition of labor and civil rights groups increased pressure on city officials to ensure safe black occupancy of the project. When the incident appeared in Nazi war propaganda, local and national embarrassment removed any remaining doubts that the move would take place.[97]

The first tenants were protected by more than two thousand troops drawn from the state home guard, the state police, and the Detroit police. But after a few weeks troops left, and residents were left to defend and create a living space under siege conditions. Adam Shakoor, a member of the Sojourner Truth community, recalled this period: "They were ready to give their lives. . . . They would talk about how lights had to be put out, and they were all crouched down, standing guard in their homes. . . . People came from all over to make sure that this project stayed a project for African Americans."[98]

As with Hastings Street and Paradise Valley, the spatial sensibility attached to the Sojourner Truth community was complex and productive. Residents came from all over Detroit, and before that from places as far away as Alabama, Georgia, and Mississippi. Like Ossian Sweet, all of them learned a valuable political lesson about Detroit and other northern cities: living space was something that must be won and defended. Such battles were the making of individual and collective identities. The Sojourner Truth project was first and foremost a contested *geographical* entity, a *differential* space; its subsequent politics derived from that original fact. Former resident Gerald Blakely described the space as an embattled island: "We were a city within a city. We were an island. . . . Everything was new, even the air. The surrounding neighborhood was foreign and hostile. The parents were unaware that the children had made the administration building the dividing line. We set our own standards."[99]

Shakoor claimed that those first inhabitants had difficulty moving away. An intense "good feeling" and "closeness" was the result of "the struggle that we had in order to have this as our own."[100] Moreover, Gerald Blakely's island metaphor is an apt one. The Sojourner Truth community *was* disconnected, and it used that disconnection to create and defend a place and an identity.

But at the same time, there were both geographical and historical threads that connected that island to an archipelago of counterspaces. For example, the black suburb of Inkster provided a geographical link. Separated from the Sojourner Truth community by much of Detroit and by racist Dearborn, Inkster was rioting. Just two months after Shakoor and his neighbors moved into their hard-won new housing project, a fight between black war workers and nearby whites in Inkster turned into a local riot eventually put down by a large force of military police and state troopers. Mr.

Ford's model city was no longer peopled by docile, grateful Rouge plant workers. Inkster too was an island—its black inhabitants stranded in white suburbia were perhaps beginning to see themselves as caught up in a spatial anomaly and to question where a community of interests might be found.

The Ossian Sweet case provided an obvious historical link and context to the Sojourner Truth project. Dr. Sweet gave a profound expression of this when he described his first thoughts upon opening his front door to the angry white mob:

> I realized that for the first time in my life I stood face-to-face with the same mob that has haunted my people throughout its entire history. I knew that my back was against the wall, that I was black and that because I was black and had found the courage to buy a home, they were ready to wreak their vengeance upon me. The whole thing, the whole situation filled me with an appalling fear—a fear that no one could comprehend but a Negro, and that Negro one who knew the history behind his people.[101]

The island that was the Sojourner Truth community could only be made more painful and more joyous from the connections across time and space to other counterspaces, to places like Inkster and historical events like the Ossian Sweet case. There is nothing necessary or inevitable about these connections. They exist in the eye of the user of space; they are stories we tell ourselves in order to act in, on, and against existing space and in order to create space anew. They are the detailed incidents and everyday minutiae that allow us to restore lived experience to the abstraction of given spatial arrangements. To know that Odie Stallings wore out his shoes walking between Inkster and the Rouge plant, that the children of the Sojourner Truth project started life there crouching behind darkened windows and gradually created a home nobody wanted to leave, and that Ossian Sweet thought about southern lynchings as he defended his right to live in a white northern neighborhood—to know all these things together is to operate against the ways in which abstract space creates islands and makes us lonely. In this sense, the subversive act frequently starts as this act of knowing or remembering in order to overcome the illusions and loneliness of abstract space. Longtime activist James Boggs remembered, "Years ago, we used to laugh and say that the white folks ain't got no community. That's the thing we used to brag about, because we all got along down here. . . . And we used to say white folks don't do that."[102]

Perhaps James Boggs is just telling another Detroit story, one no less fantastic than Mr. Ford's melting pot. Or is he really underlining the importance of storytelling in the making of any community, be it Dearborn, Inkster, or Paradise Valley? If the latter is true, then such stories were the making of an increasingly explosive black Detroit.

Belle Isle

Situated in the Detroit River, just across from Detroit's Grand Boulevard, Belle Isle was a seven-hundred-acre island that, under French occupation, had been common land. Sometime after the arrival of the British in the mid-eighteenth century, the title to Belle Isle was conveyed to a Lieutenant McDougall. In 1879, the city paid $200,000 to reacquire the island for use as a public park and leisure center. Belle Isle park was designed by Frederick Law Olmsted, the landscape architect who created Central Park in Manhattan. In Olmsted's vision, leisure and metropolis were mutually exclusive. In order to play, urban people must be given a nonurban setting, yet one within striking distance of downtown. A successful urban leisure spot was one in which any traces or reminders of the city were effectively excluded. Indeed, Richard Sennett has described Olmsted's style as a "denial of meaning to the built environment."[103] Olmsted was also an early proponent of the detached spaces of suburbia, arguing that the "advantages of civilization" were best exemplified by "suburban neighborhoods where each family abode stands fifty or a hundred feet or more apart from all others, and at some distance from the public road."[104]

To cross the Belle Isle Bridge was to arrive at an island dedicated to picnics, cycling, tennis, skating, boating, and other clearly defined leisure activities. In a city in which the geographical exclusions around race were already well drawn, Belle Isle was a shared, high-contact space. On hot summer days, black and white bodies jostled for limited numbers of picnic tables, boats, and so on. Sugrue notes that wartime Detroit "simmered" with race tensions. While the Sojourner Truth project battles marked conflicts over living space, workers at many auto plants took part in wildcat strikes to protest the increased wartime hiring and upgrading of black workers. Moreover, parks, schools, and other public places witnessed "countless minor skirmishes."[105]

On June 20, 1943, summer temperatures soared, and about one hundred thousand people sought relief on Belle Isle. Sporadic fights throughout the day between black and white day-trippers turned into a small riot when everybody jammed the bridge to return home that night. Not for the first time, rumor played a powerful role in subsequent events. With the fighting audible in many parts of the city, a rumor spread through the black ghetto that a black woman and her baby had been attacked and thrown off the Belle Isle Bridge. This rumor was announced by a man impersonating a police officer who jumped onto the stage at the Forest Club, a popular black entertainment spot. An audience of seven hundred heard the announcement.[106] Stories of rape moved through black and white communities, along with reports that carloads of armed black men from Chicago were heading for Detroit.[107]

These stories provided the narrative background noise for one of the last urban disorders to be characterized by direct combat between white and black participants. Paul Gilje describes the 1943 riot as "the last of the classic race riots with extreme personal physical violence," but also as a riot that bore traces of the emphasis on property and symbols of white authority that characterized the 1960s disorders.[108] Looting and destruction of white property took place during the riot. Initially, major riot activity took place on the "two separate stages" of Woodward Avenue and Hastings Street in the Paradise Valley ghetto, thus sketching and adhering to the contours of an already highly segregated city.[109] On Hastings Street, black rioters stoned cars driven by whites along the major east-west roads that traversed the ghetto. Black moviegoers were the first victims of white gangs congregating on Woodward Avenue. In some instances, police actions were barely distinguishable from those of the white mobs, and black casualties exceeded white ones. When asked by one black man for protection, an officer replied, "You don't belong here. Get the hell back to Paradise Valley!"[110]

At first glance, the "two separate riots" appeared to take on the geography of black and white communities defending their spaces by attacking any members of the opposite group who crossed the boundaries. But there were crucial differences. The ghetto was an enforced living space: in burning and otherwise destroying white businesses, the black residents of Paradise Valley acted to de-colonize that enforced space and to define it and defend it as a home. Woodward Avenue was a business, shopping, and entertainment area. White mobs were identifying the public spaces of commerce, consumption, and culture as spaces of race exclusion, thereby reinforcing colonization and ghetto confinement. Later in the riot, the "two stages" scenario broke down, as white mobs invaded the ghetto and hurled stones and pieces of iron through the windows of houses. Black residents trying to defend their homes responded in kind. Conot described this scene as a "primitive, stone age battle."[111] White rioters were assisted by the police, who killed seventeen black participants and no whites; the total number of deaths during the riot was thirty-four. Of these, twenty-five were black, nine were white.[112]

The Passing of Belle Isle

> In the South the saying was "Come close, but don't go high." In the North it was "Go high, but don't come close."
>
> Charles Butler, in Mast, *Detroit Lives*, 191

When investigators dragged the Detroit River after the riot, no bodies were found. But the rumor of black bodies being thrown off the bridge acted as an early catalyst in a riot characterized by escalating cycles of rumor and violence. If the Belle Isle riot began as a struggle over the appropriation of leisure space and time, the politics of race soon imposed limits to any radical potential in the explosion of 1943. Instead of fighting for the right to city space, and against exclusions, Detroiters fought one another. And as we have seen, the riot's principal victims were African Americans, attacked by roving gangs of whites. Moreover, white rioters exercised a "freedom of movement" not available to their black counterparts. As Georgakas and Surkin assert, the violence "fed by the tensions of the war years, was strictly racial: whites against blacks with the whites led by a nearly all-white Detroit Police Department."[113]

By the end of the war, with the Sojourner Truth project episode and the Belle Isle riot its most recent memories, the "arsenal of democracy" looked more like an arsenal of race hatred. The "two separate stages" of the 1943 riot followed and further mapped Detroit's changing lines of apartheid.[114] Stage one referred to ghetto confinement and colonization; stage two was about access to downtown, public space, and the fruits of the capitalist city. At the same time, the Belle Isle riot marked the last period in which substantial numbers of black and white Detroiters physically engaged with each other. The violence had its origins in a contested play space characterized by high levels of visibility and contact between black and white bodies. But as we shall see in chapter 7, the "don't come close" geography of northern apartheid was being consolidated. By 1967, the very meaning of the word *riot*, the meaning of violence itself, had fundamentally shifted.

7 Postwar Space and Culture in Context

As a child in the Detroit suburb of Garden City in 1967, I heard a rumor that police fought a battle against snipers at a motel with a foreign-sounding name. Standing on the front porch at night in late July, I could see a pale glow in the sky above Detroit. By day, the kids sat on glaring, sun-baked bumpers of Fords and Chevys and repeated the rumors of a black conspiracy against our subdivisions. It was an addictive topic—like the Cuban missiles, or the death of Marilyn Monroe. We longed for the thrill of a curfew. But there was no need. In suburbia, we were safe as houses. The real conspiracy lay much closer to home, on our own doorsteps, in our safety, and in layers of self-deception.

Childhood memories of suburban Detroit in July 1967 recall the suburban preoccupation with the city that marks so many of the texts treated throughout this book. Indeed suburbanites have been unable to define themselves without having recourse to both positive and negative images of the city. In this final chapter, I examine the problem of city-suburb relations by focusing on the rapid postwar growth of Garden City in relation to changes and events in Detroit during the same period. I provide a place-specific account of processes of disinvestment and complete my project of situating the events at the Algiers Motel in a larger cultural geography of uneven development. This chapter effects a return to the Algiers Motel incident, now equipped with a more complex archive for reading the violence that occurred there in relation to the production of suburban space and culture.

"Follow the Money"

In a dark, underground car park, "Deep Throat" uttered this advice to *Washington Post* journalists seeking to unravel the Watergate mystery. The implication was that a trail of dirty money leading to higher and higher echelons of the federal government would eventually reveal the powerful source of the Watergate conspiracy and a deeply entrenched culture of government corruption. It is arguable that postwar suburbanization cannot be understood without recourse to conspiracy theory. As in all conspiracies, there is no one truth that can be grasped, no single plot to be discovered and accused. A conspiracy is not so much the product of articulated intent, but more an outcome of actions that appear to need no conscious coordination—because those actions are undertaken by disparate, nameless partisan interests. The coconspirators never really know one another; they move through their worlds like Ragle Gumm in his fantasy suburb. Their wishes are fulfilled through a series of interlocking and overlapping moves, acts, and seemingly random events. At times they sense that they are guilty, part of some problem. But most of the time, they experience themselves as simply reacting to historical events or to the *market.* They follow the money; the money follows them. Capital "flows to wherever the rate of return is highest."[1] As Auburey Pollard Sr. remarked from Detroit, "You can see the money moving."[2] In the process, a city is wounded and a race divide deepens.

If, in order to map the material and cultural space of metropolitan Detroit in the postwar period we follow the money, we arrive eventually at a more complete realization that *disinvestment* is a keyword for suburbanization and American racism. We recall that, in the aftermath of the 1950s suburban boom, William Bunge wrote that the "affluent suburbs own Detroit's heart. All told, money is sucked out of the people of Fitzgerald by the affluent white suburbanites in Grosse Pointe like lamprey eels suck the juices out of Michigan Lake trout."[3]

In Bunge's account of the Detroit neighborhood of Fitzgerald, disinvestment is a complex process that includes the suburbanization of industry, commerce, and residence. David Harvey cited urban segregation patterns as "a tangible geographical expression of a structural condition in the capitalist economy."[4]

This is the concrete and economic application of the "follow the money" thesis. But to understand the postwar history of U.S. cities, disinvestment must be viewed as a far more complicated and tangled process involving a redistribution of resources, rights, political power, and cultural authority along racist and spatially exclusive lines. If the "age of affluence" was about the postwar consolidation of capital, it was also about the negotiation of cultural identities under the "pax capitalistica." Suburbanization is an integral part of that process. But it is also the end picture, the physical mapping, and the geographical *evidence* of the disinvestment conspiracy.

Garden City occupies about six square miles of western Wayne County. It is bordered to the north by the Middle Rouge River; Dearborn Heights and Dearborn lie to the east; Inkster is just across the southern town line, and to the west and southwest is Westland. There are two locally published histories of Garden City, one narrating the early years leading up to its incorporation as a city in 1933, and the *Garden City Chronicle*, a celebratory compilation of local news clippings documenting its postwar boom period.[5] A 1950 excerpt from the latter reads:

> Joy was expressed this month by the Review, when it learned that *The American City*, a national magazine devoted to municipal news, printed an article favorable to our fair city. So often, remarked the editor of our own paper, Detroit papers had made derogatory remarks about our sewer system and horrible residential streets, where cars got stuck in holes during spring thaws and heavy rains.[6]

If Garden City's roads were substandard, the postwar flow of capital and people to the periphery promised increased resources for road improvements and maintenance. Rail and road expansion meant that "suburban residential corridors fronting the main highway arteries alternated with industrial corridors fronting the major railroad lines."[7] Darden et al. cite Inkster and Wayne (both just to the south of Garden City) as among the working-class suburbs that "clustered in the industrial corridors."[8] Garden City was situated in a kind of border zone between working-class suburbia and the more affluent suburbs to its north. Its population was a mix of white- and blue-collar workers. Accountants and Ford dealership salesmen rubbed elbows with Rouge plant workers and truck drivers. The *Chronicle* reports feature a range of newsmakers including local doctors, builders, estate agents, and tool and die makers.

Positioned as it was, Garden City stood to benefit from postwar industrial and commercial suburbanization. With its proximity to Dearborn, and with other manufacturing plants and warehouse facilities relocating from Detroit to nearby industrial corridors, Garden City's growth was assured. Complementary metal and machinery industries and retailers developed around these plant sites. These processes had a profound impact on Detroit: "Between the late 1940s and the early 1980s, Detroit's share of the region's manufacturing employment dropped from 60.3 percent to 25 percent, retail trade from 72.6 percent to 15.4 percent, services from 75.3 percent (in 1958) to 23.6 percent, and wholesale trade from 90.1 percent to 29.6 percent."[9]

In Garden City, some gains were straightforward and expected, such as the award of a $1 million contract to a local electrical parts company by the Chrysler Corporation.[10] Other benefits were more like small commentaries on the times, such as the school board purchase, in 1957, of the opulent boardroom furniture from Packard's, a Detroit car company on the skids: "Superintendent O'Leary, hearing that the Packard Motor Company was in a state of liquidation, arranged for the massive board-of-directors table, with a goodly number of carved chairs, to be purchased for our board meetings. The set of chairs and tables was originally said to have cost $700, a substantial sum back then."[11]

The Packard Company had been a major player in the automotive game, with a plant on East Grand Boulevard, stretching across many blocks.[12] In the postwar period, many plants suffered cutbacks or closures, and by the time of the 1967 riot, Detroit had lost nearly one hundred thirty thousand manufacturing jobs.[13] Following the closure of its plant in 1956, Packard's black workers experienced longer periods of unemployment than their white counterparts, as well as lower pay upon reemployment.[14] When Packard's now jobless employees hit the streets of Detroit, they found an industrial landscape increasingly in decline. As residential properties around the old plants lost value, many white workers packed up, hit the freeways, and "followed the flight of jobs to suburban and exurban areas."[15]

With new suburbanites in greater need of cars, the auto industry stood to benefit in increased sales. Indeed, there never was a public transit tax to cover the whole metropolitan area. Detroit's growing working-class suburbs were, from the start, premised on car ownership. Sharon Zukin reports that in the "downriver communities, everyone drives everywhere. Streets are marked by shopping centers and gas stations; distance is noted in miles, not blocks. Many steelworkers' families drive two cars and a recreational vehicle. Unlike in other U.S. suburbs, most cars are American. Here cars are not just a means of transport: cars mean jobs."[16]

The lack of a cohesive metropolitan-wide transportation system combined with discriminatory employment practices to limit the chances of Detroit residents seeking work in suburban locations. Car ownership was, and remains, lower in Detroit than in the suburbs. A planner with the Southeast Michigan Council of Governments (SEMCOG) states that a recent survey found that most new jobs opened up in places where there is no public transit:

> And yet 28 percent of the households in the city of Detroit have no cars. . . . We talked to the manager of a major shopping center in Oakland County about setting up a bus line between Detroit and the center. Every other store in that shopping center had a "Help Wanted" sign in the window. His reply was "No, we don't want those people because they'll arrive by bus and they'll leave by car." He meant that the whole central city black population are thieves.[17]

No postwar home development was complete without a large driveway and a large car parked there. This was the house and car package later parodied in Tim Burton's film *Edward Scissorhands* (1990), in which each pastel-shaded ranch house has a matching car. As Karal Ann Marling has shown, white Americans were "lured away from town by advertising that wrapped up family life, suburbia, and new cars in one neat and appealing package," and this was nowhere more so than in Detroit, where so many suburbanites paid for house and car with the profits and promise of the auto industry.[18] In the 1940s, a Garden City automobile trader advertised itself as "The World's Largest Suburban Dealership."[19]

Over the next decade, shops, supermarkets, gas stations, and fast-food restaurants would appear along nearby suburban strip roads. Between 1954 and 1961, twenty-nine "one stop" shopping centers opened in the Detroit suburbs.[20] Eventually, Garden City residents had several major malls within easy striking distance of home, including Wonderland, Westland, and Fairlane. In 1952, Garden City passed up the chance to annex an area of land that eventually went to neighboring Westland. *Chronicle* editor Macfie laments those "timid and cautious" residents who were against annexation: "Look-ing back, now that the Westland Shopping center and other large, taxable properties have been added within this land, we can see that the timid were wrong. But then, they nearly always are."[21]

As a "bedroom community" with no major industry located within its municipal borders, Garden City's growth relied upon the continuous creation of new "landscapes of consumption."[22] The production and consumption of suburban space took the forms of new houses, new subdivisions, new schools, new churches, and new shopping centers. This was the social and structural underpinning of postwar reconsolidation, and in this respect Garden City was indeed part of a massive national project. The acquisition of Westland not only would have increased Garden City's tax base, it would have bolstered the social power of one suburb situated in a literal and figurative field of suburban consumption. Moreover, and as Zukin points out, the sheer scale of mall building, alongside the rows of identical houses and other types of suburban building, contributed to the "structural mobility of an entire generation and a transcendence of the very idea of social class."[23]

The expansion of suburban fields of consumption was directly facilitated and financed by downtown Detroit. As the rate of return on downtown shops looked set to fall below that of suburban shopping centers, the migration of commercial capital accelerated. In 1958, Detroit had ten of the region's twenty largest shopping areas.[24] In 1959, Kern's, Detroit's second-largest department store, closed, "removing almost a whole downtown block from the tax rolls."[25] By 1977, Hudson's department store, a twenty-five-story, one-block square monumental building on Woodward Avenue was the only major shopping area remaining. In the 1940s, Hudson's downtown store "generated three times the sales of its nearest Detroit competitor."[26]

In 1951, the Hudson Company embarked on its own suburban projects, building the Northland and Eastland shopping malls, both just across the city line.[27] Hudson's downtown sales went into steady decline after 1954, but Northland and Eastland profits more than compensated for downtown losses. In 1969, Hudson's merged with Dayton, a Minneapolis corporation, and decision-making power transferred to the Minneapolis office. Finally, in 1983, Dayton-Hudson closed its downtown store. Rosa Sims remembers

> going downtown as a little girl with my mother. It was so special. She would dress me up like we were going to church. . . . It's changed so much. It's been very difficult for me to adjust to not being able to find whatever products and services that I need at the corner. I have to drive ten to thirty miles before I can find a store that has what I need. And taking my money out of the community and knowing that it's not helping Detroit. . . . When it first started happening I refused to shop any place outside of Detroit. Then it became very apparent that if I was going to have anything I was going to have to shop outside of Detroit.[28]

From the early 1950s to its final closure in 1983, Hudson's followed a gradual but definite course of urban disinvestment until the final demolition of the downtown building in 1998. The downtown store had once made monumental and geographic reference to a capitalist success story. Detroit, the flivver capital, had been a magnet for dream seekers—from industrial fat cats to line workers and powerful unions. Hudson's facade lent architectural credence to the belief that, in the Motor City, eventually everybody would get a piece of the automotive pie. James Boggs underlines the profound connection Detroiters made between an expanding auto industry and community well-being. The belief was that everybody was working, and therefore the community would take care of itself:

> There would be enough taxes paid to pay for the schools, and there would be some houses built, and so forth. . . . Suddenly, ain't nobody working, ain't nobody taking care of housing and here all the houses are collapsing all around us. We ain't working for Ford now so we ain't building houses now. We ain't doing nothing because we ain't working for Ford.[29]

In the postwar period, new houses *were* being built and on a massive scale. But as we have seen, the mechanics of VA/FHA financing combined with "white flight" to ensure that new residential construction was concentrated in the suburbs. With almost no new houses being built in Detroit, those that remained assumed great importance to the expanding black community. It is possible that Rosa Sims lived on one of Detroit's tree-lined streets with detached houses. There were many such streets in Detroit, and as the white exodus proceeded, these streets became part of the black community. Sims recalls that her father was an officer in the block club, and the entire family took part in cleanups and tree-planting projects. As Herb Boyd suggests, Detroiters have been proud of these neighborhoods and see them as integral to the development of black culture in the city:

> Detroit was unique in terms of the geographical patterns of how we lived—single-family homes, a basement, a back yard. These things figured into the relationships people have that other cities didn't have. Jazz was very important to me as a teenager. We'd meet in different basements and play instruments. We had a certain amount of privacy. We didn't have to go to a settlement. Our *homes* were points of congregation. That gave us a certain control and development that likely triggered the later development of Motown.[30]

The areas described by Rosa Sims and Herb Boyd developed into vibrant black communities in spite of resistance on the part of white Detroiters aided by a racist postwar city government. Detroit's 1949 election campaign made public housing a priority issue. The incumbent Mayor Albert Cobo drew support from the self-styled "neighborhood improvement associations," whose main purpose was to resist integrated housing. After the war, these associations spread all over the city. Cobo was opposed to public housing projects "in outlying areas where single homes are located," that is, near the newly burgeoning suburbs.[31] And of course Cobo was aided by those suburban zoning laws and redlining practices that ensured that life in the periphery remained white, detached, and profoundly antiurban. Taken together, these were the tactics that meant an expanding black population was effectively barred from the suburbs and restricted in movement within the city limits. Between 1940 and 1960, the percentage of African Americans in Detroit "rose from 10 percent to 30 percent . . . while the percentage in the suburbs decreased from 5 percent to 3 percent."[32]

Cobo's position was simply an early representation of local patterns of urban residential change that persisted throughout the postwar period. Whites (aided by local estate agents and mortgage lenders) employed a variety of legal and illegal tactics in order to prevent or delay the entry of African Americans into their neighborhoods. Eventually, one or two black families might manage to move in. At that point, whites began their exodus, often using federally backed loans to move to suburbia. "After some years, the old neighborhood had a largely black population. This drastically altered the city of Detroit."[33] Detroit's white population fell by 86 percent between 1950 and 1990: the number of whites in the city declined from 1,546,000 to 222,000. Detroit was 16 percent black in 1950 and 76 percent black in 1990.[34]

The main change was not so much that new black neighborhoods appeared, but rather that old neighborhoods expanded; in other words, the invisible walls moved. A 1962 study showed that the growing African American population "spilled out to occupy housing available in adjacent areas."[35] In the 1960s, black Detroiters occupied the same areas as their predecessors in the three previous decades: "The only difference is that, due to increasing numbers, they occupy more space *centered about their traditional quarters.*"[36] At least one observer termed Detroit's postwar population movements not as integration, but as "succession."[37] Concentric rings of succession characterized the flow of capital, power, and people away from the center. This is the uneven power in spacing rendered invisible as we speed along the freeway behind decades of commuters, all making a beeline for the suburban space of forgetting. But a Detroit pastor penetrates the layers of deception when he describes the same drive as "going into another world: no vacant storefronts, the lawns are green, the houses are occupied, and all things . . . reflect affluence and well-being. This drainage of the heart of a city seems impossible for it to have been accidental."[38]

During the suburban boom of the 1920s, Garden City had already made its mark as the "sun parlor of Detroit."[39] Estate agents and land speculators went door to door in Detroit in order to recruit customers for newly subdivided lots. Prospective buyers were told that in Garden City "children might be raised in safety, far from the maddening crowd, the factory smoke and the city's noise."[40] So when Garden City became incorporated as a home rule city in 1933, its self-differentiation from Detroit was well established.

The obvious attraction of incorporation was that it further localized municipal power over zoning and public services. Public maintenance, schools, and police and fire departments fell increasingly under the jurisdiction of the suburban municipality, which had increased its tax base as a result of exclusionary zoning practices and building requirements. Incorporation allowed for the gains of an increased tax base to be kept in local coffers. Opposition to Detroit was written into all these practices. The suburban identity was derived in part from that opposition, and from a more generalized anti-urbanism.

Despite a shrinking downtown tax base and suburban usage of downtown land, buildings, services, and other amenities, the average Garden City resident could rely on incorporation to force an arbitrary dissociation from Detroit. In this way, the suburbanite benefits from the city, while at the same time draining the city of its resources. Bunge termed suburbia "the great American tax dodge."[41] Moreover, by *not* watching how the money moves, many suburbanites located the source of urban decay not in disinvestment but in a growing inner-city black population. Thus a racist interpretation of urban decline further hardened white anti-urbanism and resistance to suburban integration.

The Garden City resident might seek a community of interests away from Detroit in the small (white) towns in the far-flung regions of Michigan. Indeed the *Chronicle* cites regular mayoral exchanges between Garden City and provincial towns smaller than itself. Moreover, the suburban worldview was bolstered by an identification with suburbanization as a national phenomenon, as the postwar trope of American success. In the 1950s, an additional twenty-two new suburban cities incorporated themselves, bringing about a proliferation of local governments surrounding Detroit, each creating a closed political entity in which the illusions of small-town life might be maintained. Indeed the winning entry in a 1956 slogan contest "designed to boost ye old Garden City" was the slogan "City Without Strangers."[42] The creation of a civic identity for Garden City rested on a precarious balance between the antiurbanist small-town ethos and local pride in the boom itself. In fact, Garden City bore no resemblance to Bedford Falls or any other idealized image of the American small town. Its look was decidedly one of tract-house sprawl.

For the most part, bordering suburbs traded on minor boundary squabbles and moments of cooperation in order to create a political landscape of suburban municipalities. A more or less friendly competition between suburbs for a share in the region's prosperity kept suburban eyes firmly fixed on their own and each other's backyards. When, in 1957, Dearborn's ubiquitous Mayor Hubbard proposed that eleven neighboring townships annex themselves to Dearborn, Garden City residents were alarmed. "If this took place, Garden City, Inkster and Wayne would find themselves lying within the Greater Dearborn City, said to be four times as large as Detroit."[43] Hubbard's plan would have created a major city of majority white residents to compete in population and area with the city of Detroit.

If Detroit did not figure as an everyday geographical reality, it remained powerful in its absence. One can only speculate as to what would have been the reaction of Garden City people if they had been included in Hubbard's proposal. But local hesitation to the idea as presented might be seen as deriving from intersuburban competitiveness and an oddly nostalgic attachment to Detroit as the city against which residents defined themselves. It must be remembered that the anti-urbanism of the fringe was not trouble free. The suburbanite traveling out of state or to Europe became an overnight *Detroiter*, expressing pride in the city's automotive history, the Institute of Arts, and the renown of Motown Records or expressing loyalty to the city baseball, hockey, and basketball teams. These cultural allegiances illustrated suburbia's own ragged sense of itself and perhaps an uncomfortable sense of cultural impoverishment experienced by sprawl dwellers.

Suburban identities have been profoundly marked by changing and ambivalent images of the city. But in the postwar period, these images were increasingly formed without any material vision of city spaces. Gone too was any tangible knowledge of downtown streets, of everyday urban life, or of the political geography that underpinned the entire region. The Fords and Chevys in 1950s driveways were the most direct visible reference to the Motor City, but increasingly these too were suburban products. With Detroit assuming a kind of ghostly, mythic quality, suburbanites sought to invent themselves. The *Garden City Chronicle* belongs to the ideological project of suburban self-invention, a project in which everyday life under the "law of uneven development" is rendered invisible unto itself.

From about 1950, the *Chronicle* records an inward-looking preoccupation with the rapid rate of growth and its associated joys and pains. But neither celebration nor grievance ever brings into question the growth process itself, or the wider social costs attached to it. As suggested earlier, Garden City had to invent its cultural identity through reference to its role as a successfully expanding suburb in an era of mass suburbanization. To suburbanize is to *be* in the postwar reconsolidation of capital.

Back to the Algiers Motel

Throughout this book, I have examined postwar suburbia as a *cultural* phenomenon, but one that can only be understood in social and historical context. Specifically, I have argued that the changing relations between city and suburb belonged to local and larger processes of disinvestment. I have grounded these insights in a series of studies of Detroit and its suburbs, culminating in a more detailed look at the postwar history of Garden City.

In the opening chapter, I argued that the road to the Algiers Motel was paved with contested narratives, from local and specific rumors concerning events in July 1967 to the larger historical and cultural representations treated in this book. Taken together, these have provided an archive for our reading of the Algiers Motel incident—a contextualization for the motel as place, event, and representation. We are now better able to locate it in the postwar cultural geography of suburbanization, disinvestment, and race. Not only is it possible to return to the scene of a material act of violence, but we are now able to consider the ways in which the events of the "long, hot summer" produced a cultural politics of space, one that contested the very place and meaning of violence itself.

In Detroit, in 1967, every incident, every street battle, was marked by competing narrative accounts and explanations, deepening the incomprehension that characterized encounters between various groups of Detroiters. For example, on the day before he raided the Algiers Motel, one police officer noticed the smiles on people's faces as they watched buildings burn, as he put it, "just like they had accomplished something. I couldn't understand that, and I asked one fellow, 'What's wrong with you people?'"[44] On their way to the motel, Auburey Pollard and his friends were stopped and searched by the police. One of them recalled, "They was searching us down. Auburey got hit then, back of the head. Auburey was just telling them he was working at Ford's. So they told us to get back in the car and go ahead on. So I said to Auburey, 'Man, what's *happened* to these people? They gone crazy.'"[45]

By the time they all converged on the motel, residents and police officers alike had entered into the narrative crisis. In order to learn from the tangled narratives, it is perhaps best to leave the mayor's institutionalized fantasy of rumor control behind and travel back to the location where they are most tangled—the Algiers Motel. If the 1967 riot can now be partly understood as an acute moment in a chronically contested representational field, the Algiers Motel gives a highly evocative sense of place to that process. As the riot exploded outward, the Algiers Motel turned violence inward, making it stagy and secretive. In its very name and decor, the Algiers Motel began its life as a piece of local theater. And everybody who entered gave performance to the spatial dislocation and the narrative crisis that was Detroit in 1967. Briefly then, here are facts of the story and a story of the facts in what came to be known as the "Algiers Motel incident."[46]

During the period of the riot, Auburey Pollard and his friends checked into the Algiers Motel in order to stay with members of the *Dramatics*, a local rhythm and blues group that had been appearing with Martha and the Vandellas at the Fox Theater. From the start of the riot, the group had been holed up in the motel Manor House, playing cards, watching TV, and generally observing the curfew. The group of young black men were joined by two white women who had recently traveled up from Ohio and taken up residence in the motel. On Tuesday morning, the police conducted an unsuccessful drug raid on the motel. Something about the TV cop show posturing of the officer who burst in and ordered the group to move into the hall provoked a momentary refusal to move, followed by laughter.

That night was the most violent of the riot. In what John Hersey called a "night of hallucination," rumors of snipers circulated the city "like a whisper grown too loud in mad imaginings, the word 'sniper' scurried around town and became a kind of roar."[47] Inside the motel, one of Pollard's friends got hold of a starter pistol and ran into the room, firing twice and mocking the police officer who had made them laugh that morning. Within minutes, there was another police raid, and the entire group was lined up and ordered to face a wall. After a prolonged episode of verbal and physical abuse, the police began to pull individuals off the line for "interrogation" in separate rooms. In the perception of the police, distorted by old narratives of white masculinist supremacy, the presence of two white women served to raise the stakes in an encounter between men: black and white men. The details of police violence and remarks made during the episode were chilling as a direct and brutal expression of a racist and phallocentric imaginary, one in which white men act against black masculinity in order to ensure domination. What's more, the police believed the women to be prostitutes and, as such, sexual predators asserting a preference for black men. Thus viewed as traitors, they were beaten and sexually abused alongside the men.

There then ensued a piece of police theater, in which each separate interrogation was accompanied by a gunshot in the air in order to convince those still on the line that their friend had been shot dead. One of the police officers present was as confused as his prisoners, and when given his turn at the murder performance, he broke the rules of the game and shot and killed Auburey Pollard. Two of Pollard's friends, Carl Cooper and Fred Temple, were also shot dead that night; the details of their deaths were even less clear than Pollard's. Nowhere in the course of the riot did the confusion of spectacle and storytelling with real matters of life and death achieve such a violent and telling outcome.

The entire episode was rooted, and multiplied itself, in fiction. None of the three centrally involved police officers reported their presence at the Algiers Motel that night. When forced to file a report, one of them wrote a "know-nothing" account for the other two to sign. The aftermath of the murders created a cultural practice of its own. The *Detroit News* reported that three youths had been killed in a gunfight between police and snipers.[48] Police admissions and denials alike were caught in a web of legal maneuvers that ensured that, increasingly, the incident itself was lost in juridical and narrative confusion. The survivors, having spent most of the incident facing a wall, being beaten from behind and forced to deny that anything was happening, gave conflicting accounts.

Initially, the police stood trial twice, once as "tragedy"—once as "farce." Not everyone agreed which was which. Ron August was the only officer to be tried in the criminal justice system. The police jammed the courtroom before it opened, taking all the front seats and turning it into an intimidating ad hoc police station. The judge casually remarked regarding the charge against August that it was "totally unlike defendant August."[49] Eventually the defense lawyers were granted a "change of venue," and the case was removed to the small town of Mason, Michigan. Mason, the town where Malcolm X's father had been murdered, was 99 percent white.[50] The all-white jury was shown a highly edited film of the riot that depicted black people looting amongst the flames, while a beleaguered police force sought to defend the city. It took the jury less than three hours to turn in the "not guilty" verdict.

In all the trial narratives, there was a conspicuous silence surrounding the police reaction to finding two white women in the Algiers Motel. Indeed, the ways in which their presence underlined the interconnectedness of patriarchy and racism has not been taken up in subsequent white or black discussions of the incident. In the racist episteme, black men had enacted what bell hooks describes elsewhere as a "dangerous masculinity," and the connection was not lost on Auburey Pollard's mother.[51] When John Hersey interviewed her, she demanded that he tell "how they killed them just because they seen the two white girls with them in the room."[52] In subsequent narratives, an encounter between the masculinities of both the dominant and oppressed ensured that the bodies of the two women were treated first to white male violence, and then relegated to relative obscurity in both communities. In that process, we may trace the contours of a limited, and limiting, race politics.

As in the trial of the Los Angeles police officers who beat Rodney King twenty-four years later, the change of venue to an all-white community, the manipulation of filmed images, the reinterpretation of the postures and gestures of black male bodies all served to reframe the victims as the site and source of the violence committed.[53] Neither the Algiers Motel incident nor the Simi Valley trial results, when viewed in the narrower context of spatial and cultural racist practice, came as a surprise. Indeed both confirmed the notion (taken from Fanon) that violence is a narrative, one in which "the individual articulates his/her relation with the nation."[54] In this sense, the Algiers Motel incident and its aftermath allow us to glimpse the positionings of murderers and victims in a racist and misogynist space economy. The storylines that converged, knotted and reemerged from the Algiers Motel, confirm the role of cultural practice in the (always contested) translation and constitution of power. Indeed the turning of the storylines to a second Algiers Motel incident trial provides evidence that cultural strategies "can make a difference," can shift "the balance of power in the relations of culture."[55]

The second trial was an unofficial one, a counternarrative posed by a coalition of black activists and held in Detroit's Central United Church. The event was originally scheduled for the Dexter Theater, but moved to the church when the theater backed out in the last minute. Named by its organizers "The People's Tribunal," this was a mock trial "patterned after one held . . . in Stockholm, in which the United States was tried in absentia and found guilty of committing atrocities in Vietnam."[56] Leaflets published by the City Wide Citizens' Action Committee invited Detroit residents to "watch accurate justice administered by citizens of the community. Witness the unbiased, legal action of skilled black attorneys. Review and watch the evidence for yourself."[57] At a rally sponsored by the *Inner City Voice* a few days before the tribunal, H. Rap Brown declared that "the brothers should carry out an execution."[58]

Attended by a huge gathering of family friends, local residents, and the press, the tribunal heard survivor statements, all of which, bar one, had been excluded from the official pretrial examination on the grounds that they were "irrelevant" to the case. The jury included Rosa Parks and author John Killens. The judge, a young black law student, ruled that the sentence be carried out by "the people." One of the organizers described the proceedings as follows: "This tribunal . . . is the beginning of a new level of thinking in Black America. Black people are telling white judges, white juries, and white newspapers that we are hip to your tricks. . . . But the *Detroit News* put us on page 1D next to the comics, and when I went up to ask the *News* about it, a Mr. Beck . . . said 'We played it like the joke it was.' I replied 'If you think it was funny, we plan to keep you in stitches.'"[59]

Who was laughing? To remove black attention from the state's judicial proceedings in the Mason courthouse, in order to create a black-owned, inner-city trial narrative was to deal an insurrectionist blow to the colonizers. Tribunal organizers argued that "the Black community needs to see that the type of justice we receive in Recorder's Courts is the same kind that is meted out in Mississippi. . . . We wanted to show Black people that if this is the law, they had better be proud of their lawlessness. . . . Our lawlessness may be the means for our survival."[60] The tribunal was a deadly serious refusal to submit to the storytelling of the dominant community. The tribunal was also a joke in the sense used by Fanon when he states that "the native laughs in mockery when western values are mentioned in front of him . . . the colonized masses mock at the very values, insult them and vomit them up."[61]

In every respect, the People's Tribunal made a direct and strategic alliance with the narrative of riot as insurrection. When Lyndon Johnson appointed the Kerner Commission to investigate the 1960s riots, he was given a critical, liberal integrationist version of events. In order to achieve this result, the Commission had to ignore black nationalist descriptions of the ghetto as an internal colony. But recall for a moment the insurrectionist counternarratives of riot participants and black activists: "Man, how can you call this place a home? This ain't no mother-fuckin' home. This is a prison. I'd just as soon burn down this damn place as any other."[62] "The Negroes in Detroit feel they are part of an occupied country."[63] "We're as organized as the Viet Cong."[64] "We are determined to control our own community."[65] "The American city is, in essence, populated by people of the Third World, while the white middle classes flee the cities to the suburbs."[66] "Anyone who has lived in a modern black ghetto knows, it is no mere figure of speech when the predominantly white police forces are referred to as a 'colonial army of occupation.'"[67]

These narratives underline a moment of particular clarity in African American political thought and practice in which local struggles located a strategic context in black nationalism and in African nationalist discourses. As the birthplace of the Nation of Islam in the 1930s, Detroit had long been an important center of black radicalism. Beyond its affiliations to Muslim activism, the city was also host to a prominent radical black Christian center. The Shrine of the Black Madonna, founded by Reverend Albert Cleage in 1967, provided a base for activists and for the development of theological ideas drawn from a radical politics of race. In the years following the riot, Detroit was at the center of arguably one of the most innovative radical movements in American history, the League of Revolutionary Black Workers. By 1970, Detroit had its own active branch of the Black Panther party, one that was particularly effective at community organization.[68]

When armed Black Panthers trailed white Californian police squads in order to monitor arrests, the assumed identity of liberation fighter was palpable. The People's Tribunal enacted a similar cultural political performance, in which the narratives of the deaths of Auburey Pollard, Carl Cooper, and Fred Temple were reclaimed. Black Detroit refused to relinquish the historical account and memory of those deaths to the violence of abstract space, to a judicial logic that would eventually find its geographical expression in the small country courthouse of Mason, Michigan. In this very narrow sense, the Algiers Motel incident and its aftermath were life-producing.

The work of the People's Tribunal and the larger history of the 1967 riot provide insight into both the lived experience of urban space and the radical potential of space politics. These events may also help us to understand Lefebvre's own political starting point. As he stated, "All subjects are situated in a space in which they must either recognize themselves, or lose themselves, a space which they may both enjoy or modify."[69] Noting the tendency to homogeneity of abstract space, Lefebvre asked that we hold to an understanding that, for every beneficiary of space, there are those who are excluded, those who are denied space. In his view, this had nothing to do with the norms and properties of space itself, but must be ascribed to the "violence intrinsic to abstraction."[70] As he put it, "The space that homogenizes has nothing homogenous about it. . . . [I]t subsumes and unites scattered fragments or elements by force."[71]

This means, in effect, that abstract space *harbors* difference, contradiction, and conflict. As such, abstract space contains within it the possibility of what Lefebvre called "counterspaces," "appropriated spaces," and "differential spaces." Throughout *The Production of Space*, Lefebvre employs these terms to suggest that a politics of space is one that works to heighten and accumulate the differences that are "subsumed" within abstract space. In his view, "a new space cannot be born (produced) unless it accentuates differences."[72] The process by which one appropriates space might be called a "rupture" or an "explosion."[73] In explosive moments, we recognize space, we act *in*, *on*, and *against* space in order to modify it. In Lefebvre's account, these are historical moments of struggle; or as he suggested, moments in which the "dialectic is resumed."[74]

Many have argued that burning, looting, and running riot are politically retrograde and ineffective. In a liberal view of race justice, such arguments may be difficult to counter. But what do we make of riot actions that constitute an appropriation of space? How does one explain the voices of participants who talked of the exhilaration of throwing a brick; who smiled at police and firemen and said, "The streets are ours"; who gazed on the burning buildings and said afterward, "I was feeling proud man, at the fact that I was a Negro. I felt like a first-class citizen"?[75]

How does one situate the ways in which participants toyed with the colonizers? For example, some people pulled looted sofas onto the pavement and became spectators in their own event.[76] In a period of television program history dominated by white sitcoms set in white suburbs, a man reported that the first image he saw on his looted TV was himself carrying that TV down a burning street.[77] The Kerner report told of rioters in their pajamas, laughing and joking and "dancing amidst the flames."[78] In his study of the role of humor in the politics of decolonization, Achille Mbembe states that "the people who laugh kidnap power and force it, as if by accident, to contemplate its own vulgarity."[79] We may recall here too the laughter of the Algiers Motel residents during the first police raid. There is drama, play, and humor in the cultural practice of a riot. This is a practice that can toy with power and hold up the idea that space is there to be taken and modified. What surprised everybody, rioters and counterrioters alike, is that however brief and however flawed, Detroit in 1967 was a critique and an appropriation of space by its users.

Burning and looting, rumors and stories are narrative interruptions of abstract space. They are autobiographical acts in which cultural identities are contested and renegotiated. For example, a young woman identified herself as a looter and further claimed that in the course of the riot, black Detroiters discovered themselves to be not Americans, but slaves.[80] The slave identity is embraced here as a source of narrative subversion and active rebellion. Riot acts and riot stories underline the historical and contingent nature of cultural identities. Old identities may be recalled and mobilized in new and productive ways. In this sense, a narrative crisis is a reinsertion of time into space; perhaps this is what we mean when we talk about "making history." And this may explain why it continues to matter how we *name* the historical events of July 1967, and why, in the memory of many Detroiters, it was not a riot, but a rebellion.

To focus on the Algiers Motel incident as a narrative crisis does not prevent us from being outraged by the reality of what occurred there. Moreover, the Algiers deaths embodied a space politics that has local and global implications and that can inform our subsequent actions. The incident raised questions about the past, present, and future of a city, and for that reason we continue to have a stake in the narratives that surround it. As for how to remember the Algiers Motel itself, we may be helped by Bunge's remark that "no stronger indication of the power of white racism can be found than its ability to hide historic geography."[81] The Algiers Motel survived for a time without the Manor House, though it changed its name to the Desert Inn. Finally demolished in 1979, its site was used as an entrance for an integrated residential community planned for the area by the city and General Motors.

If the Algiers Motel incident remains in the popular memory of Detroiters, in the suburbs it is largely forgotten or associated with those old rumors of snipers. But it is arguable that the events of 1967 did leave a permanent mark on suburban mentalities. For both city dwellers and suburbanites, the real location and meaning of violence seem less certain. Postwar suburbia may be a sunny landscape, in which residents build swimming pools and backyard ice-skating rinks and race bikes up and down. Neighbors sit on each other's porches and help each other in times of trouble. Lawns smell of cut grass and barbecues; the children stay out late playing tag under the streetlights. These are genuine and remembered benefits, suggesting an undeniable beauty and longing attached to the safety of suburbia. But there is a suggestion of violence in its very perfection: "Though seemingly secured against any violence, abstract space is inherently violent. The same goes for all spaces promising a similar security: residential suburbs, holiday homes, fake countrysides."[82]

The "conspiracy" of suburbia, the inseparable acts of disinvestment, must be seen in the widest possible framework: these are processes that involve the draining of resources, rights, and social power from a once-powerful center. Suburban estrangement is in part the guilt of the conspirator, the nagging awareness that the city is at the heart of our retreat. The only potential for a shared political project between suburbanites and city dwellers lies in a mutual realization that disinvestment cannot succeed without the penetration by capital into the everyday life of all concerned. As in July 1967, when we tell stories and repeat rumors, we underline our intense preoccupation with one another and the simultaneous centrality and abstraction of race in the organization of space. It is likely that many black Detroiters could say in a moment what it takes suburbanites so long to learn:

> If you're thinking about Detroit in the '50s, what you call the good old days is a question of who's talking. I could not possibly want to return to the Detroit of the 1950's. . . . Whites literally walked away from this city, literally abandoning all they had built, rather than make a reasonable accommodation. As a result, we have seen a pattern of economic disinvestment in this city that cannot be matched by any other major city in the United States. When I say it rides on race I absolutely mean that.[83]

Suburbia is the geography of late capitalism as it extends itself into the farthest reaches and most minute details of everyday life. But at the same time, and as Lefebvre points out, the everyday "provokes a malaise, a profound dissatisfaction, an aspiration for something else."[84] The postwar suburb, like any place, was full of "bits" that wouldn't be denied. Reminders of past lives interrupt the apparently smooth dream surface. Inhabitants might suffer the periodic estrangement of being included in a paradise built on exclusion and the denial of exclusion. A neighbor behaves in an "out of place" way. A mother gets drunk at a party; a father starts cursing the place and everyone in it. A woman refuses to enter the suburban sorority; a man builds a family room onto his kitchen, installs his wife and children there, but spends every weekend in the garage, where he sits on a lawn chair drinking beer and listening to opera. A child suddenly stops talking for a week and wanders the street wearing an expression of utter terror. There are moments of both madness and profound humanity of the type now regularly recorded and mined by cultural representations of suburbia.[85] There are brief moments of difference, of wakefulness, of mutual aid, of tiny refusals to be segregated, confirmation that there is a *lived* counterexperience of space embedded in the suburban order.

The "aspiration for something else" is, for Americans in particular, a longing for some *where* else. A commonly held belief in America has long been that if you want to change, you *move.* American transience, even as an imaginary, is in some respects a spatialized frustration with everyday existence. Utopian longings to "be somewhere else," to be "over the rainbow," even to be "at home" may be a humble precursor to an understanding that no radical social project can succeed unless it envisions and generates a new space. Yet the kind of transience available to suburbanites has long been unavailable to many black Detroiters. This too is an integral fact of the geography of uneven development. It is interesting to note that virtually none of the inner-city residents interviewed in *Detroit Lives* expressed a desire to leave. Mast's oral history reveals a critical project of urban *staying* to equal any representation of the suburban dream. Nearly all those interviewed were involved in one of the numerous Detroit groups that take as their expressed goal the redefinition and re-creation of city spaces and city life. For Rosa Sims, "Leaving Detroit would be tantamount to saying my whole life has been in vain. It's not even an option."[86]

Acknowledgments

This book was written while I was living and working in England and the Netherlands, a "geographical fact" that posed significant research challenges. In England, I had the generous support of colleagues and friends at Leeds University and Trinity and All Saints University College. In particular, I wish to thank Griselda Pollock, Deborah Phillips, Barbara Engh, Stefan Herbrechter, Derek McKiernan, Shubi Ishemo, and John Poulter. Travel funds for research in Detroit were provided by Trinity and All Saints, and I thank Tim Leadbeater for facilitating my funding application. I am also grateful for the lively discussion and interest shown by students in Cultural Studies at Trinity and All Saints, and in American Studies at Leiden University, the Netherlands. I would like to acknowledge Mark Blaug and Ruth Towse, whose ongoing encouragement as both scholars and in-laws has been immensely helpful. Rohit Lekhi generously shared ideas and sources, often at very short notice. Special thanks are due to Rachel Pyper, whose interest and support have been invaluable, and who has been the best of friends.

There are many people in Detroit and its suburbs who handled my numerous research inquiries. In particular, I wish to acknowledge the staff of the Reuther Library, the Bentley Historical Library, the Archives of the Henry Ford Museum and Greenfield Village, the Garden City Historical Museum, Inkster Public Library, and the University of Detroit Mercy Libraries. Erika Hansinger conducted numerous searches on my behalf, and in a variety of Detroit locations, uncovering important material pertaining to events in 1967. At Wayne State University Press, Jane Hoehner has been immensely patient and determined in her support of this project. Warm thanks are also due to Mary L. Tederstrom whose editorial advice has proved invaluable. Beyond contacts in Detroit, I received further helpful comments on the Algiers Motel material from Jennifer Horan, Greg Blaug, Caroline

Bath, Michael Vazquez, and Robert Gooding-Williams. Angela Dillard shared her personal knowledge of Detroit, her research expertise, and her enthusiasm.

In my visits to Garden City, I found a great number of old friends and neighbors who generously gave of their time to respond to questions and to share memories. I am particularly grateful to Charles Thompson and Bill and Trill Morgan, who offered me a place at the kitchen table and a wealth of information about life in Garden City in the 1950s. Special thanks go to my oldest friend, Dee Thompson, for keeping the faith and for helping me to photograph our old haunts, and to Dr. Mary Durbin, still sharing her gift for teaching after all these years. Although I made the strategic decision to reserve the interview and photographic material for a different project, it has nonetheless influenced this book. These encounters confirmed once again that the love of home is strong, wherever we live, and that city and suburban voices and memories are complex, varied, and deserving of greater attention than was possible within the confines of this project.

The surprise of this study was the wealth of knowledge and support gathered closest to home, in my own family. My brother Fred Kenyon and my sister Pavanne Lapham patiently responded to countless questions throughout this project. My brother-in-law, David Lapham, kindly helped me to find my way around Detroit. A further unanticipated benefit of this study was the time spent with Pavanne in her Michigan home. During our late-night searches in her "garage archive" and in lengthy conversations, I learned of the great wisdom, humor, and generosity brought by my sister to her own pursuit of personal and family history. I reserve special thanks for my parents, Raymond and Shirley Kenyon. During my return visit to Michigan, they provided a car and spent many hours helping me navigate the streets of Garden City, Dearborn, Inkster, and numerous other metropolitan locations. More importantly, their love, integrity, and spirited support have been constants in my life and have given me the courage to question a place and a world that we shared. Sadly, my mother died before this book was completed, but her tender devotion will not be forgotten.

Final thanks go to my son Isaac Kenyon Blaug and to Ricardo Blaug, the two people who live with me and have stuck with me through the highs and lows of research and writing. Having listened to my Detroit stories for years, Isaac now takes me to see *Eight Mile* and keeps me listening to music from Motown. I hope one day my English boy will visit Detroit with me. Ricardo knows me better than anyone and is still here. No one could have provided better support as a scholar, friend, and lover.

In her piece titled "Living Room," June Jordan has written that "everybody needs a home, so at least you can have some place to leave, which is where most folks will say you must be coming from." All of the people acknowledged here, along with those whose words and memories feature in this book, have helped me to gain a better understanding of the home I left and the home I carry with me.

Notes

Introduction

1. Hall, cited in Ross, *Universal Abandon?* xii.
2. Jameson, *Postmodernism*, xx and 1.
3. Ibid., 19.
4. For an important and detailed account of Detroit, and of how its manufacturing and economic history links to highly specific, local processes of racial segregation, see Farley, Danziger, and Holzer, *Detroit Divided.* The book is part of the "Multi-City Study of Urban Inequality," conducted through linked research in four cities: Atlanta, Boston, Detroit, and Los Angeles. The authors not only draw on the materials gathered by this study but incorporate material from the University of Michigan's Detroit Area Study, an annual project that, in 1976 and 1992, focused specifically on racial attitudes and residential segregation.
5. Woolf, *The Pargiters* (London: Hogarth Press, 1978), 9.
6. For an extraordinary account of post-1967 radical black politics in Detroit, see Georgakas and Surkin, *Detroit.* For a recent political and labor history of this period, see Thompson, *Whose Detroit?* Thompson specifically argues that, to a large extent, "the racially conservative whites who chose to abandon the inner cities in the 1970s and to vote for Ronald Reagan in 1980 did so as *losers*, not victors, of their battle to lead urban America into the future" (219).

Chapter 1

1. See Smith, *Dancing in the Street*, 200–201.
2. See Oliver, Johnson, and Farrell, "Anatomy of a Rebellion," 119.
3. See Gilje, *Rioting in America*, 158.
4. Fine, *Violence in the Model City*, 385.
5. Ibid., 385.
6. The concentration camp rumors were reported in the radical black community newspaper *Inner City Voice (ICV)*, first published in October 1967. *ICV*, issue number 6, contained the following headline: "Detroit's Concentration Camps Waiting for Blacks." Moreover, many black activists were aware that under the McCarran Act (1950), provisions existed for the reactivating of internment camps. See Rosenthal, "Where Rumor Raged," 40–41. In an August 1967 speech in Detroit, H. Rap

Brown claimed that the federal government was preparing thirteen camps "to do away" with "a lot of excess niggers" and called on his audience to "stop looting" and "start shooting." See Fine, *Violence in the Model City*, 372.

7. Rosenthal, "Where Rumor Raged," 35.
8. Fine, Violence in the Model City, 385.
9. See Rosenthal, "Where Rumor Raged," 35.
10. Detailed accounts of these processes may be found in Sugrue, *Origins of the Urban Crisis*, 47–51 and 181–207, and Fine, *Violence in the Model City*, 3 and 57.
11. According to Sugrue, "the area was over one-third (37.2 percent) non white in 1950. By 1960 . . . only 3.8 percent of the area's residents were white." Sugrue, *Origins of the Urban Crisis*, 244.
12. Hersey, *Algiers Motel Incident*, 369.
13. Conot, *American Odyssey*, 449.
14. See Sugrue, *Origins of the Urban Crisis*, 128. The postwar "deindustrial ization" of Detroit is treated at length in Sugrue's work and supports his central argument that current urban problems have their origins not in the aftermath of the 1960s' urban rebellions, but in the "complex and interwoven histories of race, residence, and work" in the longer postwar period (ibid., 5).
15. Bunge, *Fitzgerald*, 135.
16. Ibid., 130.
17. See Sugrue, *Origins of the Urban Crisis*, 246–49.
18. Ibid., 233.
19. The descriptor "invisible walls" is from Clark, *Dark Ghetto*, 11.
20. Stanton, "Pain and Promises." It has been noted that ghetto compression facilitates the operation of rumors: "There is probably a better system of internal communications in the ghetto than in the National Guard." Fred Powledge, quoted in Singer, Osborn, and Geschwender, *Black Rioters*, 35.
21. Dan Aldridge quoted in "Power Struggle among the Black Militants," *Detroit Scope Magazine* (May 1968), reprinted in Gordon, *City in Racial Crisis*, 116.
22. Warren, "Community Dissensus: Panic in Suburbia," in Gordon, *City in Racial Crisis*, 124.
23. Fine, *Violence in the Model City*, 356.
24. Richard Marks, addressing a 1963 Open Occupancy conference in Detroit. See "Messages about a Racially Divided Community," in Gordon, *City in Racial Crisis*, 31.
25. Morrison, *Song of Solomon*, 115.
26. See, for example, Lefebvre, *La pensée marxiste et la ville*; Lefebvre, *Survival of Capitalism*; Lefebvre, *Production of Space*.
27. The concept of abstract space is examined at length in Lefebvre, *Production of Space*, esp. 285–89, 306–21, 341–42.
28. Harvey, *Social Justice*, 237.
29. Ibid., 271.

30. Ibid., 232.
31. Sugrue, *Origins of the Urban Crisis*, 141. For a recent critical analysis of the widely used "spatial mismatch thesis," see Farley, Danziger, and Holzer, *Detroit Divided*, 59–65.
32. Malcolm X, cited in Allen, *A Guide to Black Power in America* (London: Gollancz, 1970), 28.
33. Auburey Pollard Sr., interviewed in Hersey, *Algiers Motel Incident*, 182.
34. Hersey, *Algiers Motel Incident*, 23–24.
35. Bunge, *Fitzgerald*, 2.
36. Ibid., 125.
37. Ibid., "Foreword."
38. Baldwin, *Nobody Knows My Name*, 66.
39. Thompson, *Whose Detroit?* 38. Thompson chronicles the deteriorating relations between black Detroiters and the police force throughout the 1960s. See esp. pp. 37–44.
40. Darden et al., *Detroit*, 73.
41. After his election in 1973, Mayor Coleman Young insisted that all Detroit police officers live inside the city limits. See Thompson, *Whose Detroit?* 206.
42. See Herron, *Afterculture: Detroit and the Humiliation of History* (Detroit: Wayne State University Press, 1993), 90 and 13–14.

Chapter 2

1. For a good survey of debates about suburbia, see the *American Quarterly* 46, no. 1 (1994), an issue devoted to the topic.
2. Sharpe and Wallock, "Bold New City," 1–30.
3. Jackson, *Crabgrass Frontier*, 284.
4. Sharpe and Wallock, "Bold New City," 1 and 24. The 1990 Census recorded 46 percent of the American population as inhabiting suburbia.
5. It is interesting to note the postwar popularity of *The Wizard of Oz* (1939) as an annual television event, starting in 1956. The film was not a big moneymaker for MGM until the TV broadcasts. Dorothy's lesson that she shouldn't go "seeking her heart's desire any further than her own backyard" was apposite to the suburban ethos of home and family.
6. Jackson, *Crabgrass Frontier*, 283–84.
7. Sugrue, *Origins of the Urban Crisis*, 3.
8. For discussions of other suburbanizations, see Schwartz, "Evolution of the Suburbs," 1–37; Clark, "Process of Suburban Development," 19–31; Fishman, *Bourgeois Utopias*.
9. Jackson, Crabgrass Frontier, 84.
10. See Schwartz, "Evolution of the Suburbs," 26.
11. Ibid., 29.
12. Ibid., 30.
13. Jackson, *Crabgrass Frontier*, 175.
14. Ibid.

15. This is the famous "water scandal" given fictional treatment in the Roman Polanski film *Chinatown* (1974).
16. Marsh, *Suburban Lives*, 169. See also Marsh's description of Palos Verdes as the prototypical suburb on pp. 168–81.
17. F. W. Kellogg, Palos Verdes investor, quoted in Marsh, *Suburban Lives*, 171. The *Palos Verdes Bulletin* claimed it "makes better citizens of people to own their own homes" (ibid., 171).
18. Cain, *Mildred Pierce*, 10.
19. Davis, *City of Quartz*, 37 and 38.
20. Baudrillard, *America*.
21. Fishman, *Bourgeois Utopias*, 16 and 156.
22. Schwartz, "Evolution of the Suburbs," 31.
23. Marsh, *Suburban Lives*, 153. Sugrue reports the same stagnation in Detroit, where the construction industry did not begin its recovery until the late 1940s. Sugrue, *Origins of the Urban Crisis*, 41.
24. Jackson, *Crabgrass Frontier*, 193.
25. Allen, "Big Change in Suburbia," 64.
26. Widick, *Detroit*, 50–64.
27. Ibid. See also Michael Moore's 1989 documentary film *Roger and Me*.
28. See Bradbury, *Modern American Novel*, for a discussion of works by Michael Gold, Edward Dahlberg, Jack Conroy, Richard Wright, Zora Neale Thurston, and others. Social conditions in Detroit were given pas sionate treatment in Upton Sinclair's *The Flivver King: A Story of Ford-America*, published in 1937.
29. Dos Passos, *U.S.A.*, 6.
30. Woodiwiss, *Postmodernity U.S.A.*, 3–5.
31. Ibid., 18–20.
32. Ibid. See also Sitkoff, *Struggle for Black Equality*.
33. O'Neill, *American High*, 90.
34. Woodiwiss, *Postmodernity U.S.A.*, 25.
35. Sugrue, *Origins of the Urban Crisis*, 59–63.
36. See "A Version of America" in Marsh, *Suburban Lives*, 129–55.
37. Ibid., 183.
38. Jackson, *Crabgrass Frontier*, 193.
39. Marsh, *Suburban Lives*, 153.
40. Rexford Tugwell, quoted in Jackson, *Crabgrass Frontier*, 195. See also Arnold, *The New Deal in the Suburbs*.
41. Marsh and Kaplan, "The Lure of the Suburbs," in Dolce, *Suburbia*, 37–59.
42. Abrams, *Forbidden Neighbours*, 229–35.
43. Jackson, *Crabgrass Frontier*, 197–200. In Detroit, every neighborhood "with even a tiny African American population" was redlined. See Sugrue, *Origins of the Urban Crisis*, 44.
44. Jackson, *Crabgrass Frontier*, 200.
45. See Popenoe, *Suburban Environment*.
46. Sugrue, *Origins of the Urban Crisis*, 63.

47. Rothblatt and Carr, *Suburbia*, 32.
48. Ibid., 32.
49. Michael Harbulak and Charles Johnson, quoted in Sugrue, *Origins of the Urban Crisis*, 57.
50. O'Neill, *American High*, 12; Jackson, *Crabgrass Frontier*, 232.
51. See Sugrue, *Origins of the Urban Crisis*, 42.
52. O'Neill, *American High*, 15.
53. Ibid., 10.
54. Keats, *Crack in the Picture Window*, 100.
55. Jackson, *Crabgrass Frontier*, 233.
56. Ibid.
57. Ibid., 234.
58. Rothblatt and Carr, *Suburbia*, 33; Jackson, *Crabgrass Frontier*, 234–35; Andres, "Urbanization and Architecture," 205.
59. Jackson, *Crabgrass Frontier*, 235–36.
60. Rothblatt and Carr, *Suburbia*, 33.
61. Popenoe, *Suburban Environment*, 113.
62. Quoted in Gans, *Levittowners*, 9.
63. See Lacey, *Ford*, 284. These questions (and Gans's account of life in Levittown) will be further explored in chapter 4.
64. See Herron, *Afterculture: Detroit and the Humiliation of History* (Detroit: Wayne State University Press, 1993), 89–90.
65. Ibid., 90.
66. Ibid.
67. See Jackson, *Crabgrass Frontier*, 237.
68. Lefebvre, *Survival of Capitalism*, 21. Lefebvre also remarked, "Industrialization, once the producer of urbanism, is now being produced by it." Lefebvre, quoted in Soja, *Postmodern Geographies*, 88.
69. O'Neill, *American High*, 9, and Woodiwiss, *Postmodernity*, 34.
70. Woodiwiss, *Postmodernity U.S.A.*, 35.
71. Harvey, *Social Justice*, 248.
72. Woodiwiss, *Postmodernity U.S.A.*, 37.
73. Whyte, *Organization Man*; Riesman, *Lonely Crowd*.
74. Wilson, *Man in the Gray Flannel Suit*, 109.
75. See Herron, *Afterculture*, 20.
76. William Levitt, quoted in Jackson, *Crabgrass Frontier*, 231.
77. Woodiwiss, *Postmodernity U.S.A.*, 35.
78. Packard, *Hidden Persuaders*, 23.
79. Ibid., 98.
80. Herron, *Afterculture*, 20.
81. These are privileges "which we tend increasingly to think of in spatial terms; privacy, empty rooms, silence, walling other people out, protection against crowds and other bodies" (Jameson, *Postmodernism*, 286).
82. Oates, *Expensive People*, 89.
83. Ibid., 88.
84. Sitkoff, *Struggle for Black Equality*, 15.

85. Sugrue, *Origins of the Urban Crisis*, 33.
86. Sitkoff, *Struggle for Black Equality*, 11–12.
87. Ibid., 15.
88. See Bruck, "Protest, Universality, Blackness."
89. Wright, "How Bigger Was Born": Introduction to *Native Son.*
90. Ibid.
91. The best discussion of uneven development in relation to Detroit can be found in Darden et al., *Detroit.* The term "uneven development" here refers to the inequalities that result when "disinvestment, suburbanization, and racial segregation strongly influence the status of the central city and its suburbs." See p. 6. The authors argue that the "problem in the Detroit metropolis is one of uneven regional development, rather than unmitigated regional decline" (ibid., 6).
92. Wood, *Suburbia*, 69.
93. Harvey, *Urbanization of Capital*, 120.
94. Williams, *Eyes on the Prize*, 28–29.
95. Baldwin, *Nobody Knows My Name*, 65.
96. Sugrue, *Origins of the Urban Crisis*, 8.
97. Oates, *How I Contemplated the World*, 1073.
98. Ibid., 1074.
99. Ibid., 1076.

Chapter 3

1. Dick, *Time Out of Joint*, 81.
2. Ibid., 138.
3. Ibid., 174.
4. Ibid., 181.
5. Ibid., 184.
6. Lefebvre, *Production of Space*, 393.
7. Ibid., 289.
8. Bunge, *Fitzgerald*, 152.
9. Ibid., 135–37.
10. Dick, *Time Out of Joint*, 186.
11. See Ross, *Universal Abandon?* xii.
12. Karp, *Leave Me Alone*, 52.
13. Ibid., 311.
14. Ibid., 245–46. Barney Steel is representative of a recurrent type in American fiction. Other realtors cum social commentators appear in such works as Lewis, *Babbitt* (1922); Cameron, *The Block Busters* (1964); and more recently, Ford, *Independence Day* (1995).
15. Karp, *Leave Me Alone*, 296.
16. Jackson, *Crabgrass Frontier*, 18.
17. Ibid., 17.
18. Ibid., 50.
19. See Doherty, *Teenagers and Teenpics*, 120.

20. See, for example, *Teenage Crime Wave* (1955), *Crime in the Streets* (1956), *The Delinquents* (1957), and *Dangerous Youth* (1958).
21. Suburban juvenile delinquents made their appearance at about the same time, but were a very different breed. Their problems were firmly located in the family, not the community in which the family lived. We will return to the treatment of suburban juvenile delinquency in chapter 4.
22. Cited in Doherty, *Teenagers and Teenpics*, 122.
23. Ibid., 105.
24. Gans, *Levittowners*, 22–25.
25. Ibid., 372.
26. Ibid., 37.
27. Ibid., 32–37.
28. Karp, *Leave Me Alone*, 24.
29. Ibid., 74.
30. Ibid., 128.
31. Whyte, *Organization Man*, 387, 253, and 297.
32. Ibid., 280.
33. Ibid., 350.
34. Ibid., 281.
35. Karp, *Leave Me Alone*, 65–66.
36. In 1987, a random sample of 800 New Jerseyites gave the following results: 10 percent said living in the city was very desirable compared to 38 percent the older suburbs, 50 percent small towns, and 34 percent rural areas. Eagleton poll cited in Dahl, *After the Revolution?* 140.
37. Jameson, *Postmodernism*, 314.
38. Karp, *Leave Me Alone*, 66.
39. Ibid., 75.
40. Ibid., 77.
41. Ewen and Ewen, *Channels of Desire: Mass Images and the Shaping of American Consciousness* (New York: McGraw-Hill, 1982), 235.
42. Haralovich, "Sit-coms and Suburbs," 112.
43. Whyte, *Organization Man*, 308.
44. Ibid., 302.
45. Malamud, *New Life*, 98–99.
46. Dick, *Puttering about in a Strange Land*, 209.
47. Whyte, *Organization Man*, 359.
48. Dick, *Puttering about in a Small Land*, 210.
49. Haralovich, "Sit-coms and Suburbs," 119.
50. Ibid., 111.
51. Green, *Heartless Light*, 3.
52. Housing designer Robert Woods Kennedy, quoted in Hayden, *Redesigning the American Dream*, 63.
53. See Haralovich, "Sit-coms and Suburbs," 133.
54. Jameson, *Postmodernism*, 280.
55. Shulman, *Rally Round the Flag, Boys!*, 53.
56. Whyte, *Organization Man*, 280.

57. Ibid., 356.
58. Karp, *Leave Me Alone*, 87.
59. Shulman, *Rally Round the Flag, Boys!*, 28.
60. Ibid., 33.
61. Wilson, *The Man in the Gray Flannel Suit*, 121.
62. Ibid., 73.
63. An ad agency director, quoted in Packard, *Hidden Persuaders*, 58.
64. Haralovich, "Sit-coms and Suburbs," 121.
65. In addition to *The Thrill of It All*, see *Young at Heart* (1955), *Please Don't Eat the Daisies* (1960), *Send Me No Flowers* (1964), and *With Six You Get Eggroll* (1968). For an appreciative treatment of Day's work, see "Nice Girls Do" in Williamson, *Consuming Passions*, 145–52.
66. Dick, *We Can Build You*, 110–11.

Chapter 4

1. "Our Country and Our Culture," Editorial Board, *Partisan Review* 19 (1952): 282–86.
2. Ibid., 283.
3. Ibid., 284. Along with *Dissent* and *Politics*, the *Partisan Review* attracted many anti-Stalinist intellectuals attempting to reconcile their prewar Trotskyist radicalism with Cold War formations.
4. Ibid., 284.
5. Ibid., 285.
6. Notable objectors included Irving Howe, Norman Mailer, and C. Wright Mills.
7. Ross, "Containing Culture in the Cold War," in *No Respect*, 43.
8. Ibid., 50–51.
9. Sidney Hook in "Our Country and Our Culture," 574.
10. C. Wright Mills in "Our Country and Our Culture," 447.
11. Ross, "Containing Culture in the Cold War," in *No Respect*, 52.
12. Ibid., 56.
13. Louise Brogan in "Our Country and Our Culture," 563.
14. Ibid., 592.
15. Spigel, "Installing the Television Set," 6.
16. See Spigel, "Suburban Home Companion."
17. As we have seen, the *American Quarterly* devoted an issue to suburbia in 1994. A stated goal of the lead article was to bring the debate up to date. See Sharpe and Wallock. "Bold New City," 1–30.
18. Riesman, *Lonely Crowd;* Whyte, *Organization Man.*
19. Riesman, *Lonely Crowd*, 67–68.
20. Ibid., 307.
21. Riesman, "The Suburban Dislocation," *Annals of the American Academy of Political and Social Science* (November 1957): 134.
22. Whyte, *Organization Man*, 46 and 68.
23. Ibid., 253. Peale's titles included *A Guide to Confident Living* (1948) and

The Power of Positive Thinking (1952).
24. Whyte, *Organization Man*, 276.
25. Ibid., 270.
26. Ibid., 282.
27. Ibid., 297.
28. Ibid., 299.
29. Mumford, *The City in History* (New York: Harcourt, Brace and World, 1961), 486.
30. Berger, *Working-Class Suburb*, 92
31. Ibid., 96.
32. Ibid., 82 and 84.
33. Ibid., 93.
34. Ibid., 102.
35. Gans, *Levittowners*, 166.
36. Ibid., 414.
37. Ibid., 284.
38. Ibid., 374.
39. Ibid., 373.
40. Ibid., 426.
41. Berger, *Working-Class Suburb*, 84.
42. Ibid.
43. See Cross, *Time and Money*, 190.
44. Friedan, *Feminine Mystique*, 18.
45. Ibid., 17.
46. Ibid., 55.
47. Ibid., 17.
48. Ibid., 110.
49. Ibid., 37 and 107.
50. Ibid., 15.
51. Ibid., 214.
52. Ibid., 179.
53. Douglas, *Where the Girls Are*, 124–25.
54. See, for example, Clarke, "Tupperware," 133.
55. See, for example, *The Bad Seed* (1956), *It Came from Outer Space* (1953), *The Space Children* (1958), *I Married a Monster from Outer Space* (1958), *I Was a Teenage Werewolf* (1957), and *I Was a Daughter of Dracula* (1957).
56. Ross, *No Respect*, 45.
57. Ibid., 19.
58. Biskind, *Seeing Is Believing*, 111.
59. Keats, *Crack in the Picture Window*, 7.
60. Shulman, *Rally Round the Flag, Boys!* 31–32.
61. Not until *The Stepford Wives* (1974) did we see this reversed, with men tricking their wives into the suburban trap.
62. Karp, *Leave Me Alone*, 24.
63. Ibid., 27.
64. Wouk, *Marjorie Morningstar*, 171.

65. Ibid., 265.
66. Ibid., 543.
67. Here films like *Gaslight* (1944), *Undercurrent* (1946), and *Notorious* (1946) are also relevant. See Elsaesser, "Tales of Sound and Fury."
68. It has been claimed that, in 1955, "one movie in ten contained a psychiatrist or a psychiatric problem." See Walker, "Hollywood, Freud and the Representation of Women," in *Home is Where the Heart Is: Studies in Melodrama and the Woman's Film*, ed. Gledhill, 202.
69. The Gordons, quoted in Friedan, *The Feminine Mystique*, 254. See also Gordon, Gordon, and Gunther, *Split-Level Trap.*
70. See Walker, "Hollywood," 204.
71. Friedan, *Feminine Mystique*, 266.
72. See Leed, *No Man's Land: Combat and Identity in World War I*, 163. And W. H. R. Rivers himself concluded that "neurotic symptoms correlated not with the intensity of battle," but with the degree of the soldier's "immobility." See Showalter, "Rivers and Sassoon," 62.
73. Baumgartner, *Moral Order of a Suburb*, 110.
74. Ibid., 108.
75. See Biskind, *Seeing Is Believing*, 200 and 201.
76. Thomas Doherty distinguishes between what he terms the "slum-cen tered environmentalism" associated with the Warner Brothers gangster films and a "suburban Freudianism" popularized by films like *Rebel without a Cause* (*Teenagers and Teenpics*, 122).
77. Ibid., 125.
78. Ibid., 132–34.

Chapter 5

1. Lefebvre, *Critique of Everyday Life*, 57.
2. See Lefebvre, *Production of Space*, 89.
3. Foucault, "Two Lectures," in *Power/Knowledge*, 80.
4. Ibid., 80.
5. Carver, "Menudo," in *Where I'm Calling From*, 339.
6. Ibid., 350.
7. Carver, *Where I'm Calling From*, 350.
8. Ibid., 18.
9. Ibid., 41.
10. Ibid., 43.
11. Ibid., 44.
12. Ibid., 51.
13. Ibid., 33.
14. "The substance of everyday life—'human raw material' in its simplicity and richness—pierces through all alienation and establishes 'disalienation.'" See Lefebvre, *Critique of Everyday Life*, 97.
15. Carver, *Where I'm Calling From*, 167.
16. Ibid., 167.

17. Lefebvre, *Critique of Everyday Life*, 66.
18. Raymond Carver, "What We Talk about When We Talk About Love?" in *Where I'm Calling From*, 128.
19. Lefebvre, *Critique of Everyday Life*, 180.
20. Carver, *Where I'm Calling From*, 316.
21. Cheever, "The Trouble of Marcie Flint," in *Stories of John Cheever*, 296.
22. See "The Wrysons" in *Stories of John Cheever*, 319.
23. Ibid., 320.
24. Cheever, *Stories of John Cheever*, 324.
25. Ibid., 514.
26. Two of the most popular sitcoms, *I Love Lucy* (1951–61) and *The Adventures of Ozzie and Harriet* (1952–66), featured real-life married couples, further blurring the distinction between dream and reality.
27. Cheever, *Stories of John Cheever*, 285.
28. Ibid.
29. Suburbia is, like Lefebvre's conception of the everyday, "ambiguous and contradictory. On the one hand, it provides satisfactions: it satisfies the very needs it produces. On the other hand, the everyday provokes a malaise, a profound dissatisfaction." Lefebvre, "Toward a Leftist Cultural Politics," 80.
30. Oates, *Expensive People*, 147.
31. Ibid., 171.
32. Ibid., 298.
33. Simmel, "Stranger," 402.
34. Yates, *Revolutionary Road*, 29.
35. Ibid., 30.
36. Ibid., 111 and 110.
37. Ibid., 323.
38. French, *Women's Room*, 101.
39. Ibid., 102.
40. Ibid., 107.
41. See Donaldson, *Suburban Myth*, 111.
42. French, *Women's Room*, 106.
43. It is worth noting that suburbia features (along with war, marriage, and fatherhood) in Valerie Solanis's hate list of male contributions to the world "shitpile" as set out in the SCUM (Society for Cutting up Men) Manifesto. See Morgan, *Sisterhood Is Powerful*, 578.
44. Lurie, *The War between the Tates*, 200.
45. Ibid., 200.
46. Friedan, *Feminine Mystique*, 215 and 217.
47. Lurie, *Nowhere City*, 192.
48. Dick, "The Commuter," in *Second Variety*, 180.
49. Ibid., 182.
50. Updike, *Rabbit, Run*, 7.
51. Ibid., 21–22 and 27.
52. Ibid., 29.

53. Ibid., 80.
54. Ibid., 89.
55. Ibid., 93.
56. Ibid., 91.
57. Ibid., 104.
58. Ibid., 178.
59. Ibid., 183.
60. Ibid., 229.
61. Updike, *Rabbit Omnibus*, 186.
62. Ibid., 186.
63. Ibid., 239.
64. Ibid., 206.
65. Ibid., 206.
66. Ibid., 299.
67. Ibid., 309.
68. Ibid., 300.
69. Ibid., 315.
70. Ibid., 346.
71. Ibid., 347.
72. Ibid., 370.
73. Ibid., 408.
74. Oates, *them*, 358.
75. Ibid., 384.
76. Ibid., 391–92.
77. Wright, *Native Son*, 24.
78. Ellison, *Invisible Man*, 497.
79. Carl Cooper's mother, quoted in Hersey, *Algiers Motel Incident*, 21.
80. Ibid., 21.
81. The expression, "wounds of geography" is taken from Sennett, *Fall of Public Man*, 298.
82. "Men make their own history, but they do not make it just as they please; they do not make it under circumstances chosen by themselves, but under circumstances directly found, given and transmitted from the past" (Marx, "Eighteenth Brumaire of Louis Bonaparte," in Tucker, ed., *The Marx-Engels Reader*, 595).

Chapter 6

1. Dos Passos, *Big Money*, 772.
2. See Conot, *American Odyssey*, 164.
3. Lacey, *Ford*, 120.
4. The *New York Evening Post* and the *Algonac Courier*, quoted in ibid., 118.
5. Lacey, *Ford*, 121.
6. Ibid., 122.
7. Ibid., 125.
8. Ibid., 124.

9. Cited in ibid., 119.
10. Widick, *Detroit*, 33.
11. See Lacey, *Ford*, 350.
12. From Charles Madison, "My Seven Years of Automotive Servitude," cited in ibid., 128.
13. The numbers of autoworkers climbed from 2,735 in 1904, to 67,500 in 1914, to 234,500 in 1925 (Darden et al., *Detroit*, 15).
14. Sugrue, *Origins of the Urban Crisis*, 22.
15. Lacey, *Ford*, 125–26. For a recent fictional account of the Sociological Department and the melting pot ceremony, see Eugenides, *Middlesex*, 79–105.
16. Cited in Lawson-Peebles, "Performance Arts," in Gidley, ed., *Modern American Culture*, 263.
17. From Lefebvre, *The Right to the City*, cited in Kofman and Lebas, *Writings on Cities: Henri Lefebvre*, 162.
18. Lefebvre, *Production of Space*, 423, and Kofman and Lebas, *Writings on Cities*, 151.
19. Fanon, *Black Skin, White Masks*, 111–12.
20. Ibid., 111.
21. Ibid., 115.
22. See Geschwender, *Class, Race, and Worker Insurgency*, 18–19.
23. See Sugrue, *Origins of the Urban Crisis*, 25.
24. Walter Rosser, a former Ford worker, interviewed in Moon and Detroit Urban League, *Untold Tales, Unsung Heroes*, 139.
25. James Boggs, interviewed in ibid., 150.
26. Northrup, *Organized Labor and the Negro*, 23.
27. Howe and Widick, *UAW and Walter Reuther*, 217.
28. See Geschwender, *Class, Race, and Worker Insurgency*, 24.
29. Darden et al., *Detroit*, 15.
30. Ibid.
31. Conot, *American Odyssey*, 209.
32. See Darden et al., *Detroit*, 15–16.
33. Sugrue, *Origins of the Urban Crisis*, 128.
34. Zukin, *Landscapes of Power*, 106.
35. Darden et al., *Detroit*, 38.
36. See Bostick, *Roots of Inkster*, 40.
37. Farley, Danziger, and Holzer, *Detroit Divided*, 154.
38. Ibid., 155.
39. Darden et al., *Detroit*, 98.
40. Conot, *American Odyssey*, 277.
41. Bostick, *Roots of Inkster*, 54.
42. Conot, *American Odyssey*, 278.
43. Ibid., 210.
44. Lacey, *Ford*, 222.
45. Hardin, Pretzer, and Steele, eds., *An American Invention: The Story of Henry Ford Museum and Greenfield Village* (Dearborn, MI: Henry Ford

Museum and Greenfield Village, 1999), 45.
46. Ibid.
47. Lacey, *Ford*, 246.
48. Zukin, *Landscapes of Power*, 217–50.
49. For a helpful discussion of Disneyland's relation to the 1950s suburban boom, see "Disneyland, 1955: The Place That Was Also a TV Show" in Marling, *As Seen on TV*, 87–126.
50. Ford Motor Company Archives, Oral History Section, *The Reminiscences of Mr. Edward J. Cutler*, March 1952, 159–60.
51. Georgakas and Surkin, *Detroit*, 42.
52. We may recall Carl Cooper's mother asking why he wanted to go "out there." This is a frequently used term in black inner-city descriptions of white neighborhoods and the white suburban ring. Suburbia is literally an unknown and forbidden space. In the 1995 film *Hoop Dreams*, the young basketball player recruited from the Chicago ghetto to attend a white suburban high school remarks that it is the first time he has been "out there."
53. Widick, *Detroit*, 44.
54. Ibid.
55. Ibid., 45.
56. Conot, *American Odyssey*, 285.
57. Ibid., 352. See also Howe and Widick, *UAW and Walter Reuther*.
58. For a detailed account of race and the UAW, including discussions of the divisive tactics employed by Ford Motor Company, see Meier and Rudwick, *Black Detroit*.
59. For an account of these complex and community-wide negotiations, see ibid., 82–107.
60. Ibid., 94.
61. Ibid., 155.
62. Ibid.
63. Ford Motor Company Archives: Oral History Section, *The Reminiscences of Mr. H. S. Ablewhite*, November 1951, 12.
64. The organization of Ford brought seventeen thousand new black workers into the UAW. Geschwender, *Class, Race, and Worker Insurgency*, 48.
65. Sheldon Tappes, interviewed in Moon and Detroit Urban League, *Untold Tales, Unsung Heroes*, 107.
66. Georgakas and Surkin, *Detroit*, 187.
67. Conot, *American Odyssey*, 351.
68. Moon and Detroit Urban League, *Untold Tales, Unsung Heroes*, 128.
69. For a powerful representation of the continued use (by company *and* union) of race as a divisive issue, see Paul Schrader's 1978 film *Blue Collar*, set in a Ford factory, which is clearly based on the Rouge plant.
70. See Darden et al., *Detroit*, 121.
71. Ibid., 120.
72. Ibid., 121.
73. Sugrue, *The Origins of the Urban Crisis*, 76.

74. Darden et al., *Detroit*, 122. Another useful account of the Hancock episode can be found in Abrams, *Forbidden Neighbours*.
75. Darden et al., *Detroit*, 122.
76. William Serrin, cited in ibid., 124.
77. Darden et al., *Detroit*, 135.
78. Oates, *Expensive People*, 147.
79. Morrison, *Song of Solomon*, 114.
80. Grace Boggs, interviewed in Mast, *Detroit Lives*, 11.
81. Moon and Detroit Urban League, *Untold Tales, Unsung Heroes*, 368–69.
82. Ibid., 369.
83. See Wright, "How Bigger Was Born."
84. By 1948, there were almost a half-million white southerners living in Detroit. See Widick, *Detroit*, 27.
85. See Geschwender, *Class, Race and Worker Insurgency*, 64.
86. Frank Angelo, in Moon and Detroit Urban League, *Untold Tales, Unsung Heroes*, 41.
87. Sheldon Tappes, in ibid., 105.
88. Morrison, *Song of Solomon*, 4.
89. Helen Nuttall Brown, interviewed in Moon and Detroit Urban League, *Untold Tales, Unsung Heroes*, 37.
90. Ibid., 37.
91. Dorothy Elizabeth Lawson, in ibid, 118.
92. Paul B. Shirley, in ibid., 50.
93. Kermit G. Bailer, in ibid., 181.
94. Widick, *Detroit*, 90.
95. Out of 104 people arrested for rioting, only 2 were white. See ibid., 96.
96. Darden et al., *Detroit*, 118.
97. See Geschwender, *Class, Race and Worker Insurgency*, 66.
98. Adam Shakoor, in Moon and Detroit Urban League, *Untold Tales, Unsung Heroes*, 203.
99. Gerald Blakely recalls his childhood years in the Sojourner Truth project. See ibid., 200.
100. Adam Shakoor, in ibid., 204.
101. Cited in Widick, *Detroit*, 11.
102. Mast, *Detroit Lives*, 11.
103. Sennett, *Conscience of the Eye*, 56.
104. Olmstead, quoted in Jackson, *Crabgrass Frontier*, 45.
105. Sugrue, *Origins of the Urban Crisis*, 28.
106. Widick, *Detroit*, 108.
107. Turner, *I Heard It Through the Grapevine*, 51.
108. Gilje, *Rioting in America*, 156–57.
109. Conot, *American Odyssey*, 384. Widick described the spatial division of rioting as "two separate riots." Widick, *Detroit*, 102.
110. Conot, *American Odyssey*, 383.
111. Ibid., 385.
112. See Widick, *Detroit*, 102; and Conot, *American Odyssey*, 385.

113. Georgakas and Surkin, *Detroit*, 187.
114. Denton and Massey argue that "by World War II the foundations of the modern ghetto had been laid in every northern city." See Massey and Denton, *American Apartheid*, 31.

Chapter 7

1. Harvey, *Social Justice and the City*, 112.
2. See chapter 1.
3. Bunge, *Fitzgerald*, 135.
4. Harvey, *Social Justice and the City*, 273.
5. Barikmo et al., *Early Days in Garden City*, and Macfie, *Garden City Chronicle.*
6. Macfie, *Garden City Chronicle*, 71.
7. Darden et al., *Detroit*, 18.
8. Ibid.
9. Ibid., 22.
10. Macfie, *Garden City Chronicle*, 122.
11. Ibid.
12. Sugrue, *Origins of the Urban Crisis*, 17.
13. Ibid., 143.
14. Ibid., 146.
15. Ibid., 126.
16. Zukin, *Landscapes of Power*, 106.
17. Ed Hustoles, a planner at SEMCOG, quoted in Mast, *Detroit Lives*, 156.
18. Marling, *As Seen on TV*, 132.
19. Macfie, *Garden City Chronicle*, 126.
20. Neill, Fitzsimons, and Murtagh, *Reimaging the Pariah City*, 119.
21. Macfie, *Garden City Chronicle*, 99.
22. Zukin, *Landscapes of Power*, 141.
23. Ibid., 141.
24. Darden et al., *Detroit*, 26.
25. Neill, Fitzsimons, and Murtagh, *Reimaging the Pariah City*, 119.
26. Darden et al., *Detroit*, 24.
27. See Ibid., 25.
28. Rosa Sims, interviewed in Mast, *Detroit Lives*, 33.
29. James Boggs, interviewed ibid, 18.
30. Herb Boyd, interviewed in ibid., 78. Indeed, Berry Gordy's original headquarters, "Hitsville, U.S.A.," was a converted semidetached house on West Grand Boulevard. For an important cultural and political history of Motown music, see Smith, *Dancing in the Street.*
31. Abrams, *Forbidden Neighbors*, 96–98.
32. See Richard V. Marks, "Message to the Open Occupancy Conference (1963)," in Gordon, *City in Racial Crisis*, 31.
33. Farley et al., "Stereotypes and Segregation," 754.
34. Ibid.

35. Mayer and Hoult, "Race and Residence in Detroit" in Gordon, *City in Racial Crisis*, 3.
36. Ibid., 4.
37. Marks, "Message to the Open Occupancy Conference," 31.
38. Charles Butler, interviewed in Mast, *Detroit Lives*, 192.
39. Barikmo et al., *Early Days in Garden City*, 47.
40. Ibid., 47–48.
41. Bunge, *Fitzgerald*, 179.
42. Macfie, *Garden City Chronicle*, 117.
43. Ibid., 120.
44. Robert Paille, in Hersey, *Algiers Motel Incident*, 112–13.
45. James Sortor, in ibid., 138.
46. The publication of John Hersey's book in 1968 influenced short-term legal tactics in the case and, in the long term, helped to ensure that the incident remained in the popular memory of Detroiters. See Fine, *Violence in the Model City*, 286–89; and Stanton, "Pain and Promises: The Detroit Riot's Legacy," *Detroit Free Press*, Sunday, July 19, 1987. Hersey declared that the incident drew his attention because it "contained all the mythic themes of racial strife in the United States." Hersey, *Algiers Motel Incident*, 31. Hersey's book was reissued in 1998, with a new introduction by Thomas Sugrue.
47. Hersey, *Algiers Motel Incident*, 160.
48. Ibid., 21–22.
49. Fine, *Violence in the Model City*, 285.
50. Ibid., 287.
51. bell hooks, *Yearning*, 63.
52. Hersey, *Algiers Motel Incident*, 334.
53. For a detailed exposition of this argument, see Butler, "Endangered/-Endangering," 15–22.
54. The quote is from Diawara, "Black British Cinema," 33–47. The reference here is to Fanon's agonistic treatment of violence and decolonization in Fanon, *The Damned*, 1963.
55. Hall, "What Is This 'Black' in Black Popular Culture?" 24.
56. Tribunal organizer Dan Aldridge, interviewed in Watkins, "Tribunal Stage Set," *Michigan Chronicle*, Saturday, August 26, 1967.
57. Hersey, *Algiers Motel Incident*, 349.
58. Ibid.
59. Ibid., 350–51.
60. Ibid., 348.
61. Fanon, *The Damned*, 308.
62. Sauter and Hines, *Nightmare in Detroit*, 231.
63. A 1965 statement by the president of the Detroit NAACP, cited in Fine, *Violence in the Model City*, 99.
64. Riot participant, quoted in ibid., 363.
65. Reverend Albert Cleage, cited in ibid., 372.
66. Stokeley Carmichael, cited in Allen, *A Guide to Black Power in America*

(London: Gallancz, 1970), 6.

67. Ibid., 9.
68. For a detailed examination of all these movements, and of their long-term impact on Detroit politics, see Thompson, *Whose Detroit?*
69. Lefebvre, *Production of Space*, 35.
70. Ibid., 289.
71. Ibid., 308.
72. Ibid., 52.
73. See, for example, Lefebvre, *Explosion*, esp. 101–25.
74. "To recognize space, to recognize what takes place there and what it is used for, is to resume the dialectic." Lefebvre, *Survival of Capitalism*, 17.
75. Fine, *Violence in the Model City*, 162, and National Advisory Commission, *Report of The National Advisory Commission on Civil Disorders*, 76.
76. Fine, *Violence in the Model City*, 292.
77. Ibid.
78. National Advisory Commission, *Report of the National Advisory Commission on Civil Disorders*, 51.
79. Mbembe, "The Banality of Power," 1–30.
80. National Advisory Commission, *Report of the National Advisory Commission on Civil Disorders*, 76.
81. Bunge, *Fitzgerald*, 62.
82. Lefebvre, *Production of Space*, 387.
83. Arthur Johnson, cited in Mast, *Detroit Lives*, 199.
84. Lefebvre, "Toward a Leftist Cultural Politics," 80.
85. See, for example, Amidon, *The New City* and *Subdivision;* Hoffman, *Seventh Heaven;* Eugenides, *Virgin Suicides;* Ford, *Independence Day;* Moody, *The Ice Storm* and *Purple America: A Novel.* For a recent analysis of writing about suburbia, see Catherine Jurca, *White Diaspora: The Suburb and the Twentieth Century American Novel.* In film, see, for example, *The 'burbs* (1988), *Edward Scissorhands* (1990), *Welcome to the Doll's House* (1995), *Trees Lounge* (1996), *The Ice Storm* (1997), *Happiness* (1998), *The Virgin Suicides* (1999), *American Beauty* (2000), *Crime and Punishment in Suburbia* (2000), *Ghost World* (2001).
86. Mast, *Detroit Lives*, 33.

Bibliography

Aberbach, Joel D., and Jack L. Walker. *Race in the City: Political Trust and Public Policy in the New Urban System.* Boston: Little, Brown, 1973.

Abrams, Charles. *Forbidden Neighbors: A Study of Prejudice in Housing.* New York: Harper, 1955.

Allen, Frederick Lewis. "The Big Change in Suburbia." In *North American Suburbs: Politics, Diversity, and Change,* ed. John Kramer, 57–71. Berkeley, CA: Glendessary, 1972.

Amidon, Stephen. *The New City.* New York: Doubleday, 2000.

———. *Subdivision.* London: Bloomsbury, 1991.

Andres, Glenn M. "Urbanization and Architecture." In *Modern American Culture,* ed. Mick Gidley. London: Longman, 1993.

Arnold, Joseph L. *The New Deal in the Suburbs: A History of the Greenbelt Town Program.* Columbus: Ohio State University Press, 1971.

Auchincloss, Louis. *Pursuit of the Prodigal.* London: Victor Gollancz, 1960.

Bachelard, Gaston. *The Poetics of Space.* Boston: Beacon Press, 1969.

Baldassare, Mark. *Trouble in Paradise: The Suburban Transformation in America.* New York: Columbia University Press, 1986.

Baldwin, James. *The Fire Next Time.* London: Penguin, 1963.

———. *Go Tell It on the Mountain.* New York: Dell, 1953.

———. *Nobody Knows My Name: More Notes of a Native Son.* London: Michael Joseph, 1964.

Barikmo, Nora, Rev. Eugene Friedrich, John Macfie, Winifred Palmer, and Don Pruden. *Early Days in Garden City.* Garden City, MI: Garden City Historical Commission, 1962.

Basinger, Jeanine. *A Woman's View: How Hollywood Spoke to Women, 1930–1960.* London: Chatto and Windus, 1994.

Baudrillard, Jean. *America.* London: Verso, 1988.

Bauman, Zygmunt. *Modernity and Ambivalence.* Cambridge: Polity Press, 1991.

Baumgartner, M. P. *The Moral Order of a Suburb.* New York and Oxford: Oxford University Press, 1988.

Beauregard, Robert A. *Voices of Decline: The Postwar Fate of U.S. Cities.* Oxford, UK: Blackwell, 1993.

Benjamin, Walter. *Illuminations: Essays and Reflections.* New York: Schocken, 1968.

Bennett, Tony, Colin Mercer, and Janet Woolacott, eds. *Popular Culture and*

Social Relations. Milton Keynes, UK: Open University Press, 1986.

Berger, Bennet. *Looking for America: Essays on Youth, Suburbia, and Other American Obsessions.* Englewood Cliffs, NJ: Prentice-Hall, 1971.

Berger, Bennet M. *Working-Class Suburb: A Study of Auto Workers in Suburbia.* Berkeley: University of California Press, 1968.

Bhabha, Homi. "Bombs Away in Front-line Suburbia." *Guardian,* July 8, 1995.

Biskind, Peter. *Seeing Is Believing: How Hollywood Taught Us to Stop Worrying and Love the Fifties.* New York: Pantheon, 1983.

Blair, Thomas. *Retreat to the Ghetto.* New York: Hill and Wang, 1978.

Bone, Robert. *The Negro Novel in America.* New Haven, CT: Yale University Press, 1965.

Bostick, Alice J. *The Roots of Inkster.* Inkster, MI: Public Library and Historical Commission, 1980.

Bradbury, Malcolm. *The Modern American Novel.* Oxford: Oxford University Press, 1992.

Bressler, Marvin. "The Meyers Case: An Instance of Successful Racial Invasion." *Social Problems* 8 (1960), 126–42.

Bruck, Peter. "Protest, Universality, Blackness: Patterns of Argumentation in the Criticism of the Contemporary Afro-American Novel." In *The Afro-American Novel since 1960,* ed. Peter Bruck and Wolfgang Karrer. Amsterdam: B. R. Gruner, 1982.

Bryan, Ford R. *Beyond the Model T: The Other Ventures of Henry Ford.* Detroit: Wayne State University Press, 1997.

Buck-Morss, Susan. *The Dialectics of Seeing: Walter Benjamin and the Arcades Project.* London: MIT Press, 1989.

Bunge, William. *Fitzgerald: The Geography of a Revolution.* Cambridge, MA: Schenkman, 1971.

Butler, Judith. "Endangered/Endangering: Schematic Racism and White Paranoia." In *Reading Rodney King: Reading Urban Uprising,* ed. Robert Gooding-Williams, 15–22. London: Routledge, 1993.

Cain, James M. *Mildred Pierce.* New York: Random House, 1978.

Cameron, Lou. *The Block Busters.* Bristol, UK: Robert Hale, 1964.

Carmichael, Stokely, and Charles V. Hamilton. *Black Power: The Politics of Liberation in America.* London: Jonathan Cape, 1967.

Carter, Erica, James Donald, and Judith Squires. *Space and Place: Theories of Identity and Location.* London: Lawrence and Wishart, 1993.

Carver, Raymond. *Where I'm Calling From: New and Selected Stories.* New York: Atlantic Monthly Press, 1988.

Cassill, R. V., ed. *The Norton Anthology of Short Fiction.* New York: Norton, 1981.

Castells, Manuel. *The City and the Grass-roots: A Cross-cultural Theory of Urban Social Movements.* Berkeley: University of California Press, 1983.

Chambers, Iain. *Popular Culture: The Metropolitan Experience.* London: Routledge, 1986.

Cheever, John. *The Stories of John Cheever.* London: Jonathan Cape, 1979.

———. *The Wapshot Scandal.* New York: Harper and Row, 1963.

Chinitz, Benjamin, ed. *City and Suburb: The Economics of Metropolitan Growth.* Englewood Cliffs, NJ: Prentice-Hall, 1964.

Chinoy, Ely. *Automobile Workers and the American Dream.* Boston: Beacon, 1968.

Clark, Clifford Edward. *The American Family Home, 1800–1960.* Chapel Hill: University of North Carolina Press, 1986.

Clark, Kenneth B. *Dark Ghetto: Dilemmas of Social Power.* New York: Harper and Row, 1965.

Clark, S. D. "The Process of Suburban Development." In *North American Suburbs: Politics, Diversity and Change,* ed. John Kramer, 19–31. Berkeley: Glendessary, 1972.

Clarke, Alison. "Tupperware: Suburbia, Sociality and Mass Consumption." In *Visions of Suburbia,* ed. Roger Silverstone, 132–60. London: Routledge, 1997.

Clay, Phillip L. "The Process of Black Suburbanization." *Urban Affairs Quarterly* 14, no. 4 (1979): 405–24.

Cohen, Abner. *Masquerade Politics: Explorations in the Structure of Urban Cultural Movements.* Oxford, UK: Berg, 1993.

Coleman, James Samuel. *The Adolescent Society.* New York: Free Press, 1961.

Conot, Robert. *American Odyssey: A Unique History of America Told through the Life of a Great City.* New York: Bantam, 1974.

Cripps, Thomas. *Making Movies Black: The Hollywood Message Movie from World War II to the Civil Rights Era.* New York: Oxford University Press, 1993.

Cross, Gary. *Time and Money: The Making of Consumer Culture.* London: Routledge, 1993.

Cruse, Harold. *Crisis of the Negro Intellectual.* New York: William Morrow, 1967.

Cuomo, Mario. *Forest Hills Diary.* New York: Random House, 1974.

Dahl, Robert. *After the Revolution?* New Haven, CT: Yale University Press, 1990.

Darden, Joe T., Richard Child Hill, June Thomas, and Richard Thomas. *Detroit: Race and Uneven Development.* Philadelphia: Temple University Press, 1987.

Davis, Mike. *City of Quartz: Excavating the Future in Los Angeles.* London: Verso, 1990.

———. "Uprising and Repression in L.A.: An Interview with Mike Davis by the *CovertAction Information Bulletin." In Reading Rodney King: Reading Urban Uprising,* ed. Robert Gooding-Williams, 142–54. London: Routledge, 1993.

Dear, Michael, and Allen J. Scott, eds. *Urbanisation and Urban Planning in Capitalist Society.* London: Methuen, 1981.

de Certeau, Michel. *The Practice of Everyday Life.* Berkeley: University of California Press, 1984.

Dent, Gina, ed. *Black Popular Culture.* Seattle: Bay Press, 1992.

Diawara, Manthia. "Black British Cinema." *Public Culture* 3, no. 1 (1990): 33–47.

Dick, Philip K. *Puttering about in a Small Land.* Chicago: Academy Chicago, 1985.

———. *Second Variety: Volume Two of the Collected Stories.* London: HarperCollins, 1987.

———. *Time Out of Joint.* London: Penguin, 1969.

———. *We Can Build You.* New York: Vintage, 1994.

Dobriner, William M. *Class in Suburbia.* Englewood Cliffs, NJ: Prentice-Hall, 1963.

———, ed. *The Suburban Community.* New York: Putnam, 1958.

Doherty, Thomas. *Teenagers and Teenpics: The Juvenilization of American Movies in the 1950s.* Boston: Unwin Hyman, 1988.

Dolce, Philip, ed. *Suburbia: The American Dream and Dilemma.* Garden City, New York: Anchor Press/Doubleday, 1976.

Donaldson, Scott. *The Suburban Myth.* New York: Columbia University, 1969.

Dos Passos, John. *The Big Money: U.S.A.* Harmondsworth, UK: Penguin, 1981.

Douglas, Susan J. *Where the Girls Are: Growing up Female with the Mass Media.* London: Penguin, 1994.

Duncan, Otis Dudley, and Albert J. Reiss. *Social Characteristics of Urban and Rural Communities, 1950.* New York: John Wiley, 1956.

Ellison, Ralph. *Invisible Man.* New York: Random House, 1972.

Elsaesser, Thomas. "Tales of Sound and Fury: Observations on the Family Melodrama." In *Home Is Where the Heart Is: Studies in Melodrama and the Woman's Film*, ed. Christine Gledhill, 43–69. London: BFI, 1987.

Eugenides, Jeffrey. *Middlesex.* London, Bloomsbury, 2002.

———. *The Virgin Suicides.* London: Bloomsbury, 1993.

Fanon, Frantz. *Black Skin, White Masks.* London: Pluto, 1986.

———. *The Damned.* Paris: Presence Africaine, 1963.

Farley, Reynolds, Suzanne Bianchi, and Diane Colosanto. "Barriers to the Racial Integration of Neighbourhoods, the Detroit Case." *Annals of the American Academy of Political and Social Science* 444 (January 1980): 97–113.

Farley, Reynolds, Danziger, Sheldon, and Harry J Holzer. *Detroit Divided.* New York: Russell Sage Foundation, 2000.

Farley, Reynolds, Shirley Hatchett, and Howard Schuman. "A Note on Changes in Black Racial Attitudes in Detroit: 1968–1976." *Social Indicators Research* 6 (1979): 439–43.

Farley, Reynolds, Howard Schuman, Suzanne Bianchi, Diane Colosanto, and Shirley Hatchett. "Chocolate City, Vanilla Suburb: Will the Trend toward Racially Separate Communities Continue?" In *Social Science Research* 7 (December 1978): 319–44.

Farley, Reynolds, Charlotte Steeh, Maria Krysan, Tara Jackson, and Keith Reeves. "Stereotypes and Segregation: Neighbourhoods in the Detroit

Area." *American Journal of Sociology* 100, no. 3 (1994): 750–80.

Fava, Sylvia F. "Suburbanism as a Way of Life." *American Sociological Review* 21 (1956): 34–37.

Fine, Sidney. *Violence in the Model City: The Cavanagh Administration, Race Relations, and the Detroit Riot of 1967.* Ann Arbor: University of Michigan Press, 1989.

Fishman, Robert. *Bourgeois Utopias: The Rise and Fall of Suburbia.* New York: Basic, 1987.

Ford, Richard. *Independence Day.* London: Harvill, 1995.

Foucault, Michel. *The Archaeology of Knowledge.* London: Routledge, 1992.

———. *Madness and Civilization.* New York: Random House, 1973.

———. *Power/Knowledge: Selected Interviews and Other Writings*, ed. Colin Gordon. London: Harvester Wheatsheaf, 1980.

Francaviglia, Richard. *Main Street Revisited: Time, Space and Image Building in Small-Town America.* Iowa City: University of Iowa Press, 1996.

French, Marilyn. *The Women's Room.* London: Warner, 1993.

Friedan, Betty. *The Feminine Mystique.* Harmondsworth, UK: Penguin, 1965.

Gaines, Donna. *Teenage Wasteland: Suburbia's Dead End Kids.* New York: HarperCollins, 1992.

Gans, Herbert J. *The Levittowners: Ways of Life and Politics in a New Suburban Community.* London: Penguin, 1967.

———. "Urbanism and Suburbanism as Ways of Life: A Re-evaluation of Definitions." In *North American Suburbs: Politics, Diversity and Change*, ed. John Kramer. Berkeley: Glendessary, 1973.

Georgakas, Dan, and Marvin Surkin. *Detroit: I Do Mind Dying: A Study in Urban Revolution.* New York: St. Martin's, 1975.

Geschwender, James A. *Class, Race, and Worker Insurgency: The League of Revolutionary Black Workers.* Cambridge: Cambridge University Press, 1977.

Gettleman, Marvin, and David Mermelstein, eds. *The Great Society Reader: The Failure of American Liberalism.* New York: Vintage, 1967.

Gilje, Paul A. *Rioting in America.* Bloomington: Indiana University Press, 1996.

Gitlin, Todd. *The Sixties: Years of Hope, Days of Rage.* New York: Bantam, 1993.

Gledhill, Christine, ed. *Home Is Where the Heart Is: Studies in Melodrama and the Woman's Film.* London: BFI, 1987.

Goings, Kenneth W., and Raymond A. Mohl, eds. *The New African American Urban History.* Thousand Oaks, CA: Sage, 1996.

Gooding-Williams, Robert, ed. *Reading Rodney King: Reading Urban Uprising.* New York: Routledge, 1993.

Gordon, Leonard, ed. *A City in Racial Crisis: The Case of Detroit Pre- and Post-the 1967 Riot.* Dubuque, IA: Wm. C. Brown, 1971.

Gordon, Richard, Katherine Gordon, and Max Gunther. *The Split-Level Trap.* New York, 1960.

Gottdiener, Mark. *The Theming of America: Dreams, Visions, and Commercial*

Spaces. Oxford, UK: Westview, 1997.

Green, Gerald. *The Heartless Light*. London: Longmans, 1961.

Gregory, Derek. *Geographical Imaginations*. Oxford, UK: Blackwell, 1994.

Gutman, Robert, and David Popenoe, eds. *Neighbourhood, City, and Metropolis*. New York: Random House, 1970.

Haar, Charles M., ed. *The End of Innocence: A Suburban Reader*. Glenview, IL: Scott, Foresman, 1972.

Hailey, Arthur. *Wheels*. London: Pan, 1971.

Hall, Stuart. "What Is This 'Black' in Black Popular Culture?" In *Black Popular Culture*, ed. Gina Dent, 21–33. Seattle: Bay Press, 1992.

Hall, Stuart, Dorothy Hobson, Andrew Lowe, and Paul Willis, eds. *Culture, Media, Language*. London: Hutchinson, 1980.

Halpern, Daniel, ed. *The Penguin Book of International Short Stories*. London: Penguin, 1989.

Haralovich, Mary Beth. "Sit-coms and Suburbs: Positioning the 1950s Homemaker," In *Private Screenings: Television and the Female Consumer*, ed. Lynn Spigel and Denise Mann, 111–41. Minneapolis: University of Minnesota Press, 1992.

Harrington, Michael. *The Other America: Poverty in the United States*. Baltimore: Penguin, 1963.

Hartigan, John, Jr. *Racial Situations: Class Predicaments of Whiteness in Detroit*. Princeton, NJ: Princeton University Press, 1999.

Harvey, David. *The Condition of Postmodernity*. Oxford: Blackwell, 1990.

———. *Social Justice and the City*. London: Edward Arnold, 1973.

———. *The Urbanization of Capital*. Oxford, UK: Blackwell, 1985.

Hayden, Dolores. *Redesigning the American Dream: The Future of Housing, Work and Family Life*. New York: Norton, 1984.

Hebdige, Dick. *Subculture: The Meaning of Style*. London: Methuen, 1979.

Heller, Joseph. *Something Happened*. London: Transworld, 1974.

Henrickson, William Wood, ed. *Detroit Perspectives: Crossroads and Turning Points*. Detroit: Wayne State University Press, 1991.

Herbers, John. *The New Heartland: America's Flight beyond the Suburbs and How It Is Changing Our Future*. New York: Times, 1986.

Hersey, John. *The Algiers Motel Incident*. Baltimore: Johns Hopkins University Press, 1998.

———. *The Algiers Motel Incident*. London: Hamish Hamilton, 1968.

Hoffman, Alice. *Seventh Heaven*. London: Virago, 1992.

Hollingshead, August B. *Elmtown's Youth: The Impact of Social Classes on Adolescents*. New York: John Wiley, 1967.

hooks, bell. *Black Looks: Race and Representation*. London: Turnaround, 1992.

———. *Feminist Theory: From Margin to Center*. Boston: South End Press, 1984.

———. *Yearning: Race, Gender and Cultural Politics*. Boston: South End Press, 1990.

Howe, Irving, and B. J. Widick. *The UAW and Walter Reuther*. New York: Random House, 1949.

Huyssen, Andreas. *After the Great Divide: Modernism, Mass Culture and Postmodernism*. London: Macmillan, 1986.
Jackson, Kenneth T. *Crabgrass Frontier: The Suburbanization of the United States*. New York: Oxford University Press, 1985.
Jameson, Fredric. *Postmodernism or, the Cultural Logic of Late Capitalism*. Durham, NC: Duke University Press, 1991.
Jencks, Christopher. *Heterotopolis: Los Angeles—The Riots and the Strange Beauty of Hetero-architecture*. London: Academy Editions, 1993.
Johnson, James H., ed. *Suburban Growth: Geographical Processes at the Edge of the Western City* .New York: John Wiley, 1974.
Jurca, Catherine. *White Diaspora: The Suburb and the Twentieth Century American Novel* (Princeton, NJ: Princeton University Press, 2001).
Kaplan, E. Ann, ed. *Women in Film Noir*. London: BFI, 1978.
Karp, David. *Leave Me Alone*. London: Victor Gollancz, 1957.
Keats, John. *The Crack in the Picture Window*. Boston: Houghton-Mifflin, 1956.
Keith, Michael, and Steve Pile, eds. *Place and the Politics of Identity*. London: Routledge, 1993.
Keyes, Francis P. *Joy Street*. Harmondsworth, UK: Penguin, 1950.
Klein, Michael, ed. *An American Half-Century: Postwar Culture and Politics in the U.S.A.* London: Pluto Press, 1994.
Kofman, Eleonore, and Elizabeth Lebas, eds. *Writings on Cities: Henri Lefebvre*. Oxford, UK: Blackwell, 1996.
Kuhn, Annette. *Women's Pictures: Feminism and Cinema*. London: Verso, 1994.
Lacey, Robert. *Ford: The Men and the Machine*. Boston: Little, Brown, 1986.
Lawson-Peebles, Robert. "Performance Arts." In *Modern American Culture*, ed. Mick Gidley, 262–86. London: Longman, 1993.
Lee, Alfred McClung, and Norman D. Humphrey. *Race Riot: Detroit, 1943*. New York: Octagon, 1968.
Lefebvre, Henri. *Critique of Everyday Life*. Vol. 1. London: Verso, 1991.
———. *The Explosion: Marxism and the French Revolution*. New York: Monthly Review Press, 1969.
———. "La Commune: Derniere fete populaire." In *Images de la Commune*, ed. James Leith. London: McGill-Queen's University Press, 1971.
———. *La pensée marxiste et la ville*. Paris: Casterman, 1972.
———. *La révolution urbaine*. Paris: Gallimard, 1970.
———. *Le droit à la ville*. Paris: Anthropos, 1968.
———. *The Production of Space*. Oxford, UK: Blackwell, 1991.
———. *The Survival of Capitalism: Reproduction of the Relations of Production*. London: Allison and Busby, 1976.
———. "Toward a Leftist Cultural Politics: Remarks Occasioned by the Centenary of Marx's Death." In *Marxism and the Interpretation of Culture*, ed. Cary Nelson and Lawrence Grossberg, 75–88. London: Macmillan Education, 1988.
Leggett, John C. *Class, Race, and Labor: Working Class Consciousness in Detroit*.

New York: Oxford University Press, 1968.

Lincoln, James H. *The Anatomy of a Riot: A Detroit Judge's Report.* New York: McGraw-Hill, 1968.

Lochbiler, Don. *Detroit's Coming of Age: 1873–1973.* Detroit: Wayne State University Press, 1982.

Loth, David. *Crime in the Suburbs.* New York: William Morrow, 1967.

Lurie, Alison. *Nowhere City.* New York: Avon, 1965.

———. *The War between the Tates.* New York: Random House, 1974.

Macfie, John. *Garden City Chronicle.* Garden City, MI: Garden City Historical Commission, 1976.

Malamud, Bernard. *A New Life.* New York: Farrar, Straus and Cudahy, 1961.

———. The Tenants. London: Penguin, 1972.

Malcolm X, and Alex Haley. *The Autobiography of Malcolm X.* London: Penguin, 1965.

Marling, Karal Ann. *As Seen on TV: The Visual Culture of Everyday Life in the 1950s.* Cambridge: Harvard University Press, 1994.

Marsh, Margaret. *Suburban Lives.* New Brunswick, NJ: Rutgers University Press, 1990.

Marsh, Margaret S., and Samuel Kaplan. "The Lure of the Suburbs." In *Suburbia: The American Dream and Dilemma,* ed. Philip C. Dolce, 37–59. Garden City, NY: Anchor Doubleday, 1976.

Marx, Karl. *Capital, A Critique of Political Economy.* Vol. 1. New York: International Publishers, 1967.

———. "The Eighteenth Brumaire of Louis Bonaparte." In *The Marx-Engels Reader,* ed. Robert Tucker, 594–617. New York: Norton, 1972.

———. *Grundrisse: Foundations of the Critique of Political Economy.* London: Penguin, 1973.

Masotti, Louis H., and Jeffrey K. Hadden, eds. *Suburbia in Transition.* New York: New Viewpoints, 1974.

Massey, Douglas S., and Nancy A. Denton. *American Apartheid: Segregation and the Making of the Underclass.* Cambridge: Harvard University Press, 1993.

Mast, Robert H., ed. *Detroit Lives.* Philadelphia: Temple University Press, 1994.

Mbembe, Achille. "The Banality of Power and the Aesthetics of Vulgarity in the Postcolony." *Public Culture* 4 (1992): 1–30.

Meier, August, and Elliott Rudwick. *Black Detroit and the Rise of the UAW.* Oxford: Oxford University Press, 1979.

Merrifield, Andy, and Eric Swyngedouw. *The Urbanisation of Injustice.* London: Lawrence and Wishart, 1996.

Meyer, Stephen I. *The Five Dollar Day: Labor Management and Social Control in the Ford Motor Company, 1908–1921.* New York: State University of New York Press, 1981.

Moon, Elaine Latzman, and Detroit Urban League, Inc. *Untold Tales, Unsung Heroes: An Oral History of Detroit's African American Community, 1918–1967.* Detroit: Wayne State University Press, 1994.

Morgan, Robin, ed. *Sisterhood Is Powerful: An Anthology of Writings from the Women's Liberation Movement.* New York: Random House, 1970.

Morris, Bill. *Biography of a Buick.* London: Granta, 1992.

Morrison, Toni. *Song of Solomon.* New York: Alfred A. Knopf, 1987.

Moynihan, Daniel Patrick. *Report on the American Negro Family.* Washington, DC: U.S. Dept. of Labor, 1965.

Muller, Peter O. *Contemporary Suburban America.* Englewood Cliffs, NJ: Prentice-Hall, 1981.

Murphy, Thomas, and John Rehfuss. *Urban Politics in the Suburban Era.* Homewood: Dorsey, 1976.

National Advisory Commission. *Report of The National Advisory Commission on Civil Disorders.* New York: Bantam, 1968.

Neill, William, Diana Fitzsimons, and Brendan Murtagh. *Reimaging the Pariah City: Urban Development in Belfast and Detroit.* Aldershot, UK: Avebury, 1995.

Northrup, Herbert. *Organized Labor and the Negro.* New York: Harper and Row, 1944.

Oates, Joyce Carol. *Do with Me What You Will.* New York: Vanguard, 1973.

———. *Expensive People.* London: Victor Gollancz, 1969.

———. "How I Contemplated the World from the Detroit House of Correction and Began My Life over Again." In *The Norton Anthology of Short Fiction*, 1064–77. New York: Norton, 1970.

———. *them.* London: Victor Gollancz, 1971.

———. *Wild Saturday.* London: J. M. Dent, 1984.

Oliver, Melvin L., Jr., James H. Johnson Jr., and Walter C. Farrell. "Anatomy of a Rebellion: A Political-Economic Analysis." In *Reading Rodney King: Reading Urban Uprising*, ed. Robert Gooding-Williams, 117–41. London: Routledge, 1993.

O'Neill, William O. *American High: The Years of Confidence, 1945–1960.* New York: Free Press, 1989.

Packard, Vance. *The Hidden Persuaders.* Harmondsworth, UK: Penguin, 1957.

Pearlman, M. *American Women Writing Fiction: Memory, Identity, Family, Space.* Lexington: University Press of Kentucky, 1989.

Perin, C. *Everything in Its Place: Social Order and Land Use in America.* Princeton, NJ: Princeton University Press, 1977.

Pollock, Griselda. *Vision and Difference: Femininity, Feminism and the Histories of Art.* London: Routledge, 1988.

Popenoe, David. *The Suburban Environment: Sweden and the United States.* Chicago: University of Chicago Press, 1977.

Rabinow, Paul, ed. *The Foucault Reader.* New York: Pantheon, 1984.

Rich, Wilbur C. *Coleman Young and Detroit Politics: From Social Activist to Power Broker.* Detroit: Wayne State University Press, 1989.

Riesman, David. *The Lonely Crowd.* New Haven, CT: Yale University Press, 1950.

Rose, Mark H. *Interstate: Express Highway Politics, 1941–1956.* Lawrence:

University of Kansas Press, 1979.
Rosenthal, Marilynn. "Where Rumor Raged." *Trans-Action* 8 (1971):34–43.
Ross, Andrew, ed. *No Respect: Intellectuals and Popular Culture.* London: Routledge, 1989.
———. *Universal Abandon? The Politics of Postmodernism.* Edinburgh: Edinburgh University Press, 1988.
Ross, James Robert, ed. *The War Within: Violence or Nonviolence in the Black Revolution.* New York: Sheed and Ward, 1971.
Ross, Kristin. "Streetwise: The French Invention of Everyday Life." *parallax* 2 (1996):67–75.
Rothblatt, Daniel, and Daniel Carr. *Suburbia: An International Assessment.* London: Croom Helm, 1986.
Rubenstein, Bruce, and Lawrence Ziewacz. *Michigan: A History of the Great Lakes State.* Wheeling, IL: Harlan Davidson, 1995.
Ryman, Geoff. *Was.* London: HarperCollins, 1992.
Sauter, Van Gordon, and Burleigh Hines. *Nightmare in Detroit: A Rebellion and Its Victims.* Chicago: Henry Regnery, 1968.
Schmid, David. "Imagining Safe Urban Space: The Contribution of Detective Fiction to Radical Geography." *Antipode* 27, no. 3 (1995): 242–69.
Schuman, Howard, and Shirley Hatchett. *Black Racial Attitudes: Trends and Complexities.* Ann Arbor, MI: Institute for Social Research, 1974.
Schwartz, Barry, ed. *The Changing Face of the Suburbs.* Chicago: University of Chicago Press, 1976.
Schwartz, Joel. "The Evolution of the Suburbs." In *Suburbia: The American Dream and Dilemma*, ed. Philip Dolce, 1–37. Garden City, NY: Anchor Doubleday, 1976.
Scott, Frank. *The Down Home Guide to the Blues.* Chicago: A Cappella, Chicago Review Press, 1991.
Seeley, John R., R. Alexander Sim, and Elizabeth W. Loosley. *Crestwood Heights: A Study of the Culture of Suburban Life.* New York: Basic, 1956.
Sennett, Richard. *The Conscience of the Eye: The Design and Social Life of Cities.* London: Faber and Faber, 1990.
———. *The Fall of Public Man.* London and Boston: Faber and Faber, 1986.
Sennett, Richard, and Jonathan Cobb. *The Hidden Injuries of Class.* London: Faber and Faber, 1993.
Shank, Barry. "Conjuring Evidence for Experience: Imagining a Post-Structuralist History." *American Studies* 36, no. 1 (1995): 81–93.
Sharpe, William, and Leonard Wallock. "Bold New City or Built-Up 'Burb? Redefining Contemporary Suburbia." *American Quarterly* 46 (1994):1–30.
Shields, Rob. *Places on the Margin.* London: Routledge, 1991.
Shogan, Robert, and Tom Craig. *The Detroit Race Riot: A Study in Violence.* New York: Da Capo, 1964.
Showalter, Elaine. "Rivers and Sassoon: The Inscription of Male Gender Anxieties." In *Behind the Lines,* ed. Margaret R. Higonnet and Jane

Jenson, 61–69. New Haven, CT: Yale University Press, 1987.
Shulman, Max. *Rally Round the Flag, Boys!* London: Reprint Society, 1958.
Sibley, David. *Geographies of Exclusion: Society and Difference in the West.* London: Routledge, 1995.
Simmel, Georg. "The Stranger." In *The Sociology of Georg Simmel*, ed. Kurt H. Wolff, 402–8. New York: Free Press, 1950.
Singer, Benjamin D., Richard W. Osborn, and James A. Geschwender. *Black Rioters: A Study of Social Factors and Communication in the Detroit Riot.* Lexington, MA: D. C. Heath, 1970.
Sitkoff, Harvard. *The Struggle for Black Equality: 1954–1992.* New York: Hill and Wang, Noonday Press, 1993.
Smith, Michael Steven. *Notebook of a Sixties Lawyer.* New York: Smyrna, 1992.
Smith, Suzanne, *Dancing in the Street: Motown and the Cultural Politics of Detroit.* Cambridge: Harvard University Press, 1999.
Soja, Edward. *Postmodern Geographies: The Reassertion of Space in Critical Social Theory.* London: Verso, 1989.
———. *Thirdspace: Journeys to Los Angeles and other Real-and-Imagined Places.* Oxford, UK: Blackwell, 1996.
Spigel, Lynn. "From the Dark Ages to the Golden Age: Women's Memories and Television Reruns." *Screen* 36, no. 1 (1995):16–33.
———. "From Theatre to Space Ship: Metaphors of Suburban Domesticity in Postwar America." In *Visions of Suburbia*, ed. Roger Silverstone, 217–39. London: Routledge, 1997.
———. "Installing the Television Set: Popular Discourses on Television and Domestic Space, 1948–1955." In *Private Screenings: Television and the Female Consumer*, ed. Lynn Spigel and Denise Mann, 3–38. Minneapolis: University of Minnesota Press, 1992.
———. "The Suburban Home Companion: Television and the Neighbourhood Ideal in Postwar America." In *Sexuality and Space*, ed. B. Colomina, 185–218. New York: Princeton Architectural Press, 1992.
Spivak, Gayatri Chakravorty. *The Post-colonial Critic: Interviews, Strategies, Dialogues.* London: Routledge, 1990.
Stanton, Barbara. "Pain and Promises: The Detroit Riot's Legacy." *Detroit Free Press*, Sunday, July 19, 1987.
Sugrue, Thomas. *The Origins of the Urban Crisis: Race and Inequality in Postwar Detroit.* Princeton, NJ: Princeton University Press, 1996.
Taylor, Ella. *Prime Time Families: Television Culture in Postwar America.* Berkeley: University of California Press, 1989.
Thomas, June Manning. "The Forces of Urban Heterogeneity Can Triumph." *American Quarterly* 46, no. 1 (1994):49–54.
Thompson, Heather Ann. *Whose Detroit? Politics, Labor, and Race in a Modern American City.* Ithaca, NY: Cornell University Press, 2001.
Turner, Patricia A. *I Heard It through the Grapevine: Rumor in African American Culture.* Berkeley: University of California Press, 1993.
Updike, John. *Rabbit, Run.* Harmondsworth, UK: Penguin, 1964.

———. *A Rabbit Omnibus.* London: Penguin, 1991.

Vidich, Arthur, and Joseph Bensman. *The New American Society: the Revolution of the Middle Class.* Chicago: University of Chicago, 1969.

Walker, Alice. *In Search of Our Mothers' Gardens.* London: Women's Press, 1983.

Whyte, William H. *The Organization Man.* New York: Simon and Schuster, 1956.

Widick, B. J. *Detroit: City of Race and Class Violence.* Detroit: Wayne State University Press, 1989.

Williams, Juan. *Eyes on the Prize: America's Civil Rights Years, 1954–1965.* New York: Viking Penguin, 1987.

Williams, Raymond. *Keywords: A Vocabulary of Culture and Society.* London: Fontana Press, 1983.

Williamson, Judith. *Consuming Passions: The Dynamics of Popular Culture.* London: Marion Boyars, 1986.

Willis, Susan. *A Primer for Daily Life.* London: Routledge, 1991.

Wilson, Sloan. *The Man in the Gray Flannel Suit.* New York: Simon and Schuster, 1955.

Wirt, Frederick. *On the City's Rim: Politics and Policy in Suburbia.* Lexington, MA: D. C. Heath, 1972.

Wood, Robert. *Suburbia: Its People and Its Politics.* Boston: Houghton-Mifflin, 1958.

Woodford, Frank, and Arthur M. Woodford. *All Our Yesterdays: A Brief History of Detroit.* Detroit: Wayne State University Press, 1969.

Woodiwiss, Anthony. *Postmodernity U.S.A. The Crisis of Social Modernism in Postwar America.* London: Sage, 1993.

Wouk, Herman. *Marjorie Morningstar.* London: Reprint Society, 1957.

Wright, Gwendolyn. *Building the Dream: A Social History of Housing in America.* New York: Pantheon, 1981.

Wright, Richard. *Native Son.* London: Jonathan Cape, 1970.

Wyden, Peter. *Suburbia's Coddled Kids.* Garden City, NY: Doubleday, 1962.

Yates, Richard. *Revolutionary Road.* London: Methuen, 2001.

Zukin, Sharon. *Landscapes of Power: From Detroit to Disney World.* Berkeley: University of California Press, 1991.

Index